stage scenery: its construction and rigging

stage scenery:

its construction and rigging

A. S. GILLETTE

director of the university theatre
state university of iowa

HARPER & BROTHERS, PUBLISHERS, NEW YORK

contents

XI. *BACKSTAGE ORGANIZATION AND MANAGEMENT*   275

The Student Stage Manager.   The Stage Crew.   The
Property Crew.   The Light Crew.   The Costume Crew.
Summary of Stage Manager's Duties and Operational Check
List for Running a University Theatre Production.

illustrations

preface

THIS book is offered as a text for a course in scenic construction and rigging, and in back stage organization and management. The material, as presented here, follows rather closely the pattern of presentation used in a course in technical production taught by the author in the Speech and Dramatic Art Department of the State University of Iowa.

Almost any technician with 25 years of problem solving to his credit in an active producing theatre is bound to have accumulated a certain fund of knowledge that can be valuable to others with similar, though always different, problems. Add to this knowledge the wisdom and seasoning that bright students are able to help any receptive teacher acquire—the too often accepted contrary view notwithstanding—and you have the author's reason for preparing this volume. That such a very small percentage of the information accumulated by teacher-technician has heretofore found its way into print is due, at least in part, to two causes. First, if the technician has been working in a situation where the number of productions bring him into contact with many unusual problems, the demands of his work schedule are probably so exacting that they leave him little time or energy for recording data—the information is simply tucked away in the back of his mind where it is sometimes forgotten, and where it certainly can be of little value to others. Secondly, it is difficult to describe a complicated piece of construction or an unusual method of rigging without detailed diagrams or drawings. For this reason attention has been focused on the illustrations that accompany the textual material in this book.

In addition to the basic material on scenic construction, a chapter on selected constructional and rigging problems has been incorporated into this book. In the author's experience, the solutions given have proved their worth and effectiveness on stage. They represent the effort of one individual to record some of his findings, and perhaps to encourage others to do the same.

The author is especially grateful to his editor, Lousene Rousseau of the staff of Harper & Brothers, for her helpful suggestions and coöperation in designing the format of this book.

A. S. GILLETTE

stage scenery: its construction and rigging

the organization of the production staff for the nonprofessional theatre

We had just heard some of the finest music and operatic voices in the world in a production of *Aida* as it was presented by an internationally known touring company. Like hundreds of others in the audience, we had looked forward to this occasion for weeks; we had driven most of the afternoon to reach the city in time for a leisurely dinner before curtain time; and what was the subject of our conversation at the first intermission? It was not the genius of Verdi, it did not concern the magnificence of the voices or the music we had just heard, nor did it concern any of the details of an otherwise splendid production. All of the entr'act conversation could be summed up by this one question: "Did you see the stage hand who wandered across the King's courtyard in Act I?"

It was a small enough incident in itself and certainly understandable when one realized that the traveling company had to supplement its regular stage crew with inexperienced members of the local union; but the effect remained, nevertheless. An otherwise flawless production had been marred by a technical error.

This experience illustrates the fact that while the average playgoer may know little about the intricacies of backstage organization and management, he is extremely conscious of any interruption of a production that is due to a technical cause. For the most part he is not too severe in his criticism of an actor and is willing to overlook a missed cue or an awkward bit of stage business; but his reaction to a comparable mistake by a member of the backstage personnel is instantly critical. The incident is likely to be an occasion for many amusing and cutting remarks.

It is unfortunately true that in the majority of educational and community productions, and even in some professional productions, the greatest share of attention and energy is expended upon perfecting the script, the acting, and the direction, while the technical aspects of the production are relegated to a position of secondary importance. The management has, through thoughtlessness or ignorance, delayed until the last possible hour giving any serious consideration to the problems of technical planning and then often relied on the inspiration of the moment. The risk of such a procedure is both serious and obvious. The standard of a production is lowered when avoidable technical errors occur that detract from the effectiveness of an otherwise carefully planned production.

The primary purpose of this text is to discuss the duties of the technician and the principles of planning, construction, and rigging of scenery. However, it seems advisable to begin with the topic of organization, since it is essential for the reader to understand just where the technician fits within the general framework of a production staff and to what degree his work will be influenced or affected by the needs of other staff members. This fact is given additional emphasis when it is realized that the office of the scene technician, as it exists in the educational or community theatre, has no counterpart in the production staff of the professional theatre. His duties there have been divided between the personnel of the studios specializing in the construction and painting of scenery and the stage carpenter, electrician, and stage manager of the regular production crew. In some educational theatre organizations the duties of the scene technician are further complicated by the fact that one man will often serve as both scene designer and technician. This fact alone makes it essential that the delegation of duties be understood by all of those working within the framework of a nonprofessional theatre production staff.

The director without a sound knowledge of backstage organization or a clear picture of the duties and responsibilities of various members of his production staff is poorly equipped to assume the authoritative leadership required of the individual who must synchronize all phases of a production. The material offered in this first chapter is therefore concerned with the basic problem of organization.

Within the broad field of the educational, community, and professional theatre it is obvious that there could be no standardization of backstage personnel, either as to number involved or nature of their assignments. However, whether a production is a simple one-act play produced by an overworked high school teacher or an epic Broadway offering under the supervision of a well-known director aided by a host of specialists, the elements of both productions remain the same.

The successful production of a play is not the achievement of any one or two individuals but the composite result of the work of a number of artists and craftsmen who have labored within their specified areas with a clear understanding of the importance their particular efforts give to the total effect. These areas of activity form the component parts of a production and are the elements upon which the organization of a theatrical production staff is formed.

THE ELEMENTS OF A PRODUCTION

THE PLAY, DIRECTION, AND ACTING

The nucleus around which the entire production centers is the manuscript. The individual usually responsible for breathing life into the script is the director; and he, working through the skill of the actors, gives to the production his interpretation of the playwright's ideas. Although it is recognized that the fields of playwriting, acting, and directing each demand special skills and training, they are grouped together here as one element because they are inseparably united by the one purpose of conveying the playwright's intention.

SCENERY

The element of scenery actually embraces two fields of activity—creative and technical. The creative field is represented by the work of the designer, who is concerned with the problem of interpreting the script through the medium of scenic design and of creating a visual environment for the action of the play.

The technical field is represented by the individuals who are responsible for the mechanical operations of drafting, constructing, painting, rigging, and shifting of scenery. Scenery as such may be defined as a series of two- and three-dimensional units that are usually placed on stage to enclose the acting area. When painted, rigged, and lighted, they form the background for the action of the play.

PROPERTIES

Properties include all practical or decorative parts of the design that are not structurally a part of the setting. They fall into several classifications, depending upon their size, placement within the setting, and use. Trim or decorative props usually serve no practical purpose other than to help the designer establish the period, nationality, and locale of the setting. They are usually placed against a wall or suspended from it. Set or floor props usually stand upon the stage floor and include all of the furniture normally used by the actors. Hand props are objects carried to and from the stage by the actors or used by them while on stage in the performance of established stage business.

LIGHTING

Advancement in the control of light and in the improvement and efficiency of lighting instruments has opened a new field for creative work. The lighting artist is no longer content to flood the stage with light for the sake of visibility alone. He has found that by the proper selection and placement of his lighting instruments, by the subtle use of color and intensity, he can literally "paint with light." Revelation of form, emphasis of scenic and dramatic composition, and enhancement of the emotional content of the play are among the contributions a lighting specialist makes to a production.

COSTUMES

This field is as highly specialized in its own way as is that of the scene designer; both have many factors in common and both include both creative and mechanical phases of production work. The costumer strives to incorporate within each costume design features and details that are indicative of the period and country dictated by the script and in accord with the social class and individuality of a specific character.

BUSINESS MANAGEMENT

An indispensable part of the work associated with the production of any play concerns the business transactions dealing with budgets, rentals, purchasing, and publicity. Within the professional theatre, where duties of this type are heaviest, they are usually handled by an Assistant Producer or a General Manager. In the educational or community theatre this position is filled by the Director of the Theatre or some other member of the staff who combines this work with his other assignments.

ORGANIZATION CHART FOR THE NONPROFESSIONAL THEATRE STAFF

Plate 1 illustrates the typical basic pattern used for the organization of a production staff for most educational and community theatres. This organizational plan uses the six elements of a production as its foundation. The diagram indicates the departmental heads and lists the members of the production staff whose work will be carried out under their supervision.

Obviously there will be numerous changes in such an organizational chart, due to variations in the number of permanent staff members and their particular aptitudes and abilities. Such a diagram is of value when used as a guide and as a means of checking the distribution of the work load among those responsible for specific assignments, but only when it is adjusted to the personnel of each producing group.

PRODUCTION STAFF PERSONNEL AND THEIR DUTIES

The more important members of a theatre production staff are listed below, together with a brief account of the areas in which they work, their duties and responsibilities. There is always a possibility that necessity may force the combining of one or more of these positions on a production staff. This should be done with a full understanding of the duties of each position in order to select combinations of functions that are compatible.

ORGANIZATION OF A PRODUCTION STAFF
DURING PERIOD OF PREPARATION

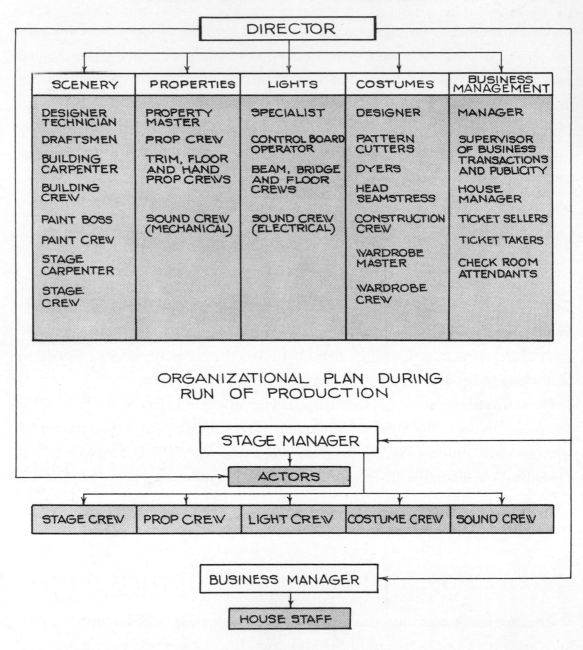

SCENERY	PROPERTIES	LIGHTS	COSTUMES	BUSINESS MANAGEMENT
DESIGNER TECHNICIAN	PROPERTY MASTER	SPECIALIST	DESIGNER	MANAGER
DRAFTSMEN	PROP CREW	CONTROL BOARD OPERATOR	PATTERN CUTTERS	SUPERVISOR OF BUSINESS TRANSACTIONS AND PUBLICITY
BUILDING CARPENTER	TRIM, FLOOR AND HAND PROP CREWS	BEAM, BRIDGE AND FLOOR CREWS	DYERS	HOUSE MANAGER
BUILDING CREW			HEAD SEAMSTRESS	
PAINT BOSS	SOUND CREW (MECHANICAL)	SOUND CREW (ELECTRICAL)	CONSTRUCTION CREW	TICKET SELLERS
PAINT CREW				TICKET TAKERS
STAGE CARPENTER			WARDROBE MASTER	CHECK ROOM ATTENDANTS
STAGE CREW			WARDROBE CREW	

ORGANIZATIONAL PLAN DURING
RUN OF PRODUCTION

STAGE MANAGER

ACTORS

| STAGE CREW | PROP CREW | LIGHT CREW | COSTUME CREW | SOUND CREW |

BUSINESS MANAGER

HOUSE STAFF

PLATE I

AUTHOR

The author is the creator of the script and the individual who, when present during the preparation of the play, assists the director by making revisions in the script or by advising on matters such as characterization or interpretation.

DIRECTOR

The director is responsible for the interpretation of the play and for the choice of style in presentation. It is through his work that acting and directing are shaped to express the idea and theme of the play. It is his responsibility to see that settings, costumes, props, and lighting are in accord with the acting and directing and that all express the idea of the play.

STAGE MANAGER

The stage manager is the director's right-hand man. His duties vary considerably with different organizations. In the professional theatre he is usually in attendance throughout the entire rehearsal period and may have some active part in rehearsing mob scenes and bit parts. In educational and community theatre he may take over his duties only a short time before final rehearsals. He is responsible to the director for synchronizing all backstage effects with the action and business of the play. He has authority over actors as well as crew members during the run of the production. On elaborate shows the stage manager may have one or two assistants.

PROMPTER

The prompter or bookholder is in attendance at all rehearsals. He aids the actors in memorizing their parts and keeps a careful record in the prompt copy of all stage business and action. An important part of the prompter's duty is the skillful feeding of lines to an actor who has "gone up" during performance.

SCENE DESIGNER

The designer provides the sketches for all the settings required by the production. He is responsible for transposing perspective sketches into mechanical drawings that describe the setting in terms of feet and inches. These drawings consist of ground plans, sight-line drawings, front elevations, and detail drawings. He provides the technician with the general scheme for shifting the settings. He supervises the painting of the settings. The designer selects the properties for each set and is responsible for the final trimming of the settings.

DESIGNER'S ASSISTANT

The designer frequently has an assistant who helps him with drafting, scene painting, and securing the correct properties and set decorations.

PAINT CREW

The paint crew is under the direct supervision of either the designer or his assistant. All of the scenery and special effects are painted by this crew.

TECHNICIAN

The technician is responsible for transposing the designer's plans into working drawings and for the division of the settings into units of scenery capable of easy handling and shifting. He perfects the designer's general scheme for shifting scenery and solves in detail the problems concerned with construction and rigging. He sees that all shop equipment is kept in good workable condition and keeps an adequate supply of building material and hardware in stock at all times. With the aid of the building carpenter and the stage carpenter the technician supervises the building, assembly, and rigging of all scenery. What sound effects and properties are to be built are constructed under his direction.

DRAFTSMEN

The technician may have one or more draftsmen to assist him in transposing the designer's plans into working drawings from which the scenery and special properties are actually made.

BUILDING CARPENTER

The building carpenter is the shop foreman whose duty it is to supervise the actual cutting, covering, and assembling of all units of scenery called for by the working drawings. He keeps the technician advised as to the amount of building materials on hand. He assigns work to each member of the building crew and checks the progress of each unit under construction. The maintenance of all hand and power tools is under his supervision. He sees to it that the scene shop is kept clean and that all building materials and hardware are properly stored.

BUILDING CREW

The building crew is usually composed of volunteer workers or students from classes in stagecraft or technical production who work on the crew as part of their laboratory requirement.

STAGE CARPENTER

In educational or community theatre productions the duties of the stage carpenter are frequently combined with those of the stage manager. The stage carpenter and his crew are responsible for the rigging and shifting and storage of all scenery during dress rehearsals and the run of the production. He plans the sequence of shifting operations, designates storage areas, and makes individual crew assignments. He must see that the scenery is kept in good condition during the run of the play and that settings are properly struck and stored at the close of the run.

STAGE CREW

The stage crew, like the building crew, is composed of either students or volunteer workers. Students are usually alternated from the building crew of one production to the stage crew of the next, to provide them with an opportunity to learn two phases of backstage work and organization.

PROPERTY MASTER

Properties that have been selected by joint agreement of the director and designer are assembled by the property master and his crew. Properties are purchased, rented, borrowed, or built by members of the prop crew under the supervision of the technician and from working drawings provided by him. Since the moving and storing of properties is carried on simultaneously with the shifting of scenery, the property master and his crew work under the supervision of the technician or stage manager and in close coöperation with stage and light crews.

PROPERTY CREW

The members of this crew, under the supervision of the property master, help in the procurement or construction of all props. During the rehearsal period and the run of the play the crew is usually divided into two sections, one responsible for the placement, shifting, and storing of all decorative and hand props, the other responsible for floor props.

SOUND CREW

Ordinary off-stage sound effects of a simple nature are usually handled by members of the prop crew. Occasionally a production may require a great many varied and complicated sound effects, or the script may be accompanied in part by a musical score. In such cases it is advisable to have a special crew that can devote its entire attention to synchronizing the sound effects, on the proper cue, to the action and business of the play.

LIGHTING SPECIALIST

The lighting specialist collaborates closely with both the director and the designer in planning the lighting of a production. More frequently than not, the duties of the lighting specialist are assumed by the designer. These duties include planning the light plot, determination of the number and types of instruments to be used, placement and mounting of these instruments, setup of the control board, and development of a control-board cue sheet.

LIGHT CREW

The work to be accomplished by the light crew is of such a nature that it forces a logical division of the crew into sections for specific purposes.

1. The control-board operators, under the direction of the lighting specialist or the designer, work out the most efficient setup of the board and plan the cue sheet. They also operate the board during rehearsals and performances.

2. The floor crew has charge of all lighting instruments mounted on or with-

in the setting or placed in off-stage areas which can be reached from the stage floor. Examples are tower spots, horizon strips, table or floor lamps, and fireplace effects. The floor crew is responsible for the proper placing and focusing of these lights, use of correct color mediums in them, and handling them during scene shifts.

3. The bridge crew controls the focusing of spotlights and changing of color mediums for all instruments and special effects mounted on the bridge.

4. The beam crew, usually consisting of but one or two members, has charge of instruments mounted in the beams over the auditorium or along the balcony front.

COSTUME DESIGNER

The costume designer submits sketches to the director for all costumes to be used in the play. These may be either rented or made in the theatre's shop. When the latter is the case, the sketches are usually accompanied by material samples and cost estimates. After the director approves the designs, the costume designer determines what stock costumes may be altered for use in the current production. He then buys the remaining fabrics and accessories and supervises the making of the costumes. When costumes are rented, the designer places the orders and supervises the adjusting and fitting of the costumes after they are received.

COSTUME CREW

The costume designer usually divides the members of his crew into two groups, construction crew and wardrobe crew. The construction crew is concerned with the actual cutting, fitting, and assembling of all costumes. The wardrobe crew assumes responsibility for the completed costumes and their maintenance from the time they are first used in dress rehearsal until the close of the run. Both crews are under the supervision of the costume designer.

BUSINESS MANAGER

The business manager keeps the books and accounts of the organization in order. Cost estimates for costumes, scenery, properties, and lighting are submitted to him by department heads, and he keeps them within established budgets. It sometimes becomes necessary to simplify or alter some phase of the production work to bring the total cost within the limits of these budgets. Changes made for this reason must be approved by the director, and notification of such changes must be given to the department heads whose work is affected by them. All advertising, news stories, and general publicity are handled by the business manager after consultation with and approval by the director. Working under the direction of the business manager is the house staff, whose duties are sufficiently described by their titles:

1. House manager.
2. Ticket sellers.
3. Ticket takers.
4. Ushers.
5. Cloakroom attendants.

NEED FOR COÖPERATIVE EFFORT

With an organization as large and as complicated as a theatre production staff the necessity for close coöperation between all department heads is obvious. Otherwise misunderstandings or differences of opinion concerning some vital part of the work may result in a performance in which some elements of the production are not in accord.

This coöperation is best achieved by conferences at which problems bearing on the production are discussed. Such meetings should occur frequently enough during the preparation of the play so that those who are responsible for the various phases of the work are conscious of the progress achieved by others, and of any changes that may affect their own work. In this manner many problems which might go unnoticed until the first dress rehearsal can be caught early and solutions found for them. The time thus saved during the dress-rehearsal period can well be devoted to the integration of the elements of a production rather than to the correction of needless mistakes resulting from lack of communication.

A well-balanced artistic production can result only when all department heads and various assistants have a complete understanding of the ultimate goal to be attained by the fusion of their individual efforts.

the relationship of the scene designer and the scene technician

PERHAPS at no place within the structure of a theatre production staff is the need of coöperation more clearly evident than between the scene designer and the technician. Actually the work of the technician is so completely dependent upon the designer's plans that little if anything can be accomplished toward the construction of scenery until the designer's plans are in the hands of the technician. There is nothing unusual about this arrangement: it is simply that those working within the theatre must follow the same pattern used by any group of individuals who are concerned with the general problems associated with designing and building. Whether the object under consideration is a bridge, a house, or a set of scenery, certain basic steps must be taken before construction can actually begin. First, of course, is the actual design of the object, by which its nature and form are determined. Once the design has been established, it is relatively easy to describe it in detail and in terms of specific measurements. These two steps are the responsibility of the designer. Although detailed discussion of the duties of the scene designer is beyond the scope of this book, it is essential that the technician understand just what the designer's plans are and what they are intended to convey, for the obvious reason that he, the technician, must convert these plans into working drawings that will supply all information needed by the building crews in constructing the scenery.

THE DESIGNER'S PLANS

The designer may present his ideas for a proposed setting to the director and to the production staff by either of two methods: (1) he may use a three-dimensional scaled model, or (2) he may represent the setting by means of a colored perspective sketch. In either case it is necessary to supplement the model or sketch with mechanical drawings that describe the setting in greater detail and with greater accuracy. These drawings are known as the designer's plans and consist of ground plans, sight-line drawings, front elevations, and detail drawings.

THE MODEL

The majority of scene designers prefer to present their ideas by colored perspective sketches rather than models, simply because they are easier and faster to make. However, there are occasions when a model is the only practical method of approaching a particularly difficult problem. Settings that are highly irregular in form or that employ forced perspective or that are unusually complicated in construction are frequently worked out in detail by the designer with models constructed of clay and cardboard. There are additional disadvantages to the use of models besides the time and skill required to build them. Models are awkward to handle and to carry about, and unless they are very well made they are constantly in need of repairs. Small, detachable parts are easily lost or broken. But in spite of these handicaps there is no question but that the scaled three-dimensional model provides the production staff and the cast with a much clearer picture of what the proposed setting will be than will a sketch. Some directors prefer to work with a model because it gives them an opportunity to try out stage pictures and groupings of actors by moving miniature scaled figures about within it.

THE SKETCH

Whether the designer expresses his ideas by means of a model or a sketch, they both serve the same purpose and form the nucleus around which is centered all of the activity associated with the process of planning and constructing scenery (Plate 2).

The sketch of a proposed setting is usually rendered in color and is drawn to represent it as it would appear to a member of the audience who is seated in the center and about halfway back in the auditorium. Usually these sketches are quite complete and represent not only the style and form of the setting but the furniture and property arrangements as well. Frequently the designer may attempt, through his rendering, to give some indication of the proposed lighting scheme. Such a sketch provides all members of the staff and cast with

PERSPECTIVE SKETCH
FOR
BLITHE SPIRIT

PLATE 2

a clear visual representation of what the finished setting will be. Although the general arrangement of the room, the location of such architectural features as doors, windows, fireplace, or stairway are all indicated, the designer's primary concern is with the problem of describing the setting. No matter how accurately the perspective has been drawn or how well rendered the sketch may be, it is nevertheless totally inadequate as a guide to the technician who is concerned with the problem of how to build it. In this respect the sketch can be compared to a photograph: both give a clear picture of what the finished object should look like, but neither provides the necessary information required for its construction.

Perhaps the most critical step in the whole process of designing comes at this point. The sketch or model is complete and it has been approved by the director and the rest of the production staff; yet it in no way gives the technician the necessary specifications and dimensions that will permit him to start construction. If the sketch were his only guide, the best he could possibly do would be to guess at the dimensions the designer might have had in his mind, with the result that the completed setting would be only a rough approximation of the designer's intentions. Since this would be a foolhardy procedure at best, the designer must transpose his sketch or model into terms of actual feet and inches by means of ground plans, elevations, and detail drawings.

GROUND PLANS

Scenery is designed not only for a specific play but for a particular stage. It is probably redundant to say that the designer must know the physical characteristics and dimensions of the stage on which he is to work just as thoroughly as a tailor must know the measurements of an individual for whom he is making a suit. Neither can hope for a well-fitted product unless these factors are constantly kept in mind.

There is no agreement among designers as to just when the details of the ground plans should be worked out. Some maintain that the ground plans should be made first and the sketches or models based upon these; others declare that they conceive the ideas for their setting in sketch form and then adapt them to the dimensions of the stage. It makes little difference which method is used just so long as it is done, for the ground plans form the key plates on which all other drawings are based.

The ground plan is a scaled mechanical drawing representing the setting in top view as it appears in relation to the stage on which it is to be presented. Perhaps the best way to visualize it is to imagine that one is in a position directly above the setting, from which the ceiling has been removed; what one would see from this vantage point is represented on the ground plan. Such a view should show the exact shape and size of the setting in relation to the proscenium arch and the curtain line, the width and angle of all wall sections, the location and width of all doors and the direction of their swing. The exact placing and dimensions can be shown for such architectual features as windows, stairways, columns, nitches, alcoves, and fireplaces. The location and width of all masking backings that will be seen through windows or doorways can be clearly shown in this drawing. In addition, the amount of available storage

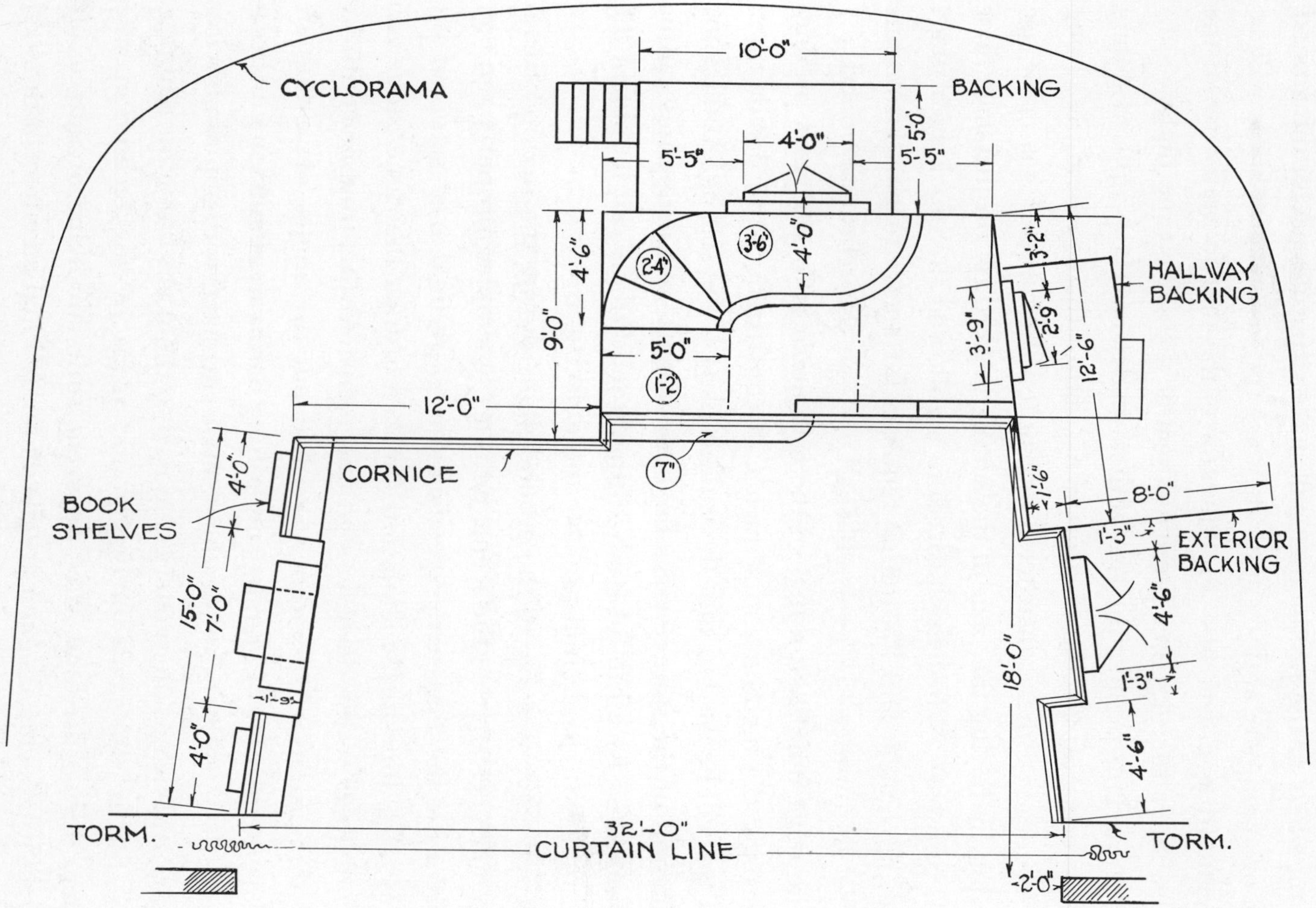

CYCLORAMA

BACKING

HALLWAY
BACKING

EXTERIOR
BACKING

10'-0"

5'-0"

5'-5"

3'-9"

3'-2"

12'-6"

2'-9"

8'-0"

1'-3"

4'-6"

1'-3"

4'-6"

5'-5"

4'-0"

4'-0"

(36)

(24)

5'-0"

(12)

1'-6"

18'-0"

2'-0"

TORM.

4'-6"

9'-0"

(7")

12'-0"

CORNICE

32'-0"
CURTAIN LINE

4'-0"

15'-0"

7'-0"

4'-0"

1'-3"

BOOK
SHELVES

TORM.

GROUND PLAN FOR
BLITHE SPIRIT
Scale ¼" = 1'-0"

PLATE 3

space for scenery or properties or for the location of lighting instruments can be determined with accuracy (Plate 3).

Since all members of the production staff make extensive use of the ground plans, the more complete and accurate they are the less chance there will be for misunderstandings or errors. The director is the first to make use of the ground plans, since the designer presents them at the same time that he submits his sketches. This permits the two of them to discuss the proposed setting or settings in terms of specific measurements rather than generalities. Long before the scenery is either constructed or painted the director has made use of this drawing by having the plan of the setting marked off on the stage floor for rehearsal purposes. When this procedure is followed the blocking of stage business and movement and the timing required for actors to move from one part of the set to another can be established early in the rehearsal period.

One of the most important duties of the technician is to analyze a production to determine the method and sequence of construction and decide upon what technique will be used to shift the various parts of the setting. At the same time the location of the storage areas for both scenery and properties can be decided upon. Only by a careful study of the ground plans can he obtain the information that will enable him to make these decisions.

Constant reference is made to the ground plans during the period of construction to make certain that the scenic units are assembled properly and that they comply with the designer's specifications. The final trial setup of the scenery is usually done in the shop and checked against the dimensions and notations contained on the designer's ground plans. At this time not only are the overall dimensions of the scenery verified but the angles of joining are checked, as is the placing of bracing and lashing hardware. Faults in construction or rigging detected by this procedure can be corrected with a minimum loss of shop hours and before the scenery is moved to the paint frame for painting.

Extensive use is also made of the ground plans by the technician, who employs them during the time when the scene shifts are being organized and in order to clarify specific assignments given to individual members of the stage crew. This subject will be treated in detail in a later chapter.

Much of the preliminary planning of two other members of the production staff is based on the information contained in the ground plans; these are the lighting specialist and the head of the property crew. Using a duplicate plan of each setting, the lighting specialist can locate all major areas of the stage that are to receive light and determine the number, type, and mounting positions of the lighting instruments to be used. The property master, usually in consultation with both the director and the designer, also uses the ground plans, to establish the exact location and size of all practical and decorative floor properties.

SIGHT LINES

Have you ever watched a production from a seat in the auditorium when the setting is so placed on stage that you can see but a part of it, or when some vital scene is played just beyond the limits of your visibility? If so, you will appreciate the importance of adequate sight lines. Determining satisfactory sight lines for a setting is the responsibility of the designer. This step must be taken early in the process of designing, usually at the time the ground plans are formulated. Sight-line drawings assure the designer that all important parts of the setting and all acting areas are within the range of visibility of each member of the audience.

Two separate drawings are required to test the sight lines of any proposed setting. One is a horizontal sectional plan and the other a vertical sectional elevation. Both must be carefully scaled mechanical drawings representing different views of the auditorium with the set in position on stage (Plate 4). By locating the position of the extreme side seats in the first and last row in the orchestra and in the first and last row of the balcony, it is possible to test the sight lines of a setting with surprising accuracy. A straight line drawn from one of these seats past the edge of the proscenium arch and to the setting will reveal how much or how little of the setting is visible to a person seated at that point. If it becomes apparent from this test that an important entrance will be lost to view to a good portion of the audience, the setting should be adjusted until the sight lines are considered satisfactory.

From the horizontal sectional drawing the designer can not only test for good sight lines but he can determine the width and proper placement for the tormentors, returns, masking backings, groundrows, and cutouts.

The vertical sectional elevation is used in much the same manner. If a sight

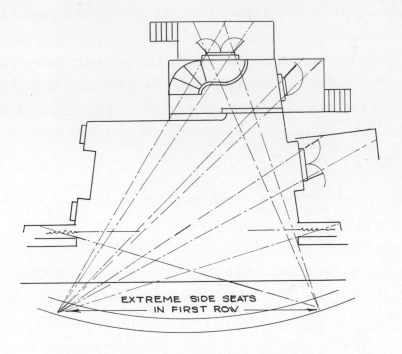

HORIZONTAL SIGHT-LINE DRAWING

EXTREME SIDE SEATS
IN FIRST ROW

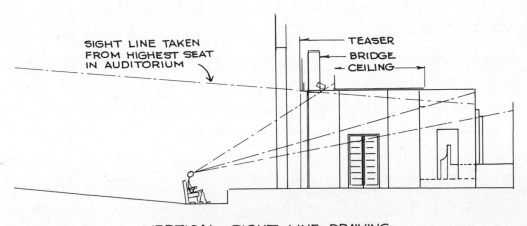

SIGHT LINE TAKEN
FROM HIGHEST SEAT
IN AUDITORIUM

TEASER
BRIDGE
CEILING

VERTICAL SIGHT-LINE DRAWING

PLATE 4

line is drawn from the highest seat in the house past the lower edge of the teaser, it will reveal how much or how little can be seen of an actor standing on the highest level of the setting. If this test indicates poor sight lines, these may be corrected by adjusting the teaser height, the depth of the setting, or the height of the levels. This drawing makes it possible to establish the height of the teaser, the light bridge, and the depth and placement of the ceiling and of all masking backings. This is especially valuable in testing the sight lines of exterior settings when it is essential to know the exact height and placement of possible foliage borders, tree silhouettes, and drops.

Unfortunately, some theatres have been so poorly planned in regard to sight lines that no amount of set adjustment and rearrangement can possibly result in satisfactory sight lines. It has been the author's experience to work within a theatre where, if sight lines were extended from the two extreme side seats past the proscenium arch, little or no acting area could be seen. In such situations there is only one satisfactory solution—rope off the extreme sides of the auditorium and do not sell such seats.

FRONT ELEVATIONS

No matter how complete and accurate the ground plans are, such drawings are lacking in one vital respect: they provide no opportunity for indicating vertical measurements. The designer's elevations are scaled mechanical drawings representing a front view of the setting as it would appear when drawn in a single plane. Such drawings present the designer with a means of establishing, and showing, all vertical measurements. Drafting these elevations must not be looked upon as so much "busy work," or a phase of designing that could just as well be omitted, for these drawings form one of the most critical steps in the process of designing. By their means the designer can construct a drawing that will be a proportional reduction of the finished setting. He will be able to see and adjust the relationship and proportion of wall areas to doors, windows, and other architectural features. Through the use of elevations he can establish exact dimensions of such details as the size and number of repeats of a wall-paper pattern, the proper yardage of material needed for window draperies, the size and placement of all wall hangings. Every part of the setting visible to the audience should be shown on the elevations and should be personally checked

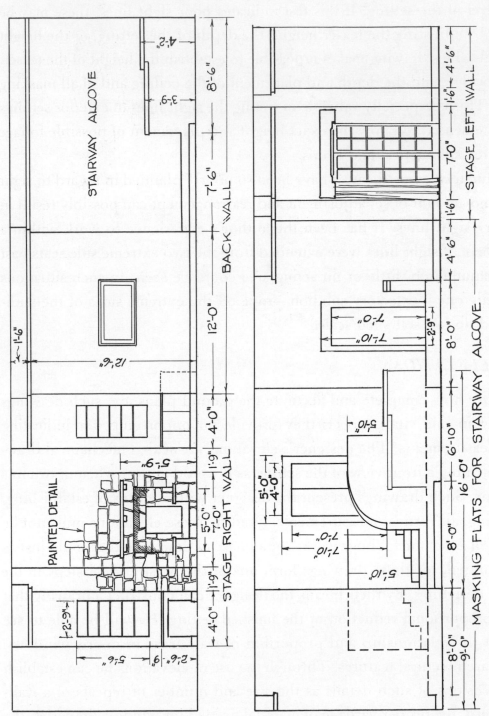

FRONT ELEVATIONS
BLITHE SPIRIT
Scale ¼"=1'-0"

PLATE 5

by the designer as to proper size, proportion, and position. If he is pleased with the compositional arrangement of the setting as it appears in the elevations, and if he has accompanied it with accurate dimensions and concise notations, he may reasonably expect to be pleased with the finished setting (Plate 5).

DETAIL DRAWINGS

Owing to the large size of most stage settings the scale used for both ground plans and elevations is of necessity small. Usually they are drawn on a scale of $\frac{3}{8}''$ or $\frac{1}{2}''$ to $1'$-$0''$, which permits the designer to draw the entire setting on a single sheet of drafting paper and still keep all dimensions large enough to be easily read. These scales, while quite adequate for plans and elevations, are not satisfactory for showing details and dimensions of smaller three-dimensional units of the setting, such as a fireplace or a stairway. These objects are redrawn on a much larger scale, usually $\frac{3}{4}''$, $1''$, or $1\frac{1}{2}''$ to $1'$-$0''$, and are known as detail drawings. These drawings represent an object by showing its top, front, and side views and occasionally a sectional or cutaway drawing. The most commonly used methods of shape description used for this purpose are orthographic projection and isometric drawings (Plate 6). More rarely oblique and cabinet drawings may be used for the same purpose.

A study of Plates 2–6 will reveal how completely the setting for a production of *Blithe Spirit* is described. It will also be noted that while the shape, form, and size of the setting has been given in detail, there is nothing about these drawings that tells the carpenter how the set is to be built. The technician and his assistants are responsible for the working drawings from which the scenery will actually be constructed.

THE TECHNICIAN'S ANALYSIS OF A PRODUCTION

The work of the technician cannot really begin until all the designer's plans are in his hands: sketches, ground plans, elevations, and detail drawings. The technician may have had earlier consultations with the designer to consider problems of construction, rigging, or cost, or perhaps to discuss the advantages offered by one method of shifting over another for the immediate production, but there remains very little that the technician can do until the designer has completed most of his work.

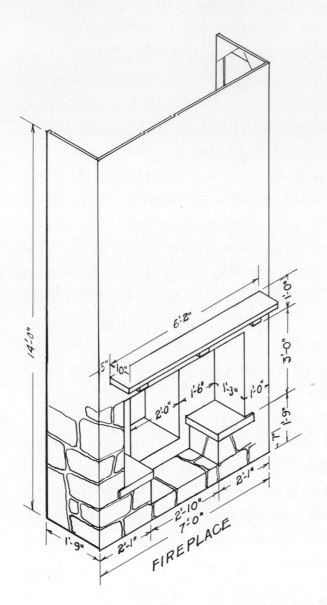

14'-0"

6'-2"

1'-0"

5" 10"

3'-0"

2'-0" 1'-6" 1'-3" 1'-0"

1'-9"

7"

1'-9" 2'-1" 2'-10" 2'-1"

7'-0"

FIREPLACE

PLATE 6

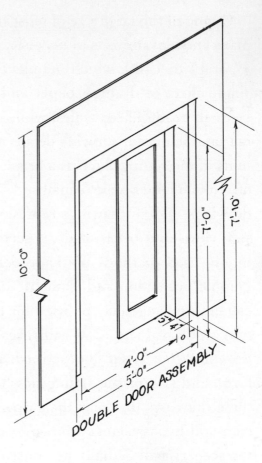

10'-0"

7'-0"

7'-10"

3"
4"
0"

4'-0"

5'-0"

DOUBLE DOOR ASSEMBLY

DETAIL DRAWINGS
BLITHE SPIRIT
Scale ½"=1'-0"

As was mentioned earlier in this chapter the first, and one of the most important, of the technician's duties is his analysis of the production. From his study of the designer's plans he learns the number of settings required, the complexity of the building job, and the general scheme by which the scenery will be shifted. He must anticipate the need for special building materials and order them in time so that delivery can be made before they are required in the shop. It is on the basis of this study that he determines the sequence of construction. The experienced technician does not necessarily begin construction on the first set simply because it will be seen first by the audience. Experience has proved that if the order of construction is governed by the general rules listed below, the time required for completing the construction and rigging of the scenery can be noticeably reduced.

THE SEQUENCE OF CONSTRUCTION

1. List for immediate construction the practical parts of the setting that could be used to good advantage by the actors during early rehearsals.
2. Follow these by constructing units that will be shifted by flying. Additional time is usually required for rigging and trimming flown units. This operation can best be done when the stage is comparatively clear of other scenery.
3. Next in order of construction should be parts of settings scheduled for an elaborate and time-consuming paint job.
4. The order in which the remaining scenery is built is determined by its degree of complexity, the more easily and rapidly built pieces being reserved for the last.
5. Allow adequate time for a trial setup of the scenery and for adjustments in the rigging and stage hardware.

WORKING DRAWINGS

It has been pointed out that the designer's plans are mechanical drawings used for the express purpose of describing the setting. The designer is interested in representing the front, or on-stage side, of the scenery and in the adjustment and placement of the features that will contribute to the compositional effect of the design. Since the details of construction can be shown only by a drawing representing the rear, or off-stage side, of the scenery, the techni-

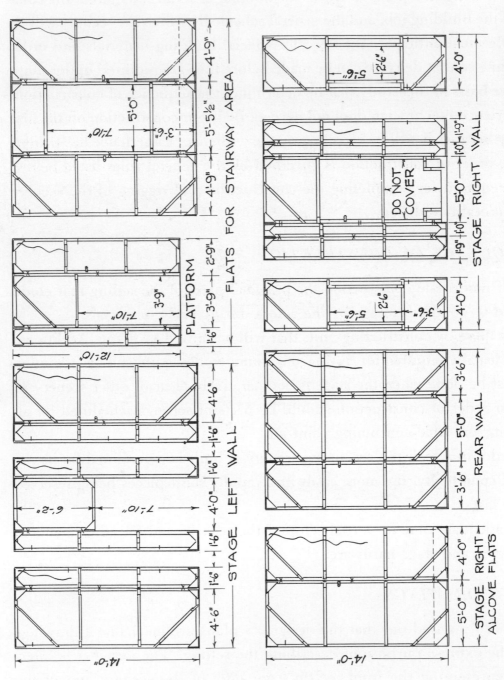

WORKING DRAWINGS
OF FLAT WORK FOR
BLITHE SPIRIT

Scale ¼" = 1'-0"

PLATE 7

cian makes a completely new set of plates called the working drawings. These are scaled mechanical drawings representing the rear view of the scenery; they indicate clearly what material should be used, size and form of separate members, and how these separate members will be joined to form the whole. They are accompanied by all necessary dimensions and specifications. There is no better way to assure a true realization of the designer's plans than to have an accurate and complete set of working drawings (Plate 7). The little additional time required to make them is more than offset by being able to detect and correct possible mistakes on the plans before they have been translated into lumber and canvas. A complete set of working drawings is especially desirable for the technician working in the educational or community theatre, where the majority of the building crew will be inexperienced students or volunteer workers.

In comparing the designer's elevations with the working drawings, it will be noticed that the latter not only represents the rear as opposed to the front view, but that the order of the flats has been reversed. The first flats drawn in the working drawings are those forming the stage left wall; successive flats are shown in their proper order and the drawing terminates with the flats forming the stage right wall. Unless this procedure is followed, the entire setting will be reversed—a mistake which happens with surprising frequency with inexperienced draftsmen. They must train themselves to visualize the setting as they will see it from backstage.

The working drawings should be complete enough to provide the building carpenter with all information he will need to build the setting without frequent conferences with the technician. Verbal instructions are all too frequently inadequate, inaccurate, and unreliable. A complete set of working drawings will show the following:

1. How the setting has been subdivided to form units for easy handling, shifting, and storage.
2. The number and size of each member composing a unit.
3. How these members are to be joined.
4. The placing and number required of all lashing, bracing, and rigging hardware.

5. Proper allowances in size of openings for detachable door or window units or in the width of units to be joined by lashing.
6. Special construction or framing required for rigging, shifting, or flying scenery.
7. Explanatory notes or specifications concerning building materials or procedures other than standard.

WORK SCHEDULE

In many theatrical-producing groups the approach of the opening date for a production is accompanied by a feverish increase of activity in the scene shop and on stage, often culminating in one or two all-night sessions for members of the paint, stage, and light crews. In some weird fashion such activity is associated with the old cliché of "The show must go on!" It is looked upon as something of a lark and an indispensable part of the business of producing a play. Nothing could be farther from the truth. Rather, it can be looked upon as proof that the technical work has been poorly planned, or more likely not planned at all.

In the majority of cases the technician can avoid this type of complication by planning his work in advance and then sticking to the dates established by his work schedule. It requires only a little time to make out such a schedule, and there is no greater aid to an even distribution of the work load over a period of time than the utilization of such a plan. A work schedule is simply a calendar in reverse. It begins with the date that the production is to open, then, working backwards, it lists the days set aside for dress rehearsals and technical rehearsal, the days required for rigging, painting, construction, etc. A sample of the work schedule for a single-set production such as *Blithe Spirit* is given below:

October 24	Opening of production.
October 23	Dress rehearsal.
October 22	Dress rehearsal.
October 21	Dress rehearsal.
October 20	Sunday.
October 19	Technical rehearsal, final adjustment of lights, properties, and setting.
October 18	Assemble setting on stage, adjustment

	of lights, touch up painting. Assemble floor properties.
October 17	Complete painting.
October 16	Painting.
October 15	Begin painting. All scenic construction to be completed. Start construction of props.
October 14	Construction.
October 13	Sunday.
October 12–7	Construction. Begin assembly of hand properties.
October 6	Sunday.
October 5	Begin construction.
October 4	Finish working drawings. Complete cost estimates.
October 3	Begin drafting of working drawings.
October 2	Sunday.
October 1	Receipt of designer's plans. Analysis of production. Order building materials.

As the number of settings or their complexity is increased, the greater becomes the need for a carefully planned work schedule. The technician will soon learn that it is possible to carry on several phases of the work simultaneously. For example, the construction of the first setting can be under way at the same time that he is completing the working drawings for the second set, or the scenery for act II can be painted while the completed setting for act I is being rigged.

The dress rehearsals are used by the director to bring together and synchronize all elements of the production. This process of polishing the production should not be handicapped by frantic last-minute operations by members of the technical staff and their crews. The technician who has pride in his work will have so planned and executed his assignment that the dress rehearsals can be used for the purpose for which they were intended.

chapter III

the scene shop

THE material offered in this chapter and in Chapter IV is basic to an understanding of scenic construction. Before any detailed account can be given of construction or rigging techniques, it is advisable for the student to understand to what a great extent his work can be improved and made easier by having a properly planned scene shop and by knowing the characteristics and peculiarities of the tools and materials with which he will be working. This is not meant to imply that good work cannot be done under conditions that are less than ideal—such a statement could be belied by the work of too many producing theatre groups. However, some of the suggestions made here can be adapted and used to improve existing shop conditions and to make possible a better selection of tools and materials.

A recent study conducted at the University of Iowa reveals that there has been little standardization within colleges and universities in planning and equipping the scene shop—in fact, it would appear that very little thought has been given to the subject. Answers to a questionnaire that was a part of this study indicated that the theatre's scene shop could be found in such unlikely locations as an old two-car garage, a church, abandoned barracks, unused class-rooms, under the stadium, or in the basement under the stage. Apparently it is felt that any space left over after all other activities of the theatre have been housed is quite satisfactory. This attitude has seriously impaired the efficiency of some otherwise well-planned theatre plants. The scene shop is much more than just a space where scenery can be built; it is in every sense a classroom or laboratory where students are taught the fundamentals of stagecraft and are provided an opportunity to learn the importance of organization and coöperation—a place where they may develop a sense of responsibility.

Thought and care is as important in planning a scene shop as it is in planning laboratories used for physics or chemistry. A fact not appreciated by some who have been responsible for planning our educational theatres is that the number of student hours spent in the shop in building, painting, and assembling scenery will equal or exceed the total time spent by the cast in rehearsing the production. The efficiency and safety of all operations performed within the shop is dependent upon how well the shop has been planned.

PHYSICAL REQUIREMENTS OF THE SCENE SHOP

The construction of scenery parallels the pattern of operations found in the manufacture of any product; that is, raw materials enter one end of the shop and after a series of progressive steps the finished product emerges from the other. A list of the operational steps normally accomplished within the limits of the scene shop provides the basis for determining the actual size and form of the space devoted to these purposes. Several of these constructional operations demand much floor space to be accomplished expeditiously. Probably more than any other factor the failure to understand or appreciate these basic requirements has resulted in shops so limited in floor space or height that their efficiency has been greatly reduced (Plate 8). The chart that follows lists both the operational steps and the type of space needed to accomplish them.

Operational Steps	*Type of Space Required*
1. Storage of new materials	Horizontal and vertical
2. Storage of stock scenery	Vertical
3. Marking and cutting lumber	Horizontal
4. Framing and alteration	Horizontal
5. Covering	Horizontal
6. Joining	Horizontal
7. Placement of hardware	Horizontal
8. Trial setup	Horizontal and vertical
9. Painting	Vertical
10. Storage of hand tools	Vertical
11. Storage of theatrical hardware	Vertical
12. Placement of power tools	Horizontal

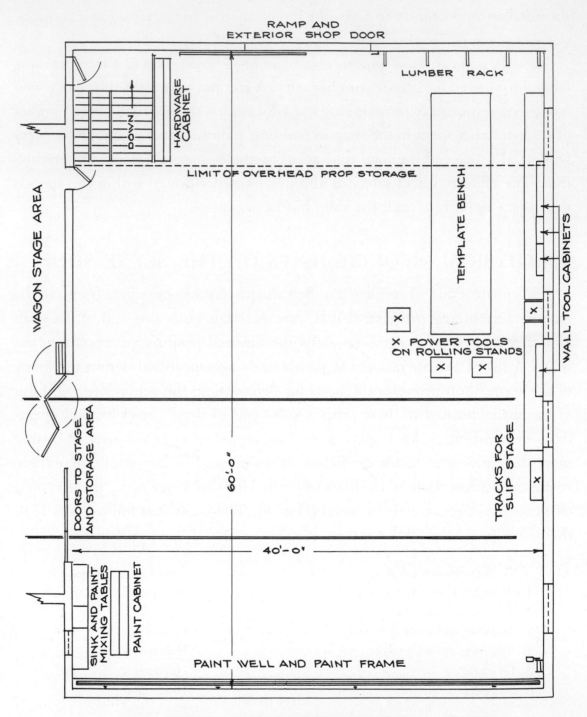

RAMP AND
EXTERIOR SHOP DOOR

LUMBER RACK

HARDWARE CABINET

DOWN

LIMIT OF OVERHEAD PROP STORAGE

WAGON STAGE AREA

TEMPLATE BENCH

X POWER TOOLS
ON ROLLING STANDS

WALL TOOL CABINETS

DOORS TO STAGE
AND STORAGE AREA

60'-0"

TRACKS FOR
SLIP STAGE

40'-0"

SINK AND PAINT
MIXING TABLES

PAINT CABINET

PAINT WELL AND PAINT FRAME

THE SCENE SHOP AT THE UNIVERSITY OF IOWA

PLATE 8

STORAGE OF NEW MATERIAL

Lumber and compositional and covering material constitute most of the new material for which storage facilities should be provided. Of these the placing and space required for the storage of lumber is the most important. The lumber rack should be placed as near the shop loading door as possible to avoid interrupting building operations that may be in progress at the time the lumber is delivered. Less floor space is required for this storage if some type of lumber rack is developed. One of the better types is a series of shelves formed by strap-iron brackets bolted solidly to the wall. Several comparatively narrow shelves are better than one or two deep ones, as this conserves floor space and provides individual spaces for varying widths of lumber.

Where space permits, compositional material such as plywood and beaver-board is stored on its face. Since this material is sold in sheets 4'-0" wide and 8'-0" to 10'-0" long, it may not be possible to allow adequate floor space for storing it. In this case the following substitute can be used: two rigid wood frames about 6'-0" high and 3'-6" wide and bolted 8" apart at right angles to a wall. The compositional material is slipped between these supporting frames and stored on end.

Canvas or muslin covering material is usually sold in rolls of 50 or 100 yards. A pipe slipped through the center of the roll and supported on brackets attached to the end of the template bench makes a convenient way of storing and handling this material.

STORAGE OF SCENERY

One of the heaviest cost items in the production of plays is the construction of scenery. The personnel of educational and community theatres have wisely tried to keep this item at a minimum by reusing scenery built for previous productions. However, the number of times stock scenery can be reused is largely dependent upon the degree of care given it in handling and the kind of storage provided for it.

There are two basic requirements for scenery storage docks: they should be in or near the scene shop, and they should be designed in such a manner that flats may be taken from them or stored in them with a minimum of effort. Scene docks located on a floor level different from the shop or in some distant building are not only inconvenient to use but have a tendency to defeat the very purpose for which scenery is stored, namely, its reuse. To prevent damage resulting from mildew, water stains, and warping, care must be used to select a dry, well-ventilated storage space. There is less danger of torn canvas or warped frames if the flats are stored in a vertical position and at right angles to a wall. Pipe or 2″ x 4″ framing partitions divide the storage area into compartments for different types of flats. Such an arrangement makes it easy to slip a flat in or out of the dock.

The extent of available storage space will determine the amount of bulky three-dimensional scenery that can be kept for possible reuse. Units such as doors, windows, fireplaces, or stairways that are both heavy and space-consuming are normally dismantled at the close of a production and all reusable material salvaged. Experience has proved that units of this type are seldom reused without major alterations.

Both rigid and folding platforms are usually kept as part of the stock scenery. Rigid platforms and the tops of the parallels can be stored vertically by leaning them against a wall. Supporting frames of the parallels are best stored by stacking them on top of each other.

MEASURING AND CUTTING LUMBER

Most new lumber used in the construction of scenery is ordered in the proper width for a specific purpose rather than in a wider width that must then be ripped to size. There are two advantages to this procedure: it eliminates the work of having to rip and dress the lumber, and it is less expensive. (The price of white pine increases about 1¢ a board foot for stock 10″ and 12″ wide.)

It is important that lumber can be moved from its storage rack to the work table and the power saw where it will be cut without interfering with other shop operations. The actual selection and marking of material is done by the shop foreman, who, because of his knowledge of building procedure and materials on hand for reuse, is better qualified to make such decisions. Each piece so marked for cutting is given an identification number or letter that aids in the assembly of the unit and helps avoid possible loss.

Most power sawing of lumber is crosscutting, which can be best accomplished by a pull-over or radial saw. When these saws are mounted with the cutting table flush with the top of the adjacent work benches, an ideal surface is provided for both measuring and cutting.

Unless there are adequate crew members available to assemble the flat frames as the lumber is cut, it is well not to precut more than two or three flats at a time. This will avoid the possibility of misplacing some of the cut lumber or having it used for other purposes.

FRAMING AND ALTERING

The process of assembling the cut lumber into flat frames can be greatly speeded and made less tiring for crew members if a template bench is used. This is a heavy work table 6'-0" wide and 18'-0" or 20'-0" long. A raised edge along two sides of the bench forms an accurate right angle that can be used to good advantage in aligning flat frames. When the template bench is located near the measuring and cutting table, minimum time is required to move cut material from one to the other. It is extremely important that the template bench be placed in such a position that working space is available on all four sides.

There are two types of templates: one has a solid work top; the other has a partial or skeletal top and is used in many professional studios. While the latter is admirably suited for mass production of standard flats, it is poorly suited for general work. A template bench with a solid worktop is best suited for the nonprofessional theatre, where as much work is done in altering old flats and in building properties as in constructing new scenery.

COVERING

One of the most critical steps in the construction of scenery is the process of covering the flat frames with canvas or muslin. This operation demands adequate floor space, as the flats must be placed in a horizontal position to receive the covering material. Should the template bench, which is ideal for the purpose, be in use, the flats can be supported on a series of saw horses or placed on the shop floor. Details of the various steps used in the process of covering flats will be discussed in a later chapter.

JOINING

The parts of a stage setting consisting of unbroken wall areas are usually formed by joining two or more standard plain flats edge to edge. Such flats are usually joined by hinging them on the face and concealing the junction and hinges with a strip of canvas or muslin tacked and glued into position. This procedure reduces the number of individual flats that must be handled and the number of lashings that must be made during the shift. The hinged flats form a compact unit that can be folded for easy handling and storage.

PLACEMENT OF HARDWARE

After the flats have been joined, they are turned face down to receive the lashing and bracing hardware. This is another operation demanding adequate floor space, as many of the larger units will be composed of two, three, or even four flats hinged together. The exact position for each piece of hardware has been determined by the technician and is clearly shown on the working drawings. However, it is a wise precaution to check the placement of all hardware to make sure that all items have been properly installed and are correctly aligned. Normally the hardware is not attached to the scenery until the flats have been covered and joined, as the lash lines, stiffening battens, and stop blocks prevent the flats from lying flat and complicate the process of covering and joining.

TRIAL SETUP

Whenever the nature of the design will permit, and there is the necessary floor space within the shop, the technician will arrange for a trial setup. This provides him with the opportunity of seeing that all parts of the setting have been built, that they are of the correct size and shape, and that they fit properly. It also provides him with an excellent chance to double-check the placement of all lashing and bracing hardware and to see the various parts of the setting standing in a vertical position as they will when placed on stage. Frequently he will find that some hardware has been omitted, that lash cleats have been placed too close to toggle bars, making it difficult for the thrown lash line to engage them, or he will find junctions between flats that need additional stop blocks or stop cleats to close them properly.

The trial setup insures the technician, before the painting is started, that he is delivering all parts of the setting to the designer. There is probably no omission quite so disturbing to the designer as the discovery that some small but critical flat has been overlooked in the building and its absence not noticed until the finished scenery is being assembled on stage for the first time. Corrections that must be made in the finished paint job due to such omissions and to unforseen alterations are difficult to accomplish and costly in time and effort. Such mistakes can be detected in advance by the trial setup and the necessary steps taken to correct them. Should there be inadequate space within the shop to accommodate a full set of scenery, the same information can be obtained by a partial trial setup. Adjacent units of scenery are tested one against the other for proper fit and size.

SCENE PAINTING EQUIPMENT

Contrary to the practice followed in the professional theatre, where the scenery is built in one studio and painted in another, the scene shop of the majority of educational and community theatres is planned to provide the necessary facilities for both construction and painting of scenery. The reason for this arrangement is twofold: it not only conserves space, but, more important, it allows one person to supervise both operations.

The painting of scenery is the last operation to be performed in the shop before the scenery is moved to the stage. This means that in order to reduce the distance the finished scenery must be moved and to avoid interrupting other building operations, the paint frame should be located as near to the stage entrance as possible.

The amount of equipment needed for painting is comparatively modest but extremely important. There must be an unbroken expanse of wall area where the paint frame can be located, there must be a sink with hot and cold running water, and there must be a mixing table with storage bins for brushes and scene paint.

THE COUNTERWEIGHTED PAINT FRAME

The counterweighted paint frame (Plate 9, Fig. 1) is a large wooden frame, usually made of $1\frac{1}{4}''$ x 6" lumber, to which the scenery can be temporarily

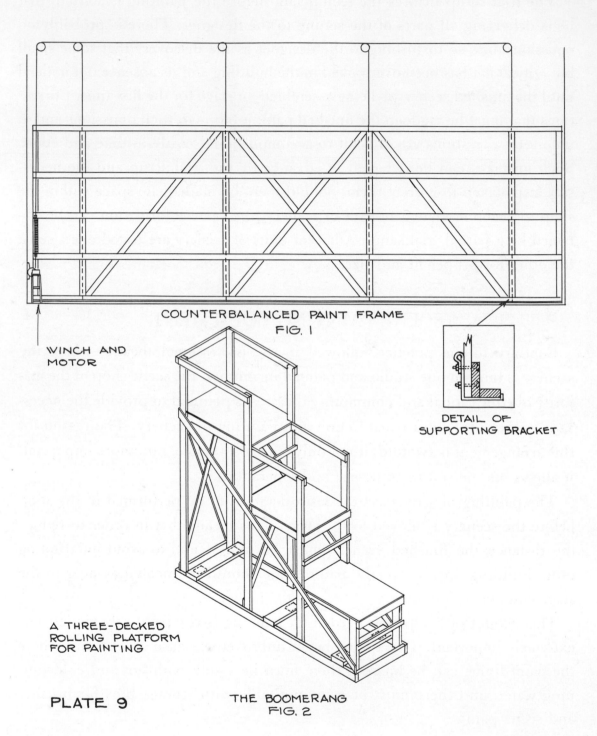

COUNTERBALANCED PAINT FRAME
FIG. 1

WINCH AND
MOTOR

DETAIL OF
SUPPORTING BRACKET

A THREE-DECKED
ROLLING PLATFORM
FOR PAINTING

PLATE 9

THE BOOMERANG
FIG. 2

nailed to hold it in a vertical position while it is being painted. The paint frame is suspended from a series of steel cables running over loft and head blocks to a counterweight arbor. A hand-powered or electrically driven winch can be used to lower and raise the frame through a slot in the floor. This arrangement permits the scenery to be lowered to a point where the tops of the flats can be painted from the shop floor. The counterweighted paint frame provides marked advantages over any other method of painting: it requires very little shop space, it affords a much faster method of painting, and it is much safer as it eliminates the need for ladder painting.

THE STATIONARY PAINT FRAME

Should circumstances prevent the use of the counterweighted paint frame, a substitute stationary paint frame can be used. Horizontal battens of 2″ x 2″ stock are spaced 3′ or 4′ apart and toggle-bolted to the wall. The scenery is nailed in a vertical position to the battens, and the painting is done from a two- or three-level rolling platform called a boomerang.

THE BOOMERANG

This rolling platform (Plate 9, Fig. 2) can be easily constructed in the scene shop of $1\frac{1}{4}″$ x 3″ stock. The height and the number of painting levels is determined by the height of the stock scenery. The top level of the platform should be high enough to permit a painter to reach the top of the flats, while the lower levels are spaced to permit an easy overlap of the painter's work. There should be adequate space on each level for the painter's brushes and equipment, with guard rails fitted to the upper levels. In spite of the floor space occupied by the boomerang when it is not in use it proves to be an invaluable and flexible piece of equipment. It is not only safer and much easier to paint from than ladders, but it can be rolled on stage and used as a rigging platform, a temporary off-stage stairway, or a rolling platform for tower lights.

ROLLING PAINT PALETTE

One of the most useful pieces of paint shop equipment is the rolling paint palette, which is used in detail painting and as a mixing table for small quantities of scene paint (Plate 10, Fig. 6). This is a work table mounted on castors, with the top surface covered with sheet aluminium or copper. Along one side of the table top is a series of small, covered compartments, each holding $\frac{1}{2}$ or 1 pound of dry scene paint. The painter charges a brush with sizing water and dips it into the desired pigment which is then worked to the proper painting consistency on the table top in much the same manner that an artist uses a hand palette. When it is not being used for detail work, the palette can be employed as a convenient work table on which heavy buckets of paint can be placed and rolled to the point of work. The lower portion of the table can be built to form compartments for the storage of brushes, paint containers, and other equipment.

MIXING TABLES

Flanking the sink with its faucets for hot and cold water are the mixing tables. These are sheet metal covered drain boards providing work table surface for mixing scene paint, washing brushes and paint containers. A gas burner stove or an electric double-boiler glue pot is usually kept on one of the mixing tables. Space under the mixing tables should not be used for storing dry scene paint, as there is too much risk of spoilage due to water or glue seepage. The sink should be equipped with an easily accessible oversized trap that can be cleaned readily, as all waste paint is disposed of by diluting it with water and allowing it to drain from the sink.

PAINT BINS AND BRUSH STORAGE

The paint bins should keep pigment dry and free of dust, they should be conveniently located to the mixing table, and each bin should be capable of holding 35 to 40 pounds of dry pigment. If wall space is not available for the bins, a rolling storage rack can be constructed to serve the same purpose. Several types of bins have proved satisfactory and can be housed in the rack. They may be of regular drawer construction, or compartments hinged at the bottom and capable of tipping out at the top, much like the old-fashioned flour bins. (See Plate 10, Fig. 5.) Small covered garbage cans make excellent bins when stored at an angle in the rack. Good, inexpensive substitutes for these are reclaimed 20-gallon lard tins.

A section of the upper part of the storage rack can be built with ventilated locked cupboards for storing brushes. Drill a hole in the handle of each brush

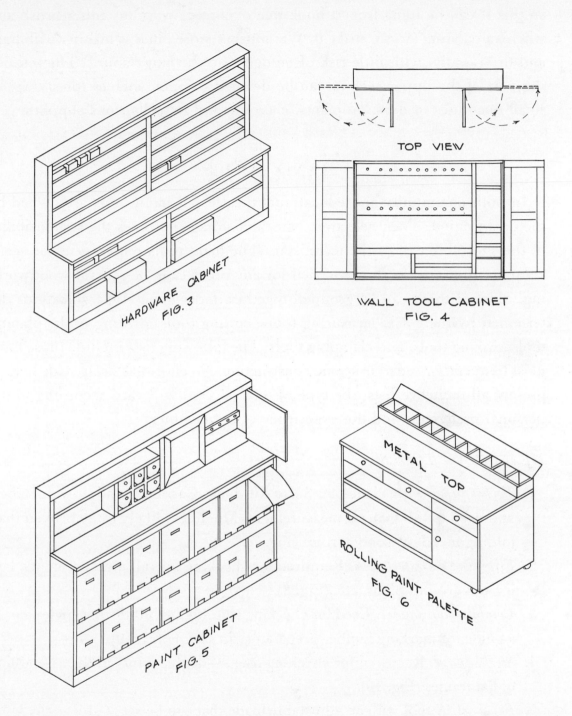

HARDWARE CABINET
FIG. 3

TOP VIEW

WALL TOOL CABINET
FIG. 4

METAL TOP

ROLLING PAINT PALETTE
FIG. 6

PAINT CABINET
FIG. 5

PLATE 10

so that it can be hung from a hook free of contact with any other brush and where circulating air can strike it. Wet brushes stored in this manner will drain and dry rapidly, with little risk of mildew or of turning "sour." The remaining part of the upper section can be devoted to open shelves for storage of small quantities of dyes, oil paints, charcoal, and miscellaneous supplies.

HAND TOOLS

In both community and educational theatres all hand tools are owned by the organization. Their selection, care, and storage becomes the responsibility of the shop foreman or the technician. The hand tools required in the scene shop are the same as those needed for any other type of general woodworking. Most of them can be grouped together under general classifications determined by their use: measuring tools, cutting tools, drilling tools, planing tools, driving tools, and clamping tools. The following lists include those tools most frequently needed in scenic construction. No effort has been made here to present all-inclusive lists; the type of tool selected will vary according to the personal preference and the experience of the technician.

MEASURING TOOLS

1. *Pocket tapes* with blades 6′, 8′, or 10′ long. Carried by all crew members and used for all general measurement. Much less likely to be broken than folding metal or wooden rules (Fig. 7).
2. *Fifty-foot roll-steel tape.* Required for checking overall measurements, laying out ground plans, etc. (Fig. 8).
3. *Combination square.* Used for checking true 45- and 90-degree angles and as a guide for marking lumber preparatory to sawing (Fig. 9).
4. *Steel square.* Required for checking true 90-degree joints in the assembling of flat frames (Fig. 10).
5. *Bevel set.* A tool with an adjustable blade that can be set at any angle. Used as an aid in marking lumber and checking the accuracy of angular joints (Fig. 11).
6. *Mortise gauge.* A measuring tool used in scribing a line parallel with the length of lumber or across the width and thickness of stock (Fig. 12).

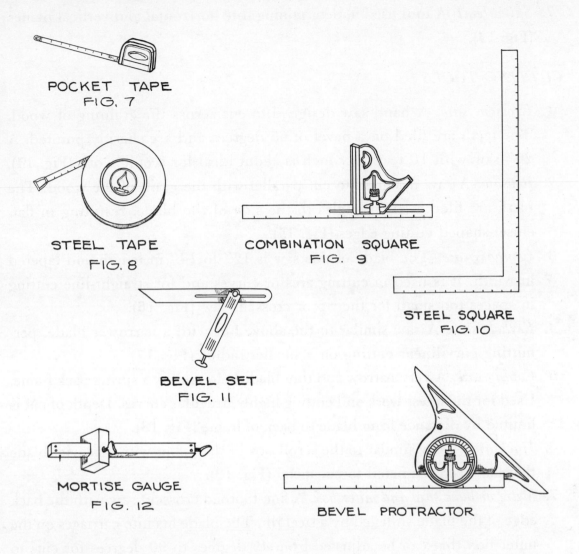

POCKET TAPE
FIG. 7

STEEL TAPE
FIG. 8

COMBINATION SQUARE
FIG. 9

STEEL SQUARE
FIG. 10

BEVEL SET
FIG. 11

MORTISE GAUGE
FIG. 12

BEVEL PROTRACTOR

SPIRIT LEVEL
FIG. 13

MEASURING TOOLS

PLATE 11

7. *Spirit level.* A tool used in determining true horizontal and vertical planes (Fig. 13).

CUTTING TOOLS

1. *Crosscut saw.* A hand saw designed to cut across the graining of wood. The teeth are filed on a bevel of 65 degrees and are sharply pointed. A 26″-saw with 10 teeth per inch is about ideal for scenic work (Fig. 14).

2. *Ripsaw.* A saw designed to cut parallel with the grain of the wood. The teeth are filed at right angles to the side of the blade, resulting in flat, chisel-shaped cutting edges (Fig. 15).

3. *Compass saw.* The blade of this saw is 12″ to 14″ in length and tapered in width. It is used in cutting arcs or curves and for straight-line cutting in spaces too small for the rip or crosscut saw (Fig. 16).

4. *Keyhole saw.* A saw similar to the above but with a narrower blade, permitting curvilinear cutting on a smaller radius (Fig. 17).

5. *Coping saw.* A very narrow and thin blade held taut by a spring back frame. Used for the finest work and cutting highly irregular curves. Depth of cut is limited by distance from blade to back of frame (Fig. 18).

6. *Hacksaw.* A saw similar to the scroll saw in shape but with a heavier blade that has been tempered to cut metal (Fig. 19).

7. *Miter or back saw and miter box.* A fine-toothed crosscut saw with the back edge of the blade stiffened by a steel rib. The blade fits into carriages on the miter box that can be adjusted from 45 degrees to 90 degrees for cuts to either left or right. The carriages hold and guide the saw in making accurate right-angle or angular cuts (Fig. 20).

8. *Tin shears.* A cutting tool similar to a pair of scissors but differing from them in the greater length of the handles from the pivot point (for greater leverage) and by the fact that the cutting blades have been tempered to cut metal (Fig. 21).

DRILLING TOOLS

1. *The brace.* A tool designed for clamping and turning a wood bit. It is provided with two handles, a pivot handle, and an offset crank handle by which the bit is rotated. Better-quality braces are fitted with a ratchet,

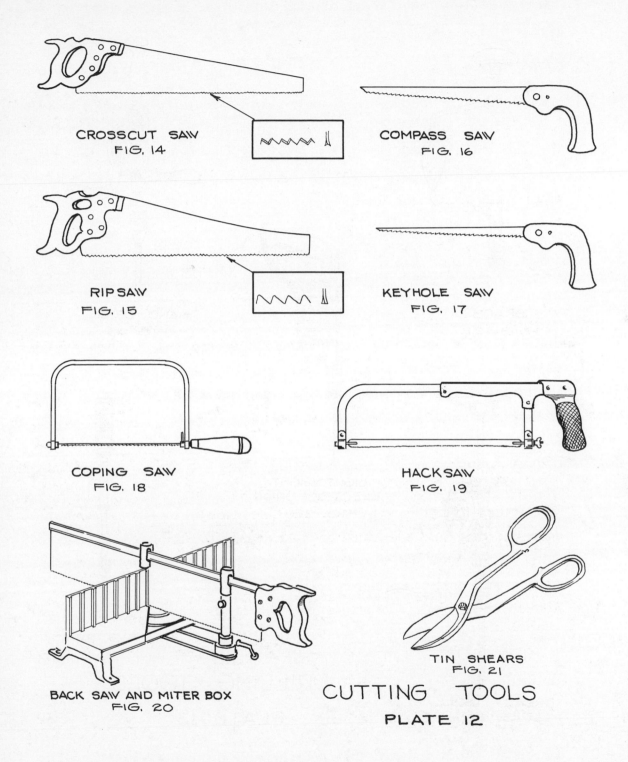

CROSSCUT SAW
FIG. 14

COMPASS SAW
FIG. 16

RIP SAW
FIG. 15

KEYHOLE SAW
FIG. 17

COPING SAW
FIG. 18

HACK SAW
FIG. 19

BACK SAW AND MITER BOX
FIG. 20

TIN SHEARS
FIG. 21

CUTTING TOOLS
PLATE 12

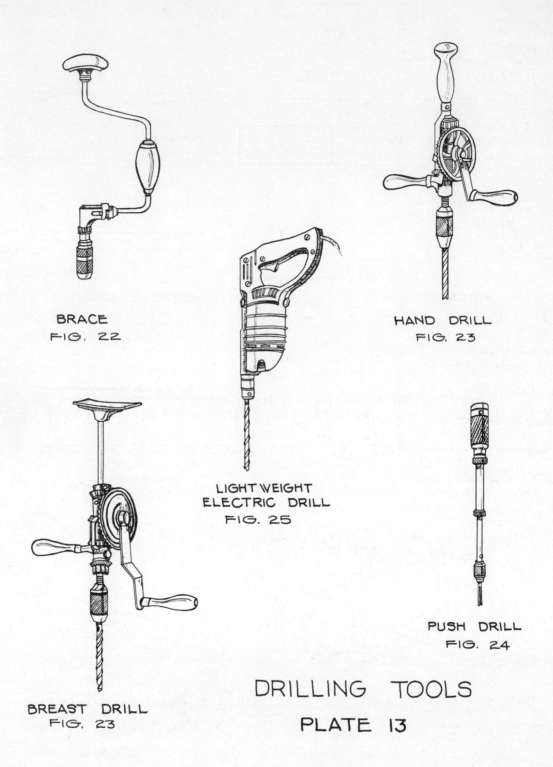

BRACE
FIG. 22

HAND DRILL
FIG. 23

LIGHT WEIGHT
ELECTRIC DRILL
FIG. 25

PUSH DRILL
FIG. 24

BREAST DRILL
FIG. 23

DRILLING TOOLS
PLATE 13

needed for work in close quarters, that permits the bit to be driven forward with a back-and-forth motion of the crank handle. Wood-cutting bits increase in diameter size by $\frac{1}{16}''$ and may be obtained in sizes from $\frac{1}{4}''$ to $1''$. Expansion bits, with an adjustable cutter blade, can be used for drilling holes from $\frac{7}{8}''$ up to $3''$ in diameter (Fig. 22).

2. *Hand drill.* Straight-shanked twist drills are clamped tightly by the jaws of this tool and rotated by turning a small geared wheel. The chuck of the average hand drill will not accommodate drills with a diameter larger than $\frac{1}{4}''$. Twist drills are tempered for work in both metal and wood (Fig. 23).

3. *Breast drill.* Similar to the hand drill but heavier in construction and capable of handling drills up to $\frac{1}{2}''$ in diameter. The gearing of this drill can be shifted from slow to fast speed and the frame is equipped with a bracket or strap against which the workman can lean to gain greater cutting pressure (Fig. 23).

4. *Push drill.* A straight-shafted tool fitted with spring return spirals that rotate the chuck and bit by pressure on the handle. Designed for light work (Fig. 24).

PLANING TOOLS

1. *Canvas knife.* Any good-quality straight-shafted knife with a blade $2''$ or $3''$ long has innumerable uses in the shop besides that of trimming the excess canvas from flat frames.

2. *Wood chisel.* Straight-shafted cutting or paring tool fitted with wooden handles, used by tapping the handle with a mallet or the heel of the hand. Chisels come in a variety of widths from $\frac{1}{4}''$ to $1\frac{1}{2}''$. They are not used extensively in rough construction work but become essential in hand working many wood joints (Fig. 26).

3. *Cold chisel.* Resembles a wood chisel but is made without a wooden handle and has a cutting edge tempered to be used on metal (Fig. 27).

4. *Drawknife.* Has an elongated cutting edge with handles at either end placed at right angles with the blade. Used for rough shaping or planing (Fig. 28).

5. *Spokeshave.* The cutting blade of the spokeshave is housed in a metal

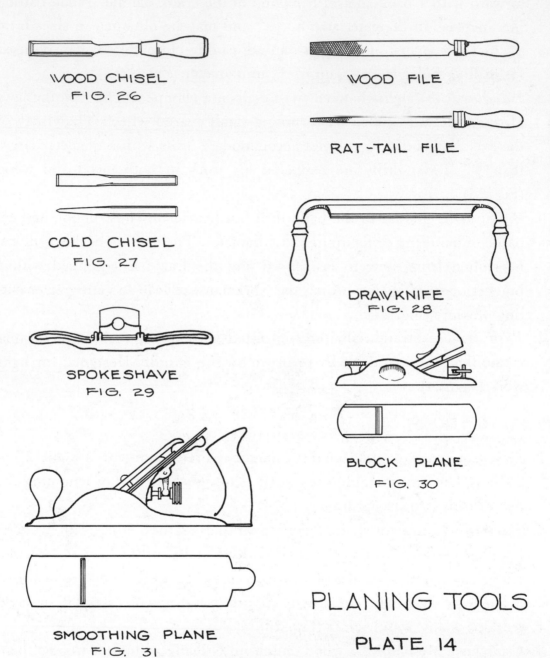

WOOD CHISEL
FIG. 26

WOOD FILE

RAT-TAIL FILE

COLD CHISEL
FIG. 27

DRAWKNIFE
FIG. 28

SPOKESHAVE
FIG. 29

BLOCK PLANE
FIG. 30

SMOOTHING PLANE
FIG. 31

PLANING TOOLS

PLATE 14

frame with adjustments for regulating the depth of the cut. It is capable of finer work than the drawknife (Fig. 29).

6. *Block plane.* The cutting blade of the block plane is set in the housing frame at a 20-degree angle and is capable of fine adjustment. Used for cutting at right angles with the grain of the wood (Fig. 30).

7. *Smoothing plane.* Similar in design to the block plain but has a wider blade and a longer and heavier frame. Used for smoothing faces or edges of lumber. There is a great variety of planes designed for specific purposes, but there is little need for them in the normal construction operations of the scene shop (Fig. 31).

DRIVING TOOLS

1. *Claw hammer.* The two curved jaws extending out from the back of the head are designed for pulling nails and are better suited to this purpose than those found on the rip hammer (Fig. 32).

2. *Rip hammer.* The straighter claws of this type of hammer are well suited to prying apart joined lumber (Fig. 33).

3. *Ball peen hammer.* A machinist's hammer. In place of claws this hammer has a second rounded striking face, used in shaping metal or in riveting (Fig. 34).

4. *Upholsterer's tack hammer.* Has a light, double-faced head with one face magnetized to hold tracks (Fig. 35).

5. *Engineer's hammer.* A heavy (1 to 3 pounds) double-faced hammer with one face wedge-shaped, used for pounding and bending strap iron into shape (Fig. 36).

6. *Spring-driven staple tacker.* A stapling gun that operates by pressing a lever which cocks and releases a spring that drives the staple. Easier for the beginner to operate than the staple hammer, as the tacker can be carefully positioned before the staple is driven (Fig. 37).

7. *Stapling hammer.* Holds a magazine of staples that are automatically placed in position and driven home with each blow of the hammer (Fig. 38).

8. *Nail puller.* A tool for pulling nails whose heads have been driven flush with the surface of the wood. The jaws are driven down on either side

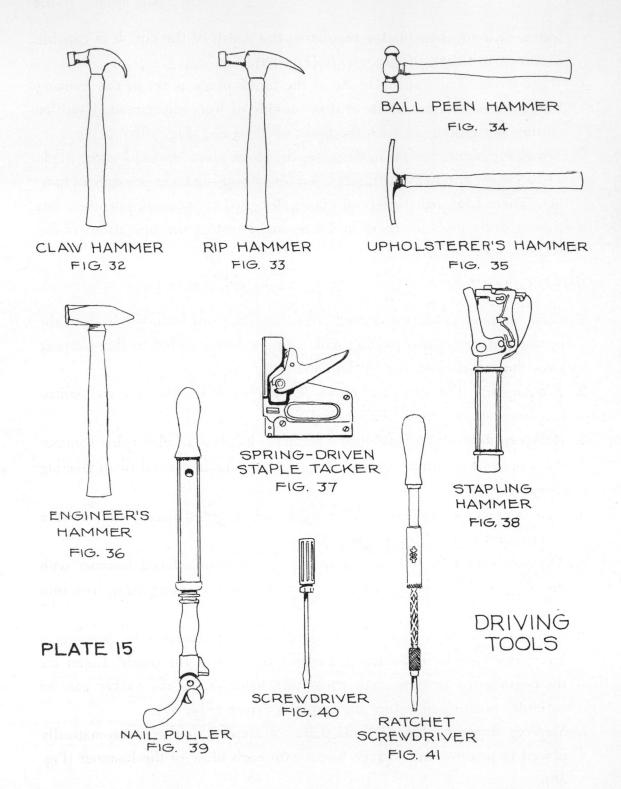

BALL PEEN HAMMER
FIG. 34

CLAW HAMMER
FIG. 32

RIP HAMMER
FIG. 33

UPHOLSTERER'S HAMMER
FIG. 35

SPRING-DRIVEN
STAPLE TACKER
FIG. 37

STAPLING
HAMMER
FIG. 38

ENGINEER'S
HAMMER
FIG. 36

PLATE 15

DRIVING
TOOLS

SCREWDRIVER
FIG. 40

RATCHET
SCREWDRIVER
FIG. 41

NAIL PULLER
FIG. 39

of the nail head by striking the hollow metal handle sharply against the stops. The leverage offered by the long handle makes it easy to remove nails (Fig. 39).

9. *Screwdriver*. A shaft of metal fitted with a wooden or plastic handle; the end of the shaft is shaped to fit the slot in the head of a screw (Fig. 40).

10. *Ratchet screwdriver*. One of the most useful tools in the scene shop. The spiral shaft of this tool permits screws to be driven or extracted by direct pressure on the handle rather than by rotation of the tool (Fig. 41).

CLAMPING TOOLS

1. *Pliers*. For holding, clamping, gripping, cutting, or bending and for working in restricted quarters too small to be reached by fingers. Slip-joint sheep-nosed pliers (Fig. 42), needle-nosed pliers, diagonal-cutting pliers, and electrician's pliers are considered essential for scene shop work.

2. *Adjustable-end wrench*. By turning a knurled screw the jaws of this wrench can be fitted to different sized bolts and nuts. The 6″, 8″, and 10″ sizes are satisfactory for most shop needs (Fig. 43).

3. *Monkey wrench*. A wrench with adjustable jaws; in the 12″ size it can be used for heavier work than the smaller end wrenches (Fig. 44).

4. *Stillson pipe wrench*. The jaws of this wrench are made with corrugated teeth to grip a cylindrical form without slipping. It is well to have two of these wrenches on hand, one to hold the pipe, the other to turn the fitting (Fig. 45).

5. *C clamp*. This tool takes its name from the shape of the frame. It is designed to hold an object or to apply pressure to it by turning the threaded shaft which forces the object against the rigid jaw (Fig. 46).

6. *Jenson wood clamp*. The wooden jaws of this clamp are activated by two threaded shafts. By adjustments of these shafts the jaws may be set at various angles. Although designed to hold wood joints together while the glue dries, they have many other uses both in the shop and on stage (Fig. 47).

7. *Bar clamp*. A clamp, working on the same principle as the C clamp, but which can be extended to apply pressure across a greater distance (Fig. 48).

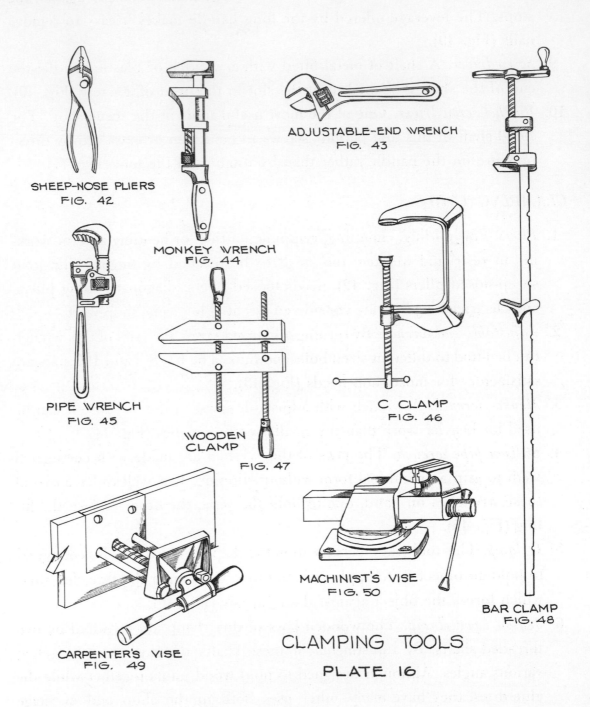

SHEEP-NOSE PLIERS
FIG. 42

ADJUSTABLE-END WRENCH
FIG. 43

MONKEY WRENCH
FIG. 44

PIPE WRENCH
FIG. 45

WOODEN
CLAMP
FIG. 47

C CLAMP
FIG. 46

MACHINIST'S VISE
FIG. 50

BAR CLAMP
FIG. 48

CARPENTER'S VISE
FIG. 49

CLAMPING TOOLS

PLATE 16

8. *Carpenter's vise.* This indispensable clamping or holding tool is used in a fixed position on the work bench. One or both of the steel jaws are lined with wood to prevent marring the objects held (Fig. 49).

9. *Machinist's vise.* Similar to the carpenter's vise, but of much stronger construction. Intended for metal work (Fig. 50).

MISCELLANEOUS TOOLS

1. *Pinch bar.* This tool is a lever of steel with one end shaped to form a tapering chisel-like prong and bent to provide a fulcrum foot. It is used for prying apart pieces of heavy lumber or moving an object by a series of short lifts. The opposite end of the bar is semicircular in shape and equipped with claws for extracting large nails.

2. *Clinch plates.* Six or eight of these plates are needed in even a modestly equipped shop. The clinch plate is made of $\frac{3}{16}''$ or $\frac{1}{4}''$ thick sheet iron cut about 12″ wide and from 14″ to 18″ long. As the frame of a flat is being assembled the clinch plate is slipped under the frame to bend over, or clinch, the projecting points of the clout nails.

3. *Electric glue pot.* Basically a double boiler with a thermostatically controlled heating element that makes it impossible to burn the glue.

STORAGE

STORAGE OF HAND TOOLS

The purchase of the hand tools listed above represents an investment of several hundred dollars. Since the care and maintenance of the tools is the responsibility of the technician, he must prevent them from being misplaced, lost, or stolen. Some technicians have attempted to solve this problem by maintaining a tool room with an attendant who issues tools to crew members as they are needed and later checks them in as they are returned. This scheme has not been too successful because of the difficulty and expense of keeping an attendant in charge at all times. Other technicians have tried issuing tool boxes containing the most commonly used tools to crew members and holding them responsible. Such a kit of tools would include a hammer, try square, rule, ratchet screwdriver, pliers, adjustable-end wrench, and a small hand drill.

However, since students are usually in a hurry when they leave the shop and not always careful about picking up their tools, tool kits are often checked in with some items missing or with a duplication of some tools.

A plan that has proved more satisfactory than most has been used in situations where a graduate student or full-time shop supervisor is in attendance in the shop throughout the day. Hand tools are under his immediate supervision and are kept in wall cabinets, from which they are selected by workers as they are needed (Plate 10, Fig. 4). The supervisor sees that tools are replaced when they are no longer needed and at the close of the work period makes sure that all tools are checked in before the students leave or the cabinets are locked.

STORAGE OF HARDWARE

Open-shelf storage for theatrical and joining hardware is usually satisfactory even in situations where it is impossible for the shop to be locked off from other parts of the theatre. Lightweight wooden boxes 4" high by 7" wide and 9" long are made for each type of item to be shelved (Plate 10, Fig. 3). The face of each box is clearly labeled with the name and size of the item and the boxes are placed on the shelves in alphabetical order. This method of storage provides for easy identification of the item and serves as a good teaching aid in giving the students an opportunity to see and handle all types of hardware.

POWER TOOLS

There is no question but that scenery can be built by the use of hand tools alone. However, with the purchase of a few carefully selected power tools the same results can be produced with a tremendous saving in both time and energy. The power tools listed below are mentioned here because experience has proved that these particular tools have been used extensively enough in the construction of scenery to warrant the money invested in them (Plate 17).

THE RADIAL SAW

The radial or "pull-over" circular saw (Fig. 51) is one of the most useful and flexible of all power tools. It is both safer and easier to use than the conventional table saw and it is ideally suited for crosscutting lumber. The motor and blade of this type of saw are mounted on a supporting arm which places them above the cutting table. This feature permits the saw to be placed near a wall with the tops of flanking work benches flush with the height of the saw's cutting table. Lumber laid on the work bench, preparatory to cutting, is then parallel with the wall and occupies a minimum of space. While the lumber is in this position, it can be measured and marked, then either ripped or crosscut without moving it from one part of the shop to another. Special accessories can convert this tool into a planer, a shaper, a router, a sander, a grinder, a wood drill, or a polisher.

THE BAND SAW

One of the most tedious and time-consuming hand-tool operations is curvilinear sawing. Since the narrow-bladed band saw is designed for this purpose, it becomes a power tool high on the technician's preference list (Fig. 52).

THE DRILL PRESS

Although designed for drilling holes in metal and wood, this tool is similar to the radial saw in that it can be adapted by the proper accessories for planing, sanding, carving, routing, shaping, or cutting either dovetail or mortise and tendon joints (Fig. 53).

THE PORTABLE SABRE SAW

Within the last few years this saw has been developed and perfected to a point where it is preferred by many to the larger space-consuming jig saw. The sabre saw was designed for cutting highly irregular shapes that cannot be cut on the band saw. Its narrow blade and its portability make it ideally suited for scenic construction (Fig. 54).

ELECTRIC HAND DRILLS

Much of the heavy drilling that must be done on stage in rigging scenery, or on large units such as rigid platforms, cannot be done with the conventional drill press because of its lack of portability. For this reason both lightweight and heavy-duty electric hand drills are considered essential tools by many technicians (Fig. 55 and Plate 13, Fig. 25).

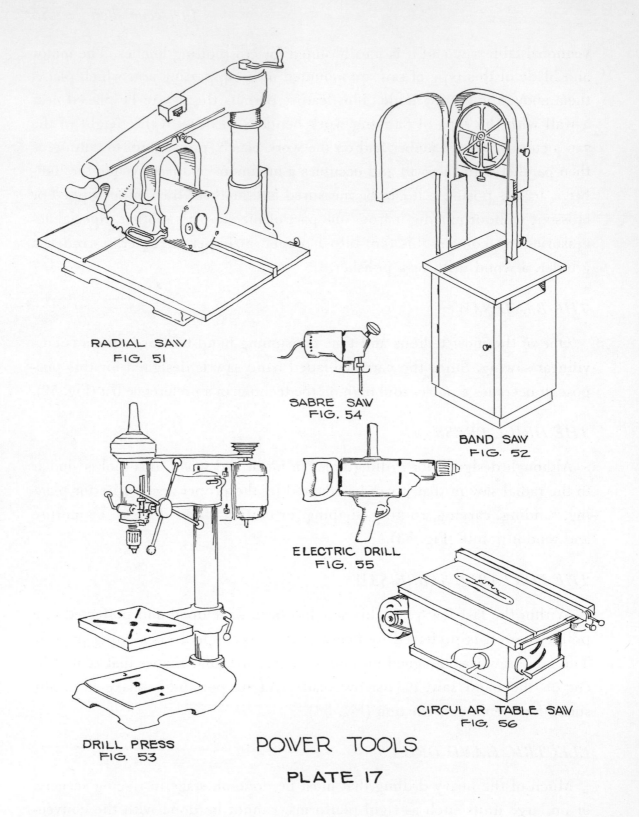

RADIAL SAW
FIG. 51

SABRE SAW
FIG. 54

BAND SAW
FIG. 52

ELECTRIC DRILL
FIG. 55

CIRCULAR TABLE SAW
FIG. 56

DRILL PRESS
FIG. 53

POWER TOOLS

PLATE 17

PLACEMENT OF POWER TOOLS

Because of the wide variety in form and size of stage settings and the resulting need for flexibility of floor space in the shop, every effort is usually made to avoid mounting power equipment in fixed positions. With the possible exception of the radial saw, all power equipment is mounted on castored tables with lock drawers capable of holding all of the accessories used by that particular tool. As a safety precaution, lock castors or a lift jack should be used to prevent the tool from creeping as it is being used. The flexibility offered by these rolling units makes it possible for power equipment to be moved from one part of the shop to another in order to clear floor space for certain constructional operations, or simply to bring the tool closer to the point of work.

chapter IV

building materials, wood joinery, and theatrical hardware

THE appearance and the life expectancy of a unit of stage scenery is dependent in part on the quality of the building materials from which it is made and in part on the skill and care used in the joining of its various parts. The technician who understands this and, more important, puts it into practice, has taken several important steps toward the following goals:

1. Improving the general standard of production.
2. Increasing the life expectancy of stock scenery.
3. Reducing the prorated cost of productions.
4. Reducing the time required for repair work.
5. Increasing the safety factor.

The more thoroughly the technician is acquainted with the characteristics of various kinds of building materials, the better qualified he is to make wise selections of the proper materials for specific jobs. A practice followed by many technicians is to make periodic visits to local lumber dealers to become familiar with the many new building materials being introduced to the market. Some of these products are adaptable for stage purposes and may prove to be excellent substitutes for heavier, weaker, or more expensive materials in current use.

The materials normally used in the construction of scenery fall into three general groups: (1) the lumber from which all supporting frames are constructed, (2) the joining materials used in holding the various parts of the frames together, and (3) the covering materials used to conceal the supporting frames.

LUMBER

Lumber to be suitable for scenic construction must be light in weight, strong, straight-grained, easily worked, well seasoned, free from any tendency to warp, and inexpensive. From the many woods normally handled by local lumber dealers only a few possess all of these characteristics. Among these are the following:

1. *Northern white pine.* This is excellent in all respects, but unfortunately, the supply is extremely limited and very little of it can be obtained in some areas, such as the Midwest.

2. *Idaho white pine.* Though the supply of this wood is somewhat limited, it may be obtained by special order or even found in local markets in certain areas. It is comparable to Northern white pine in its suitability for scenic work.

3. *Ponderosa pine.* Ponderosa pine, or West Coast yellow pine as it is sometimes called, is well suited for use in scenic construction, although it is somewhat heavier than either of the white pines mentioned. There is an adequate supply of this wood, and it sells at reasonable prices. Ponderosa pine should not be confused with other fast-growing, coarse-grained yellow pines that are too heavy and hard for anything but the roughest kind of stage work.

4. *Redwood.* This wood, like the Ponderosa pine, is a West Coast product and is usually carried in stock by most dealers. Although it meets most of the requirements for stage lumber, some of it is too soft and it has a slight tendency to splinter and split.

5. *West Coast red cedar.* This is a coarse-grained, lightweight wood that can be used for framing and in the construction of properties and trim. Some of it is too brittle to be used for large framing units.

6. *Douglas fir.* This is a coarser-grained and heavier wood than the others men-

tioned, but it is also the strongest and sells for about half the price of the others. It is used extensively for weight-bearing supports and platform framing. Standard sizes of this wood have a thickness of 2″.

QUALITY OF LUMBER

Variations in the quality of lumber are designated by a system of grading that uses "A" for perfect, "B" for next best, "C" for lumber with some slight imperfections, such as pin knots, and "D" for lumber with larger but sound knots. Below the grade of D the classifications continue with No. 1 Common, No. 2 Common, etc. So little available lumber falls within the A and B classifications that for all practical purposes they may be ignored. Not only are these grades almost impossible to obtain, but the price asked for them is prohibitive to all but those with the most expansive budgets. Most scenery is made from C-grade lumber. A few shops may make limited use of D-grade, but it is poorly suited for large framing units or weight-bearing structures.

DIMENSIONS OF STOCK LUMBER

Lumber is obtainable in a variety of standard sizes and dimensions. Thickness and width are designated in inches while length is specified in multiples of two feet. A length of stock lumber 1″ thick by 3″ wide and 14′-0″ long is written as 1″ x 3″ x 14′. Lumber for a specific job is ordered from standard sizes such as 1″ x 3″ or 1″ x 6″ in lengths that will produce the least wastage in cutting. It is well to understand that the lumber will not measure either a full 1″ in thickness or a full 3″ or 6″ in width, though the length will be full measure. Approximately $\frac{1}{4}$″ is lost from both thickness and width of all stock lumber during the process of finishing or dressing. Finished or dressed lumber has been planed smooth on both faces and edges.

The following chart lists the common stock sizes of lumber and the purposes for which they are normally used in scenic construction.

Stock Size *Thickness and Width*	*General Use*
1″ x 2″	Small flat frames, diagonal braces, small cutout frames
1″ x 3″	Standard flat frames

1″ x 4″	Large framing units, battens for drops and ceilings
1″ x 6″, 1″ x 8″	Door and window units, fireplaces, architectural trim
1″ x 10″, 1″ x 12″	Stairways, sweeps, properties, furniture
1¼″ x 3″	Oversized flats, heavy-duty parallel frames
2″ x 4″, 2″ x 6″, 2″ x 8″	Weight-bearing supports, frames, trusses
1″ x 4″, 1″ x 6″ (Tongue and groove flooring)	Platform flooring
1″ x 8″ (Car siding)	Platform flooring

COMPUTING THE COST OF LUMBER

The price of lumber varies according to its grade and is usually quoted per 1000 board feet. The board foot is a unit of measure that represents a piece of wood 1″ thick by 12″ wide by 12″ long. Given the price per 1000 board feet the price per single board foot is found by moving the decimal point three places to the left. For example, assuming that the quoted price for C-grade Ponderosa pine is $400.00 per 1000 board feet, the price per single board foot is found to be $.40.

Although lumber is sold by board feet, the technician invariably figures the amount of lumber he will need to complete a given job in terms of linear measurement or, for example, how many pieces of 1″ x 4″ x 16′-0″ would be required. It is then necessary for him to turn these linear measurements into board feet to find the cost.

To find the price of an order of 24 pieces of 1″ x 4″ x 16′-0″ C-grade white pine at 40¢ a board foot proceed as follows. Multiply the number of pieces by the length of one piece to get the total number of linear feet. Since a piece of 1″ x 4″ 1 foot long is $\frac{1}{3}$ of a board foot, divide the total number of linear feet by 3 to obtain the number of board feet. Multiply the number of board feet by the price per single board foot.

Example: Find the price of 24 pieces of 1″ x 4″ x 16′-0″ @ 40¢ per board foot.

$$24 \times 16 = 384$$
$$1″ \times 4″ \times 1′\text{-}0″ = \tfrac{1}{3} \text{ of a board foot}$$
$$384 \div 3 = 128$$
$$128 \times 40¢ = \$51.20$$

An alternate method may be used for determining the price of a lumber order. Find the number of board feet in one length of stock lumber, multiply this by the number of pieces ordered, and multiply this product by the price per board foot. Use the following formula:

$$T = \text{Thickness}$$
$$W = \text{Width}$$
$$L = \text{Length}$$

$$\frac{T \times W \times L}{12} = \text{Board feet}$$

Example: Find the price of a lumber order of 24 pieces of 1″ x 4″ x 16′-0″ @ 40¢ per board foot.

$$\frac{1 \times 4 \times 16}{12} = \frac{64}{12} = 5\tfrac{1}{3} \text{ board feet}$$
$$5\tfrac{1}{3} \times 24 = 128$$
$$128 \times 40¢ = \$51.20$$

WOOD JOINTS COMMONLY USED IN SCENIC CONSTRUCTION

The speed with which scenery can be built and its strength depends to a great extent upon the types of wood joints used in its construction. For this reason certain types of wood joints have been found more suitable than others for scenic construction (Plates 18 and 19).

In selecting the proper joint for any construction problem some thought should be given not only to the strength of the joint but to the strength of the lumber itself. The strength of any piece of stock lumber varies according to the position in which it is used and to the direction in which the force or load is applied to it. Consider the following example. A length of 1″ x 4″ placed so that a force is applied against its face is in its weakest position because this force is at right angles to the smallest dimension of the piece of lumber, its thickness. If the position of the 1″ x 4″ can be changed so that the force is against the edge, it will be many times stronger because the force will then be at right angles to the 4″ width. The same 1″ x 4″ is at its strongest position when the force is applied against its ends or parallel to its length.

LAP JOINT (Fig. 57)

A lap joint is the simplest of all wood joints to construct. Two pieces of stock lumber are joined face to face by bolts, screws, or nails. This joint is used in

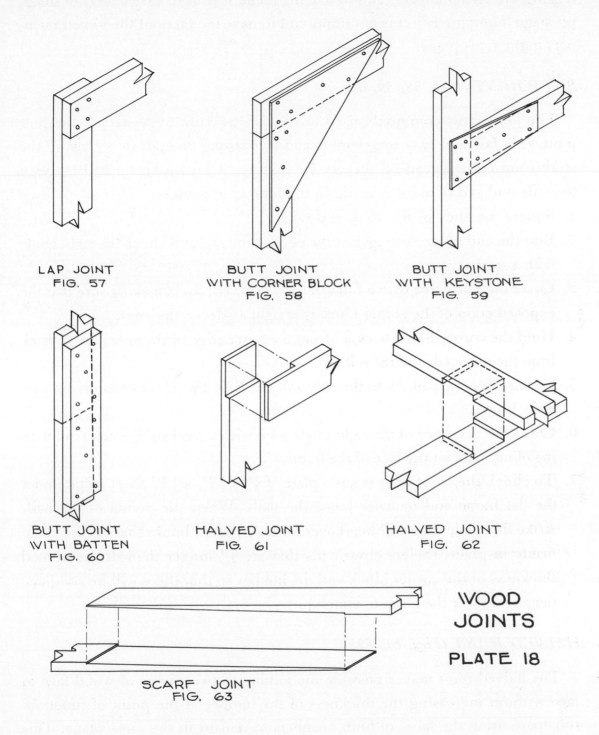

LAP JOINT
FIG. 57

BUTT JOINT
WITH CORNER BLOCK
FIG. 58

BUTT JOINT
WITH KEYSTONE
FIG. 59

BUTT JOINT
WITH BATTEN
FIG. 60

HALVED JOINT
FIG. 61

HALVED JOINT
FIG. 62

SCARF JOINT
FIG. 63

WOOD
JOINTS

PLATE 18

legging up rigid platforms and in bracing them. It is used extensively in rough off-stage framing when it is not important to have the faces of the joined members in the same plane.

BUTT JOINT (Figs. 58, 59, 60)

The joint most commonly used in the construction of scenery is the butt joint. It is fast and easy to assemble and it is strong enough to withstand the strains normally placed on scenery by shifting. A butt joint formed between the stile and rail of a flat is made in the following manner:

1. Square the ends of the stiles and rails.
2. Butt the end of the stile against the edge of the rail and check the right angle with a steel square.
3. Cover the butt joint with a full-size (10″) corner block, making sure that the exposed grain of the corner block is at right angles to the joint.
4. Hold the corner block back $\frac{3}{4}$″ from the outer edge of the stile and $\frac{1}{4}$″ back from the outer edge of the rail.
5. Fasten the corner block to the stile and rail with $1\frac{1}{4}$″ clout nails driven partially home.
6. Check the accuracy of the right-angle joint with a steel square before clinching clout nails on the face of the frame.
7. To clinch the clout nails insert a plate of $\frac{1}{4}$″ x 12″ x 12″ sheet metal under the flat frame and hammer home the nails. When the points of the nails strike this plate they will bend over forming partial hooks that anchor them firmly in place. (Select clout nails that are $\frac{1}{4}$″ longer than the combined thickness of the corner block and the lumber so that there will be adequate penetration for the point to clinch.)

HALVED JOINT (Figs. 61, 62)

The halved joint makes possible the joining of two pieces of wood face to face without increasing the thickness of the lumber at the point of junction, thus permitting the faces of both members to remain in the same plane. This joint is much stronger than a butt joint; it can be made easily with a radial saw equipped with a dado head, or it can be worked with hand tools without requiring too much time. To join two lengths of 1″ x 3″ at right angles by use of a halved joint proceed in the following manner:

1. Square the ends of both pieces of 1″ x 3″.
2. Measure back from the ends of each 1″ x 3″ a distance equal to their width. Using a try square, mark a line at right angles across the faces and edges of both pieces.
3. With a marking gauge set at $\frac{1}{2}$ the thickness of the 1″ x 3″ scribe a line along the edges and ends until it joins with the width measurement.
4. With the dado blade on a radial saw set for a cut equal to $\frac{1}{2}$ the thickness of the 1″ x 3″ remove the marked section.
5. Cover the exposed cuts with glue and allow it to dry long enough to become tacky. Then assemble the joint and check the angle for accuracy with a steel square.
6. Allow the glue to set under pressure provided by clamps, screws, or clout nails.

SCARF JOINT (Fig. 63)

It is difficult to obtain white pine in lengths greater than 18′-0″. This makes the scarf joint one of the most useful of all joints to the technician, as it provides him with a method of joining two lengths of lumber end to end without increasing the thickness. Stiles of flats with a height greater than 18′-0″, lengthwise battens of ceilings, and battens used for foliage borders and drops all are made with the aid of scarf joints. To make a joint of this type proceed as follows:

1. Square the ends of the lumber to be joined.
2. Measure 1′-6″ in from the ends of each board and draw a right-angle line across the widths of the boards at this point.
3. Cut a $\frac{1}{8}$″ deep saw kerf on this line.
4. Draw a diagonal line on each edge of the board beginning at the bottom of the saw kerf and terminating on the end at a point $\frac{1}{8}$″ in from the outer face.
5. Remove all wood above this line by using a drawknife and finish the cut with a block plane or a wood file. Make sure that the face of the taper is perfectly smooth without noticeable high or low points. The faces of both tapers should meet along their full length to insure a strong joint.
6. Cover the faces of both tapers with glue and allow it to dry until it becomes tacky. Then place the tapers face to face, check alignment of the edges to in-

sure perfect straightness of the joint, and allow the glue to dry under pressure provided by clamps, clout nails, or screws.

DADO JOINT (Fig. 64)

The dado joint provides a method of joining two pieces of wood end-to-face in a way that is many times stronger than the same junction formed with butt joints. Bookcase shelves, stair treads, and structures that may be subjected to heavy loads are frequently made by use of this joint. To make it proceed as follows:

1. Mark the vertical member at the desired height with measurements corresponding to the width and thickness of the horizontal member.
2. Remove the wood within the limits of the marks by the use of a dado blade that has been adjusted for the proper width and depth of cut.
3. Cover the face of the notch with glue, insert the end of the horizontal member, and fasten with a cleat, nails, or screws.

NOTCHED JOINT (Fig. 65)

The joint is similar to the dado joint in both construction and use, the difference being that the notch is usually cut in the edge of the supporting member rather than in its face.

MORTISE AND TENON JOINTS (Figs. 66, 67)

Since open and closed mortise and tenon joints are among the strongest of all wood joints, they are used extensively in the construction of furniture and are used by most professional scenic builders for the assembly of all flat frames. However, their shops usually have power equipment designed specifically for cutting this type of joint. The time required to cut and fit it with hand tools alone makes it almost prohibitive for the average unskilled student. As can be seen in the illustration, the open mortise and tenon joint is distinguished from the closed joint by the fact that its tenon, or tongue, is partially exposed on both end and edge when the joint is assembled. When the closed mortise and tenon joint is assembled, the tenon is completely hidden. To make the open mortise and tenon joint with hand tools proceed as follows:

1. Square the ends of both members.

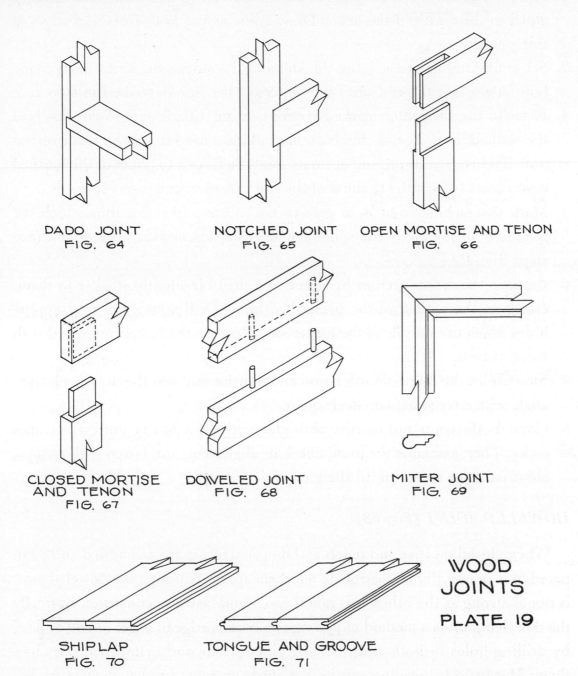

DADO JOINT
FIG. 64

NOTCHED JOINT
FIG. 65

OPEN MORTISE AND TENON
FIG. 66

CLOSED MORTISE
AND TENON
FIG. 67

DOVELED JOINT
FIG. 68

MITER JOINT
FIG. 69

SHIPLAP
FIG. 70

TONGUE AND GROOVE
FIG. 71

WOOD
JOINTS
PLATE 19

2. Mark the tenon by measuring back from the end of one member a distance equal to the width of the other. Draw a line across both faces and edges at this point.

3. Set a marking gauge at $\frac{1}{4}$ the thickness of the stock and scribe lines along both edges and the end until they intersect the line described in step 2.

4. Remove the two outer marked sections, using a back saw to cut down to the scribed lines. Wood chisels and a mallet are used to complete the operation. To insure a strong and accurate joint the faces and edges of the finished tenon must be parallel to those of the stock from which it was formed.

5. Mark the member that is to receive the mortise (the slot into which the tongue fits) in exactly the same manner used for marking the tenon. (See steps 2 and 3.)

6. Remove the center section by selecting a drill bit slightly smaller in diameter than the widths of the prescribed lines. Drill a series of overlapping holes down the middle of the center slot. Remove the remaining wood with wood chisels.

7. Smooth up the faces of both tenon and mortise and test the fit. Check right angle with a try square or steel square.

8. Cover both tenon and mortise with glue and allow to dry until it becomes tacky. Then assemble the joint, check its alignment, and fasten with clamps, clout nails, or screws until the glue is dry.

DOWELED JOINT (Fig. 68)

When closed mortise and tenon and doweled joints are assembled and compared, it is practically impossible to tell them apart. Although the doweled joint is not as strong as the other, it is much easier and faster to construct. Basically the doweled joint is a method of joining two boards edge to edge, or end to face, by drilling holes in both and inserting glued hardwood cylindrical pegs into them. Hardwood doweling can be bought from most lumber dealers in 30" lengths and in diameters from $\frac{1}{8}''$ to $\frac{3}{4}''$. The proper diameter of the dowel is usually one-half the thickness of the stock to be used. Two boards can be joined edge to edge by the use of the doweled joint as follows:

1. Place both boards face to face in a wood vise and align their upper edges.

2. Plane the edges of both boards until they are square with the faces.

3. Remove one board from the vise and place its squared edge down on the squared edge of the second board. Check for high and low places. Plane until both edges fit tightly together.

4. Realign both boards in the vise with the planed edges flush. With a marking gauge set for $\frac{1}{2}$ the thickness of the stock, mark a center line down the edges of both boards.

5. Draw lines at right angles to the center lines with a try square to mark the position for the dowel holes. It is very important that the dowel holes be exactly the same distance apart on both boards. Otherwise the resulting misalignment of the dowels makes it impossible to draw the board edges together.

6. Drill holes about $1\frac{1}{2}''$ deep at each marked position. Be sure that the holes are drilled parallel with the faces of the boards and at right angles with their edges.

7. Cut the doweling into $3''$ lengths. Cover one-half of each dowel with glue and tap them into the holes along the edge of one of the two boards. Cover the exposed ends of the dowels and the edge of the board with glue.

8. Lay both boards face side down on the work bench. Fit the dowels into the holes of the second board and force the two board edges together with pressure supplied by bar or pipe clamps.

9. Wipe off excess glue squeezed from between the boards and allow them to dry. Plane or sand the surfaces to a smooth finish.

JOINING MATERIAL

Plywood is probably the most useful single building material used in a scene shop. Used primarily as a joining material, it is also used extensively in making irregular contours for a two-dimensional cutout and as a substitute for solid stock lumber when great strength is needed. Plywood is a manufactured product made by bonding together an uneven number of thin sheets of wood. Each sheet is glued to the next, with the graining of one sheet usually at right angles to the adjoining one. It is this alternation of graining that gives plywood its unusual strength. If you test a small piece of $\frac{1}{4}''$ plywood for strength by bending it over the edge of a table, you will notice that when the exposed graining is parallel with the table edge it is possible to bend, or even break it. This does not happen when the graining runs at right angles to the edge of the table. Plywood is much stronger when placed in this position, and for this reason the exposed grain of the corner block or keystone should always be placed at right angles to the junction of the butt joints.

Panelboard, as plywood is sometimes called, is sold by the square foot. It comes in sheets 4'-0" wide and is obtainable in different lengths, though the 8'-0" length is most commonly stocked. Plywood made of fir is the least expensive; it is made in thicknesses of $\frac{1}{4}''$, $\frac{3}{8}''$, $\frac{1}{2}''$, $\frac{5}{8}''$, $\frac{3}{4}''$, and $\frac{7}{8}''$. Plywood made from soft woods such as basswood is obtainable on order in thicknesses of $\frac{3}{32}''$ or $\frac{1}{8}''$.

CORNER BLOCKS, KEYSTONES, AND STRAPS

The wood joint used most frequently in the construction of scenery is the butt joint. When this joint is formed by butting the end of one piece of lumber against the edge of another, it must be reinforced by fastening a third piece over the other two. These reinforcing pieces are made from $\frac{3}{16}''$ or $\frac{1}{4}''$ thick plywood and are called corner blocks, keystones, and straps. The corner block is triangular in shape, with the two right-angle sides 10" in length. The keystone is 8" long, 4" wide at one end and tapers to $2\frac{3}{4}''$ at the other. Straps are rectangles of plywood 8" long by $2\frac{3}{4}''$ wide. Ready-made corner blocks and keystones can be purchased from any theatrical supply house, but there is a noticeable saving in cost if the technician cuts them himself.

STRAP IRON

Strips of malleable iron, $\frac{3}{16}''$ or $\frac{1}{4}''$ thick by $\frac{3}{4}''$ wide are used to join the two lower rails of a standard door flat. Strap iron can be easily cut with a hacksaw and bent to the desired shape by placing it in a machinist's vise and striking it with a heavy hammer.

COVERING MATERIALS

There is hardly a fabric made that has not been used at one time or another for some purpose on stage. Some fabrics, of course, have been found so completely satisfactory for a particular purpose that their use in that capacity has become standard procedure. It is extremely important in selecting a fabric for stage use that it be wide enough for the purpose. The three fabrics listed below are manufactured in widths of 68″, 72″, 81″, and 108″ and sold in bolts containing 50 to 60 yards. They are priced by the running yard rather than by the square yard. If less than a full bolt is ordered, it is necessary to add 10 percent to the current price. Materials that have been flame-proofed will cost an additional 10¢ or 12¢ a yard.

LINEN CANVAS

This is probably the best material that can be used for covering flats. It is expensive, but is remarkably strong, does not snag or tear easily, and will last indefinitely when stored under proper conditions.

COTTON CANVAS DUCK

An excellent substitute for linen canvas, cotton canvas is used much more extensively than linen for covering flats, because it is less expensive and can be easily found on the market. It is manufactured in various weights and is specified by the weight in ounces of a square yard. Eight-ounce canvas is normally used for most scenic work.

MUSLIN

Heavyweight unbleached muslin is used as a covering material by many technicians who must operate with a limited budget. It is not strong and will stretch and tear rather easily; but since it is lighter in weight and thinner than canvas, it is well suited for the patching needed in altering and reusing stock scenery. Several coats of paint will completely conceal all patches. In spite of its weakness, muslin is surprisingly durable when used as a covering for flats or when made into drops; but it must be shifted and stored with care.

SISALCRAFT

This is a substitute for conventional covering fabrics when economy is a prime consideration. Sisalcraft is a building paper made from two sheets of brown craft paper with a layer of asphalt between them. Threads of sisal intermixed with the asphalt give great strength to the product. Sisalcraft comes in widths of 3', 4', 5', 6', and 8'. While it is heavy and not as easy to apply to a flat as a fabric, it can be used for covering frames of an irregular shape or those that will not be kept as stock scenery.

COMPOSITIONAL COVERING MATERIALS

Any unit of scenery that will be subjected to hard usage either on stage or in shifting is ordinarily covered with some stiff, self-supporting, compositional material capable of withstanding the stress that will be placed upon it. Plywood is ideal for this purpose, but if cost is a consideration it is essential that the technician become familiar with the characteristics of less expensive compositional materials and learn which are locally available. Such rigid materials, or "boards" as they are sometimes called, are standard building materials used in general construction and cabinet work and so are stocked by lumber dealers. They are sold by the square foot and come in sheets or boards of varying lengths, usually, however, they are 4'-0" wide. They are manufactured from a wide variety of materials—paper pulp, fibers, wood, plaster, asbestos, and even cement. Some have soft finishes, others have hard surfaces, and a few will bend without breaking. Uses of these boards on stage are limited only by one's willingness to experiment with them.

COVERING MATERIALS FOR WINDOW SASH

Real glass is rarely used on stage because it reflects too much light, is too heavy and too expensive, and there is too much danger of breakage. Numerous substitute materials provide varying degrees of transparency or translucency. Any one of these materials can be attached to the back of the sash frame by either tacking or stapling it into place.

1. *Bobinette.* A very lightweight netting with an open hexagonal weave. It is available in several different colors and should be used when transparency is more important than opacity.
2. *Sharkstooth scrim.* The weave of this material is rectangular in pattern and tighter than bobinette, which makes it more suitable for effects demanding greater opacity.
3. *Marquisette.* Another type of netting with a tighter weave than bobinette but a little less transparent.

4. *Screen wire.* Obtainable in either galvanized or japanned finish. Both are transparent. The galvanized finish gives a slight haze to the appearance of the window.

5. *Cel-o-glass.* A galvanized screen wire treated with a coating of cellophane to make it completely translucent.

6. *Cel-o-cloth.* A thin sheet of cellophane with a backing of loosely woven netting and a little less translucent than Cel-o-glass.

7. *Polyethylene sheeting.* This reflects some light and care must be used in tacking it to the frames to prevent it from wrinkling. This material is sold in varying thicknesses, the thinner sheets being more transparent.

8. *Cellulose acetate.* A perfect imitation of glass, but it possesses all glass' disadvantages for stage use except that it will not break.

COVERING MATERIALS FOR GENERAL STAGE USE

The materials listed below, while not normally used for covering flat frames, have all been used for that purpose. The term "covering material" is used in a broad context here, and applies to fabrics especially suitable for draperies, curtains, and borders used primarily for concealing or masking various parts of the stage.

1. *Cotton rep.* This is a heavy-duty cotton fabric with a ribbed weave not unlike that of fine pinwale corduroy. Its characteristics make it the favorite of many technicians. It is inexpensive, available in many colors, strong, drapes well, hangs free of wrinkles, has good opacity, and may be cleaned with either a broom or a vacuum cleaner. It is used primarily for drapery settings, masking drapes of all types, and on occasions when a special draw or fly curtain is needed as part of a setting. Rep has neither the weight nor the opacity needed for the main front curtain or teaser.

2. *Velour.* Heavy-duty cotton velour is characterized by a pronounced pile that gives the material a rich appearance. It is available in various colors and in different qualities. As it is one of the heaviest and longest-lasting materials obtainable, the main front curtain and the teaser are usually made from it. However, it is not suitable for stage draperies or cyclorama sets which must be taken down and stored after each use. It is bulky and heavy and wrinkles when stored for any length of time. Both wrinkles and dirt

picked up in the process of storing or hanging the material are difficult to remove.

3. *Sateen.* This is an inexpensive, lightweight cotton material manufactured in many colors. One face of the material is finished with a high sheen. Sateen does not possess any great degree of opacity and shows at its best under front lighting. Its light weight makes it difficult to handle as a draw or fly curtain without excessive "fish-tailing" or billowing when the curtains are operated. A chain weight inserted into the lower hem of such curtains will reduce these objectionable effects.

THEATRICAL HARDWARE

Much of the hardware used in the construction or rigging of scenery is of standard manufacture and can be purchased from local hardware stores. However, a number of hardware items have been designed and manufactured to meet specialized theatrical needs. The majority of the items in the following list must therefore be ordered from theatrical supply houses (Plates 20, 21). The prices quoted below are based on current quotations; while subject to change, they serve as a general price index.

1. *Batten clamp or drop holder* (Plate 20, Fig. 72). A clamp used for attaching drops or borders to a set of lines in preparation for flying them. The jaws of the clamp are designed to open and fit around the wooden batten at the top of a drop. They may be attached or removed rapidly and without damage to the canvas ($2.00 each).

2. *Brace cleat* (Fig. 73). The cleat is screwed to the stile of a flat and provides a fast and easy method of engaging the hooks of a stage brace required for bracing standard scenery (20¢ each).

3. *Corner plate* (Fig. 74). Corner plates are 1″ or 1⅛″ wide with 6″ sides and are cut from solid plate. They are used to reinforce the joints of a detachable door or window unit or as a substitute for corner blocks (40¢ each).

4. *Ceiling plate* (Fig. 75). Used in joining cross battens to the lengthwise battens of a book or roll ceiling and to provide the necessary rings by which the ceiling can be flown (80¢ each).

5. *Eye bolt* (Fig. 76). Used to provide a solid anchor for lines, piano wire, or turnbuckles. Varies in price according to size (25¢ to $2.50 each).

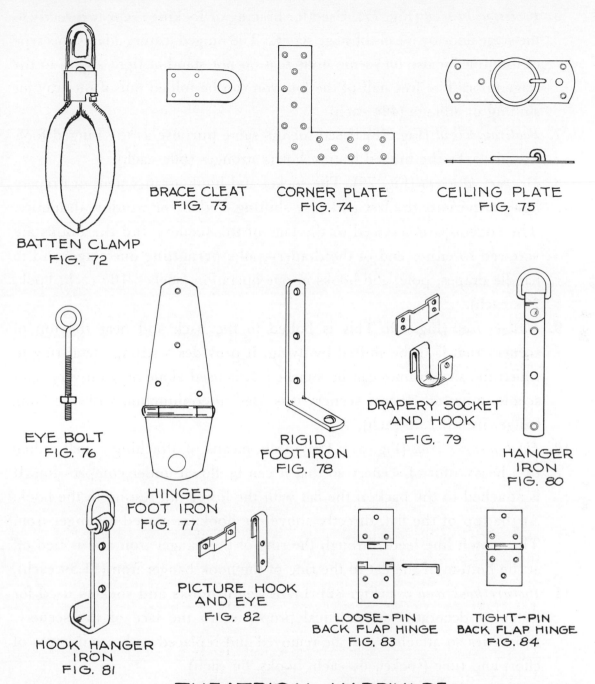

BATTEN CLAMP
FIG. 72

BRACE CLEAT
FIG. 73

CORNER PLATE
FIG. 74

CEILING PLATE
FIG. 75

EYE BOLT
FIG. 76

HINGED
FOOT IRON
FIG. 77

RIGID
FOOT IRON
FIG. 78

DRAPERY SOCKET
AND HOOK
FIG. 79

HANGER
IRON
FIG. 80

HOOK HANGER
IRON
FIG. 81

PICTURE HOOK
AND EYE
FIG. 82

LOOSE-PIN
BACK FLAP HINGE
FIG. 83

TIGHT-PIN
BACK FLAP HINGE
FIG. 84

THEATRICAL HARDWARE

PLATE 20

6. *Footiron, hinged* (Fig. 77). Used for bracing or locking scenery directly to the stage floor by means of stage screws. The hinged feature adapts this type of footiron for use on scenic units that do not stand at right angles to the stage floor. The free half of the footiron can be folded out of the way for shifting or storage (40¢ each).

7. *Footiron, rigid* (Fig. 78). Used for the same purpose as the hinged footiron, it lacks the hinged feature but is stronger (60¢ each).

8. *Drapery hangers* (Fig. 79). The socket and hook arrangement of drapery hangers permits the fast and easy shifting of door or window draperies. The sockets are screwed to the face of the scenery and the hooks are screwed to either end of the drapery pole, permitting one stagehand to handle drapes, pole, and hooks in one operation (socket, 10¢ each; hook, 20¢ each).

9. *Hanger iron* (Fig. 80). This is bolted to the back and near the top of scenery that is to be shifted by flying. It provides a strong metal ring to which the snatch lines can be attached. It is used alone only on very light scenic units; on heavier scenery it is used in conjunction with the hook hanger iron ($1.50 each).

10. *Hook hanger iron* (Fig. 81). Provides a means of attaching a snatch line to a heavy unit of scenery so that it can be flown under compression. It is attached to the back of the flat with the lower rail resting in the hook. At the top of the flat, directly above the hook, is placed a hanger iron. The snatch line feeds through the ring of the hanger iron and is tied off at the bottom of the flat to the ring of the hook hanger iron ($1.30 each).

11. *Picture hook and eye* (Fig. 82). Lightweight hooks and sockets used for fastening decorative or practical properties to the face of the scenery. Properties so attached may be removed and replaced with a minimum of effort and time (socket, 6¢ each; hooks, 6¢ each).

12. *Back flap hinge, loose pin* (Fig. 83). The loose-pin hinge is used when a temporary union is required between two pieces of scenery that must be separated during a scene shift or for storage. Removal of the pin makes this operation both easy and fast. These hinges are available in two sizes, $1\frac{1}{2}''$ x $3\frac{1}{2}''$ and $2''$ x $4\frac{1}{2}''$. The smaller size is used on units made of $1''$

x 2″ framing and the larger on frames constructed from wider stock (small, 55¢ each; large, 65¢ each).

13. *Back flap hinge, tight pin* (Fig. 84). These hinges are employed when a permanent union is required, such as that between two or more flats joined edge to edge to make up an expanse of unbroken wall. Junctions between flats and hinges are concealed by a strip of canvas glued and tacked in place over them. Available in the same sizes as loose-pin hinges (small, 37¢ each; large, 56¢ each).

14. *Lash-line cleat* (Plate 21, Fig. 85). Attached to the inner edges of flat stiles and used when a temporary joining of two flats is to be made by lashing (22¢ each).

15. *Lash-line eye* (Fig. 86). Used for attaching the lash line to the flat. The eye is attached to the inner edge of the stile just beneath the upper corner block; one end of the lash line is passed through the eye and knotted to provide a firm anchor for the line. Use of this cleat can sometimes be avoided by drilling a $\frac{3}{8}$″ hole in the corner block, inserting the lash line, and knotting it (22¢ each).

16. *Lash-line hook* (Fig. 87). A substitute for a conventional lash cleat when the structural nature of the flat prohibits the use of the latter (20¢ each).

17. *Latch keeper* (Fig. 88). Two or more latch keepers are placed over the toggle bars on the rear of a two- or three-fold flat. A stiffening batten placed in the open halves of the hooks serves to keep the flats rigid and in a single plane (50¢ each).

18. *Snap hooks* (Fig. 89). These provide a fast and safe method of attaching one object to another, eliminating the risk associated with hastily tied knots (varies in price according to size, 50¢ to $1.75).

19. *Stage screw* (Fig. 90). A heavy, hand-operated floor screw used in conjunction with a brace cleat and stage brace in bracing scenery (steel, $12.35 dz.; malleable iron, $9.90 dz.).

20. *Stop cleat* (Fig. 91). Used to assure the perfect vertical alignment of two flats that are to be joined by lashing. The cleats are screwed to the back of the stiles with their ends projecting $\frac{3}{4}$″ beyond the outer edges. This arrangement prevents one flat from slipping past the other (10¢ each).

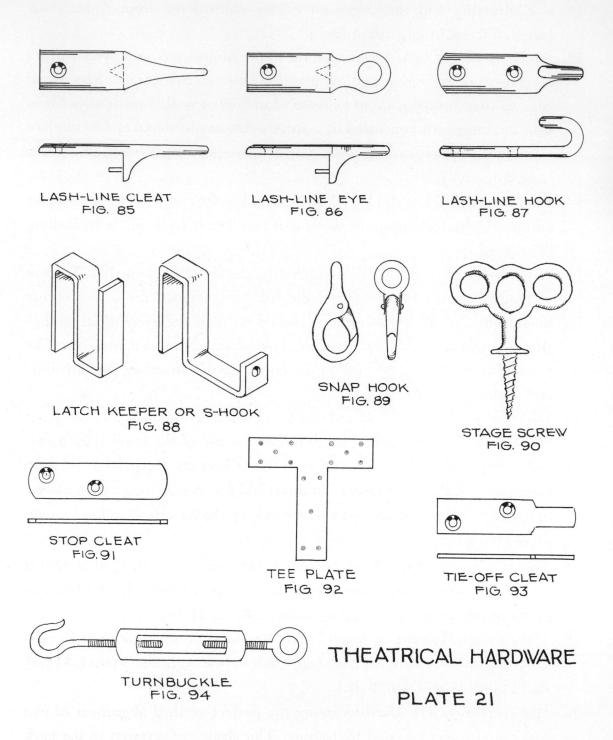

LASH-LINE CLEAT
FIG. 85

LASH-LINE EYE
FIG. 86

LASH-LINE HOOK
FIG. 87

LATCH KEEPER OR S-HOOK
FIG. 88

SNAP HOOK
FIG. 89

STAGE SCREW
FIG. 90

STOP CLEAT
FIG. 91

TEE PLATE
FIG. 92

TIE-OFF CLEAT
FIG. 93

TURNBUCKLE
FIG. 94

THEATRICAL HARDWARE

PLATE 21

21. *Tee plate* (Fig. 92). A substitute for a keystone in the assembly of a butt joint. It is cut from solid plate and is $1\frac{1}{8}''$ x 6" x 6" (60¢ each).

22. *Tie-off cleat* (Fig. 93). Two cleats placed opposite each other at the 3'-0" level on two flats to be joined by lashing; the lash-line knot is formed around them. The angular edges of this cleat prevent the lash line from slipping during the process of tying off (10¢ each).

23. *Turnbuckle* (Fig. 94). Turnbuckles are sometimes attached to the end of snatch lines, thus making easy the final trim of a flown unit. More frequently the turnbuckle is used for stretching taut a wire or rope. Varies in price according to size (75¢ to $2.00 each).

chapter V

two-dimensional scenery

IF one would pause long enough to analyze a complicated realistic stage setting in terms of how and from what it is constructed, he might be surprised to learn that from 75 to 85 percent of it is formed by the use of comparatively simple structures known as flats. The flat is a basic commodity of stagecraft and is simply a light wooden frame covered with cloth. To all intents and purposes it has but two dimensions, width and height. The $\frac{3}{4}''$ thickness of the lumber from which it is made is disregarded in classifying it as a standard piece of two-dimensional scenery.

In spite of the spectacular developments and improvements that have been made in almost all phases of production work during the 2500-year history of drama, there has been no noticeable improvement in one of the simplest devices introduced to the stage by the Greeks, the pinak. Our present-day flat remains essentially the same in construction, a light wooden frame covered with cloth. Modern technicians have tried to improve upon the original Greek pattern by constructing flats from a host of new building materials. They have experimented with lightweight metal frames; they have covered these frames with plywood, beaverboard, compositional materials of all kinds, and with various plastics and fabrics. In a few cases these experimental flats possess certain worth-while features; but the good points are, more often than not, offset by limitations imposed by the materials from which they are built. The acceptability of any device proposed as a substitute for a flat must be tested by the factors governing the construction and rigging of scenery.

FACTORS GOVERNING THE CONSTRUCTION AND RIGGING OF SCENERY

The only points of similarity between stage carpentry and general carpentry or construction work are in the tools employed and some of the wood joints and building materials used. In all other respects there is very little in common. The characteristics of scenic construction which dictate the method by which scenery is built are the following:

1. Scenery is constructed to be used for a comparatively short time.
2. Scenery must be planned for rapid construction.
3. Scenery is often planned for possible alteration and reuse.
4. Scenery is usually built in one place and used in another.
5. Scenery is constructed in easily portable units and assembled on stage by temporary joining.
6. Scenery is generally finished on one side only.
7. Scenery must be light in weight and capable of compact storage.
8. Scenery must be strong enough for safe usage and safe handling.
9. Scenery must be as inexpensively constructed as possible and still comply with the above requirements.

SIZE LIMITATIONS OF STOCK FLATS

Actually there is no limit as to how wide or how high a flat can be made except the limit placed upon it by the dimensions of the shop and stage where it is built and used. On one occasion the author constructed flats 36'-0" high, so high in fact that they had to be pulled upright by the counterweight system. (These flats were later cut in half to become part of the 18'-0" set of stock scenery.)

Normally the width of a standard flat is limited to 5'-9", which is the maximum width of most readily available canvas or muslin. Flats wider than 5'-9" are difficult to handle or store and usually require that strips of the covering material be sewed together before it can be attached to the frame. The minimum width of a flat is usually 1'-0", occasionally even as little as 9" or 10". A narrower width is supplied by using solid stock lumber.

The height of stock scenery used in the educational and community theatres is determined in part by the sight lines from the auditorium to the stage and in part by the fact that such scenery will be built and shifted by inexperienced personnel. Stock scenery 12'-0", 14'-0", or 16'-0" high is most commonly used. Flats 18'-0" high or over are not only awkward to shift and store, but should be constructed from stock lumber with greater rigidity and strength than that provided by 1" x 3" stock. This additional rigidity can be obtained by building the frame from 1" x 4" or 1¼" x 3" stock. In many parts of the country it is difficult to obtain 1" x 3" white pine in lengths greater than 16'-0", which necessitates the use of scarf-jointed stiles for all flats over 16'-0" in height. The ease with which a flat over 20'-0" in height can be handled can be increased by building scarf-jointed stiles that taper in thickness. The lower sections of the stiles are made from 1¼" x 3", while the upper parts are made from 1" x 3" stock.

THE STANDARD FLAT (Plate 22)

The conventional flat consists of the following members: rails, stiles, toggle bars, and diagonal braces. The rails are the top and bottom horizontal members, the stiles the outside vertical members. Toggle bars are the inside horizontal members that hold the stiles equidistant. Diagonal braces are placed at the top and bottom on the same side of the flat at an angle with rails and stiles to give the flat greater rigidity and strength. The various parts of a standard flat may be assembled by the use of mortise and tenon or halved joint, but most flats are made by using butt joints reinforced with corner blocks and keystones. To build a standard flat frame 5'-0" wide by 14'-0" high, proceed as follows:

1. Cut all rails, stiles, and toggle bars from 1" x 3" lumber, grade C or better.
2. Cut the two rails each 5'-0" in length.
3. Cut the two stiles 14'-0" minus the combined widths of the two rails.
4. Butt the ends of the stiles against the edges of the rails. This method of assembly forms a skid of the lower rail and eliminates the possibility of splitting the end grain of the stile by having it come in contact with the floor.
5. Place a 3-ply corner block over the butt joint with the exposed grain of the corner block at right angles to the joint. Test the accuracy of the joint with a steel square. Hold the corner block back from the outer edges of the stiles

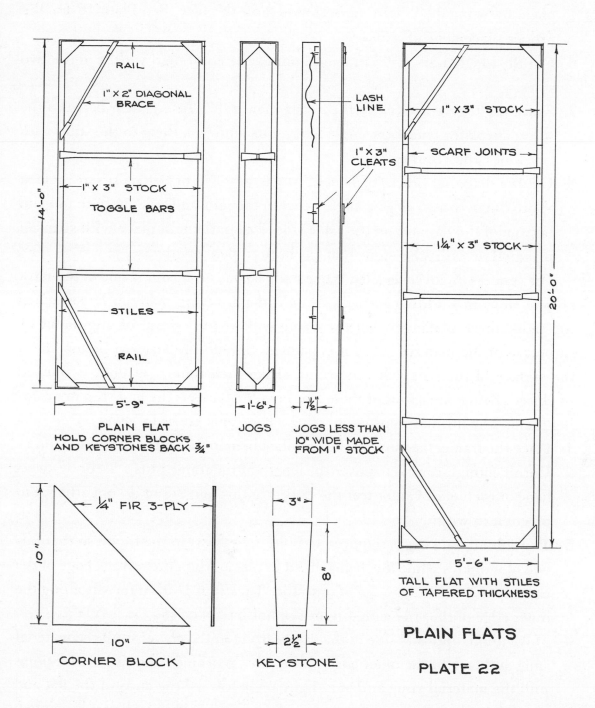

RAIL

1" X 2" DIAGONAL BRACE

1" X 3" STOCK

TOGGLE BARS

14'-0"

STILES

RAIL

5'-9"

PLAIN FLAT
HOLD CORNER BLOCKS
AND KEYSTONES BACK ¾"

JOGS

1'-6"

LASH LINE

1" X 3" CLEATS

7½"

JOGS LESS THAN
10" WIDE MADE
FROM 1" STOCK

1" X 3" STOCK

SCARF JOINTS

1¼" X 3" STOCK

20'-0"

5'-6"

TALL FLAT WITH STILES
OF TAPERED THICKNESS

¼" FIR 3-PLY

10"

10"

CORNER BLOCK

3"

8"

2½"

KEYSTONE

PLAIN FLATS

PLATE 22

by $\frac{3}{4}''$ and from the outer edges of the rails by $\frac{1}{4}''$. Nail the corner block in place by using $1\frac{1}{4}''$ clout nails clinched on the face. See Plate 18 for the proper placement of nails.

6. Cut the toggle bars 5'-0" in length minus the combined widths of the two stiles.

7. Space the toggle bars no farther apart than 5'-0". Insert them between the stiles, check for true right-angle butt joints, and join them to the stiles with keystones and clout nails.

8. Cut the diagonal braces of 1" x 2" stock, grade C or better. Insert them at approximately a 45-degree angle between the rails and stiles at both top and bottom of the flat and on the same side. Fasten them in place with strips of plywood or with a keystone that has been ripped lengthwise.

The process of covering a flat frame with canvas or muslin is one of the most critical steps in building scenery. Should the covering material be stretched too tight, there is danger that the frame will be pulled out of alignment by shrinkage of the material when it is painted. Should the material be too slack, the surface of the flats will billow and shake each time a set door is opened or closed. Being conscious of these two possible faults is the first step in avoiding them. The normal steps in covering a flat frame are as follows:

1. Place the frame, face up, on the template bench, saw horses, or the floor.

2. Unroll enough canvas to cover the length of the frame plus a 2" or 3" overhang at each end. Cut or tear the canvas to this length but do not attempt to precut it in width.

3. Preliminary tacking is required to hold the canvas to the frame so that it is free of wrinkles while it is being glued in place. Align the selvage edge of the canvas with the outer edge of one stile. Tack it at 1'-0" intervals along the inner edge of the stile with 4-ounce upholsterer's tacks.

4. Move to the opposite side of the flat. Starting in the center, pull the material snug and tack to the inner edge of the stile. Working from this center point pull the material snug and at a slight angle toward the ends of the flat and tack. Make due allowance for the shrinkage of the material when it is painted. Small semicircular wrinkles will appear around the heads of the tacks when the material has been pulled too tight.

5. Complete the preliminary tacking at either end of the flat by tacking along

the inside edge of each rail. Make what adjustments are necessary to elimi-nate any wrinkles appearing within the area now enclosed by tacks. Tacks whose heads have been driven flush with the canvas may be removed easily by inserting the corner of a screwdriver under the head and prying.

6. Turn back the loose flap of canvas over one of the stiles and apply canvas glue directly to the wood. Smooth the flap down over the glue and press it firmly into place with the heel of the hand or with a small block of wood. Work one side of the flat at a time to avoid having the glue congeal before the canvas can be pressed into it.

7. Tack along the outer edges of the stiles and rails with 4-ounce upholsterer's tacks, spacing them so that they fall between those already in the flat. This method will space the tacks about 6″ apart, alternating between the inside and the outside of the stiles and rails.

8. Allow the glue to dry before attempting to trim excess canvas from the flat. This can best be done by running a sharp knife along the outer edge of the frame while pulling the excess canvas taut with the other hand.

There are three formulas which are most commonly used in mixing a good canvas glue. Full-strength glue cannot be used without running the risk of hav-ing it seep through the canvas and darken or discolor the paint job.

1. *White-flake glue.* This is the strongest of the three mixtures and the easiest to prepare, but it is also the most expensive. To prepare it place dry-flake glue in the upper container of a double boiler, cover the glue with water, and heat until it has dissolved. This glue must be applied to the frames while it is hot, as it congeals rapidly when allowed to cool. Care must be taken to avoid getting this glue onto the face of the canvas, because it will stain or "bleed" through and darken any paint placed over it.

2. *Ground amber glue and whiting.* A very satisfactory canvas glue can be made from a mixture of 50 percent whiting and 50 percent ground amber glue. Prepare the glue by covering it with water and heating it in a double boiler as described above. Place the dry whiting powder in a separate container and add sufficient water to work it into a heavy paste that is free of all lumps. Add the hot liquid glue to the paste; this will thin the latter sufficiently for immediate use. This mixture must be applied to the frames while it is hot. Both of these first two glue mixtures will congeal into a solid mass when al-

lowed to cool overnight. Reheating them in a double boiler will return them to their original consistency without the necessity of adding more water.

3. *Cold-water paste and amber glue.* Although not as strong as the first two, this formula has the advantage of being less expensive and it does not require reheating after each use. The formula is approximately $\frac{2}{3}$ cold-water paste to $\frac{1}{3}$ hot amber glue. Prepare the ground amber glue as previously described. Cold-water paste is sold in a dry powdered form and must be mixed with water before the hot liquid glue is added. To avoid the small globules and lumps of paste that sometimes form when mixing cold-water paste, be sure to stir and sift the dry paste into a bucket containing the water.

JOG

For the sake of convenience in both the cataloging and storing of scenery many technicians divide their plain flats into two groups. Flats from 5'-9" wide down to and including those 3'-0" wide are classified as plain flats. Those less than 3'-0" wide are considered jogs. The only difference in construction of plain flats and jogs is that diagonal braces can be omitted from jogs less than 2'-0" wide.

WINDOW FLATS (Plate 23)

The window flat is but a slight variation of the plain flat. The two toggle bars are adjusted in height to correspond to the top and bottom of the window dimensions and are fastened with keystones and clout nails to the stiles of the flat. The vertical sides of the window are formed by additional lengths of 1" x 3" called window stiles. These are carefully placed according to the specified dimensions, checked for true right-angle butt joints, and fastened in place with keystones and clout nails.

Covering a window flat follows the same procedure as canvasing a plain flat. The whole flat is first covered with canvas. Then tack along the outside edges of the window stiles and toggles. Cut the canvas from the window opening by running a sharp knife along the inside of the window-framing members and removing the unwanted canvas. Make a 45-degree cut about 3" long in the canvas at each of the four corners of the window opening. This will permit turning back the resulting canvas flap for the application of canvas glue to the fram-

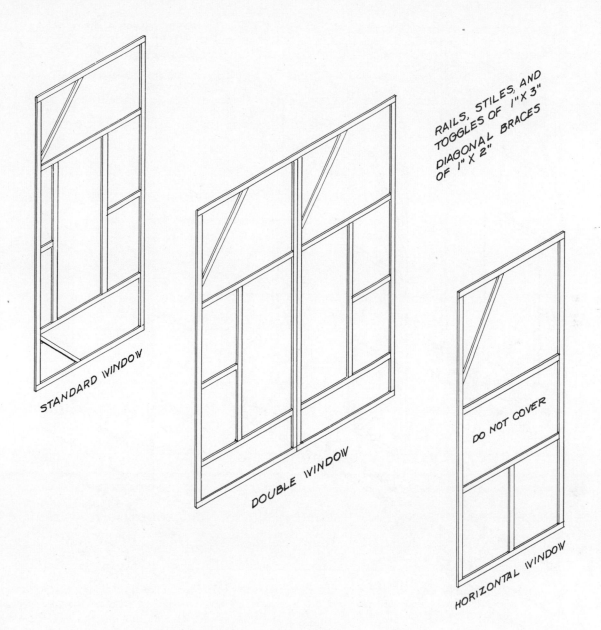

RAILS, STILES, AND
TOGGLES OF 1" X 3"
DIAGONAL BRACES
OF 1" X 2"

STANDARD WINDOW

DOUBLE WINDOW

DO NOT COVER

HORIZONTAL WINDOW

TYPES OF WINDOW FLATS

PLATE 23

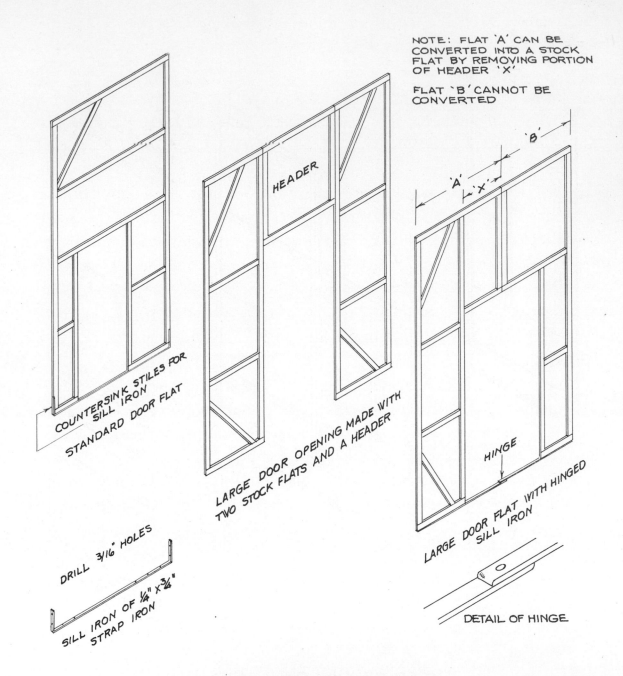

NOTE: FLAT 'A' CAN BE
CONVERTED INTO A STOCK
FLAT BY REMOVING PORTION
OF HEADER 'X'

FLAT 'B' CANNOT BE
CONVERTED

HEADER

'A'   'X'   'B'

COUNTERSINK STILES FOR
SILL IRON

STANDARD DOOR FLAT

LARGE DOOR OPENING MADE WITH
TWO STOCK FLATS AND A HEADER

HINGE

LARGE DOOR FLAT WITH HINGED
SILL IRON

DRILL 3/16" HOLES

SILL IRON OF 1/4" X 3/4"
STRAP IRON

DETAIL OF HINGE

TYPES OF DOOR FLATS

PLATE 24

ing members. Press the canvas down into the glue and tack along the inside face of the window stiles and toggles.

DOOR FLATS (Plate 24)

The only difference between constructing a window flat and a door flat is the substitution of a reinforcing band of strap iron for part of the lower rail. This band is called the sill iron and is made from $\frac{3}{16}''$ or $\frac{1}{4}''$ by $\frac{3}{4}''$ strap iron, cut 1'-6" longer than the overall width of the door flat. Each end is drilled with four to six holes, countersunk to accommodate the heads of 1" No. 9 flat-head screws. After drilling the sill iron, place it in a vise and put right-angle bends in it 9" from each end. Fit and countersink these 9" sections along the outer edges of each stile. Screw the sill iron to both the stiles and the lower rails. Make sure that the heads of the screws that were driven into the rails do not project beyond the face of the sill iron to snag or tear the floor cloth.

A door flat may be covered in one of two ways: by a single piece of material, following the same procedure outlined for canvasing a window flat, or by piecing the material together on the frame. Should the second method be used, it is well to canvas the section of the flat above the door first and then to cover the sections on either side of the door, overlapping the canvas to the full width of the toggle that forms the door top.

ARCHWAY FLATS (Plate 25)

The construction of a doorway with a rounded or arched top follows the same steps used in building a door flat. The only variation between the two is the addition of curved sweeps inserted at the top of a door opening to provide the desired shape.

Most arches, such as Roman, Gothic, or Tudor, are laid out on geometric patterns and may be easily adapted to door openings of specific sizes. Free-hand or irregular arches are transferred from the designer's plans by graph. These scaled drawings are divided into 6" or 1'-0" squares which provide a series of reference points at the intersections between the contour lines of the arch and either the vertical or horizontal graph lines. When the full-scale arch is laid out in the shop and graphed into 6" or 1'-0" squares, surprisingly ac-

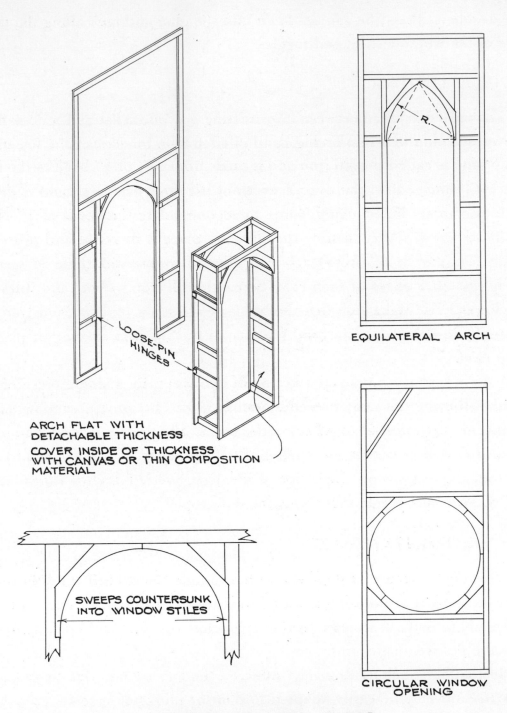

LOOSE-PIN
HINGES

ARCH FLAT WITH
DETACHABLE THICKNESS

COVER INSIDE OF THICKNESS
WITH CANVAS OR THIN COMPOSITION
MATERIAL

EQUILATERAL ARCH

R.

SWEEPS COUNTERSUNK
INTO WINDOW STILES

CIRCULAR WINDOW
OPENING

TYPES OF ARCH FLATS

PLATE 25

curate enlargements of the arch can be obtained by using the designer's graphed drawings as a guide. A heavyweight paper pattern of the arch is first made and then tested in the door opening to see that it fits properly and is of the desired shape. The pattern is then laid out and outlined on a wide width of lumber. If the arch is unusually wide, it may be necessary to have each sweep composed of two or more segments. Be sure to leave a reinforcing strip of $\frac{3}{4}''$ at the terminal points of each sweep to prevent it from splitting when nailed to the door stiles or toggle. Allow for this $\frac{3}{4}''$ reinforcing strip by an adjustment of the door toggle and by countersinking it into the door stiles. See Plate 25 for details.

IRREGULAR FLATS (Plate 26)

Flats of irregular shape include such standard stage units as wood wings, groundrows, set pieces, and profile settings. These are all two-dimensional in form and follow as closely as possible the building procedure used in constructing conventional rectangular flats. Most irregular flats fall roughly into two classifications, vertical or horizontal. In planning the framing of such units it is advisable to carry one or two framing members the full height or width of the structures for added strength and stability. The remaining parts of the frame follow as closely as possible the shape of the unit, but at the same time must adhere to the principles of good construction and sound joinery. Overlapping the full width of the outer framing members and extending beyond the frame by not more than 6″ is the lightweight compositional material or plywood. This material is nailed to the framing members, then marked and cut to give the unit its distinctive shape or profile. Beaverboard may be used for this purpose, but it will not withstand rough handling. A much stronger, but more expensive, material used for the same purpose is $\frac{3}{32}''$ or $\frac{1}{8}''$ plywood of either bass or pine. With the frame completed and the profile edges cut to shape the whole assembly can be covered with muslin or canvas. Allow the canvas glue to dry thoroughly before attempting to trim the canvas with a sharp knife.

CEILINGS

Ceiling pieces will do more toward completing the appearance of a realistic interior than any other single piece of two-dimensional scenery. No matter how

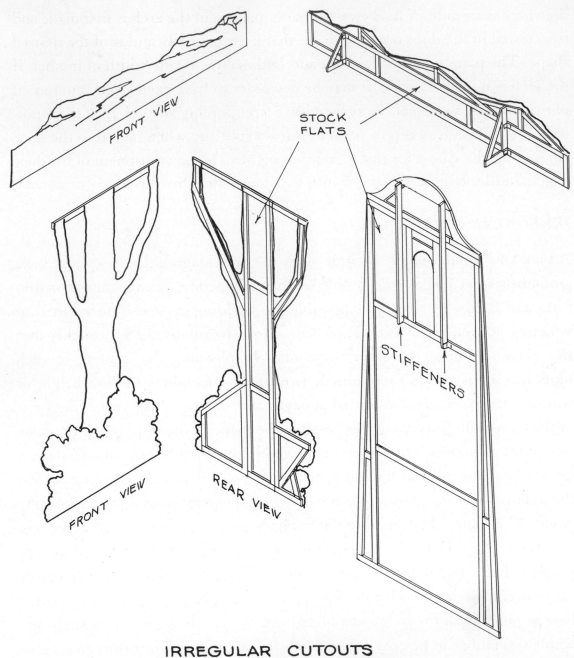

FRONT VIEW

STOCK FLATS

FRONT VIEW

REAR VIEW

STIFFENERS

IRREGULAR CUTOUTS
MADE FROM STOCK SCENERY

PLATE 26

cleverly designed and beautifully painted the setting may be, any convincing illusion of reality is shattered when a series of wrinkled cloth borders is used in lieu of a ceiling. Borders are a heritage of the old drop-and-wing setting and as such are as much out of place in today's realistic settings as kerosene headlights would be on a modern automobile.

Two other advantages to the use of ceilings should be mentioned. (1) There is a noticeable improvement in the ease with which an actor can project his voice toward the audience when a ceiling has been lowered in place on the three walls of a conventional box setting. Sound waves are reflected in part from the ceiling instead of being lost in the space overhead. (2) Additional stability and bracing is given to the setting by the weight of the ceiling resting on the flats. Most settings are braced at a point about two-thirds of the distance between the lower and upper rails by standard adjustable stage braces. This leaves the upper third of the scenery free to move or shake under the impact of a closing door or on contact by an actor. The weight of the ceiling serves to counteract this movement.

Any one of these reasons gives a sufficient justification for the construction and use of a ceiling piece. The ceiling should be considered a permanent piece of stage equipment and be designed with the idea that it will be used on any number of settings that will differ radically in both size and shape. Perhaps the most common mistake in planning a ceiling is making it too small.

The average depth of the back wall and the average angle for the placement of the side walls, as determined by the sight lines of a theatre, can be found by a study of ground plans of previous productions. With these averages established it is comparatively simple to determine the size of a ceiling. It is well to allow the ceiling to overhang the side and back walls of an average set by at least 2'-0''. This liberal allowance of overhang permits the ceiling to be shifted in any direction to provide the necessary coverage required by alcoves, niches, or bay windows that may extend beyond the average depth or width of most settings. It is unnecessary to disturb the permanent rigging of the ceiling to accomplish this shifting of position. An extended stage brace placed against one side of the ceiling just before it is lowered into place is usually adequate to shove it into the desired position.

THE ROLL CEILING.   There are two types of ceilings in common use, the roll ceiling and the book ceiling. The roll ceiling (Plate 27) is the easiest to build and rig and, as the name implies, it can be dismantled and rolled into a compact bundle for storage. Should the space set aside for the storage of the ceiling be too short, the length of the ceiling can be reduced one-half by hinging the lengthwise battens on the face with 10″ strap hinges and folding the ceiling before it is rolled. The steps in the construction of a roll ceiling follow:

1. Make the outside framework, consisting of lengthwise battens and outer cross battens, of 1″ x 4″ stock.

2. Scarf joint the lengthwise battens to the proper length. Allow an additional 1′-6″ for each scarf joint in determining the amount of lumber required.

3. Make the inside cross battens from 1″ x 3″ stock. These battens are cut to the specified depth minus the width of the two lengthwise battens.

4. Assemble the various parts of the framework in their proper positions and check the overall dimensions and angles. Mark the junction between each part with identification numbers to facilitate reassembly.

5. Place ceiling plates over each butt joint and mark their position.

6. Attach ceiling plates permanently to each end of cross batten by $\frac{3}{16}$″ stove bolts, with the heads of the bolts on the face of the ceiling.

7. Bolt ceiling plates to the lengthwise battens by a single $\frac{3}{8}$″ x $1\frac{1}{2}$″ carriage bolt fastened with a wing nut.

8. Sew the covering material into a single piece with seams running lengthwise. Allow at least a 12″ extension of the material beyond each outside cross batten.

9. Turn the assembled frame over. Then tack and glue the covering material to the two lengthwise battens only.

10. Turn the ceiling over on its face. Fold the cloth extensions into a hem and tack them to the top of the outer cross battens. An alternate method of stretching the covering material is provided by lacing it to the outer cross battens. The hem is folded and sewed, then fitted with $\frac{3}{8}$″ grommets spaced 10″ apart. A lash line threaded through the grommets engages the projecting heads of round-head screws driven into the top of the outer cross battens.

11. To dismantle the ceiling remove the tacks or unlace it from the outer cross

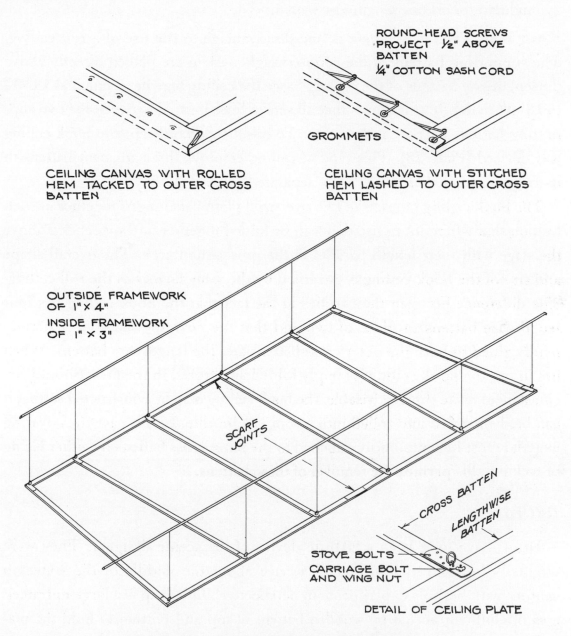

ROUND-HEAD SCREWS
PROJECT ½" ABOVE
BATTEN

¼" COTTON SASH CORD

GROMMETS

CEILING CANVAS WITH ROLLED
HEM TACKED TO OUTER CROSS
BATTEN

CEILING CANVAS WITH STITCHED
HEM LASHED TO OUTER CROSS
BATTEN

OUTSIDE FRAMEWORK
OF 1" × 4"

INSIDE FRAMEWORK
OF 1" × 3"

SCARF
JOINTS

CROSS BATTEN

LENGTHWISE
BATTEN

STOVE BOLTS

CARRIAGE BOLT
AND WING NUT

DETAIL OF CEILING PLATE

RIGGING OF A ROLL CEILING

PLATE 27

battens. Remove all cross battens. Turn the ceiling paint-side up and roll tightly around one lengthwise batten.

THE BOOK CEILING.   There is one disadvantage to the use of a roll ceiling. The supporting battens of the counterweight system are placed directly above the lengthwise battens of the ceiling. Since the ceiling may be as much as 14'-0'' to 16'-0'' in depth, this means that all sets of lines located between the two supporting battens become inoperative. To offset this handicap, the book ceiling was devised (Plate 28). This type of ceiling employs three adjacent battens in its rigging rather than two widely separated ones.

The book ceiling consists of two oversized plain flats hinged together in such fashion that when not in use they can be folded together and suspended above the stage with their length parallel to the proscenium arch. The overall shape and size of the book ceiling is governed by the same factors as the roll ceiling. The difference between the two lies in the fact that the book ceiling has four lengthwise battens in place of two and that the covering material is permanently glued to both the outer cross battens and the lengthwise battens. When not in use the book ceiling is simply folded and stored in the flies. Should circumstances make this inadvisable, the book ceiling may be constructed so that it can be dismantled and rolled into a compact bundle. In this case the covering material must be temporarily attached to the outer cross battens by either lacing or tacking; this permits the removal of these battens.

DROPS

Drops have long been a favorite device of the scenic designer. They were originally introduced into theatre service about the middle of the sixteenth century with Serlio's experiments in perspective. The drop is a large unframed area of cloth supported by wooden battens at top and bottom to hold the material free of wrinkles. Drops present the designer with a wide expanse of unbroken material upon which scenes can be painted. The advantages of a drop are obvious: they are neither difficult nor expensive to make, they require little stage space, and they may be quickly and easily shifted by flying.

The effects obtained by the use of drops can be varied greatly by the material used in their construction, the ways in which they are painted, and the manner of lighting them. The opaque or standard drop is made of muslin, canvas or

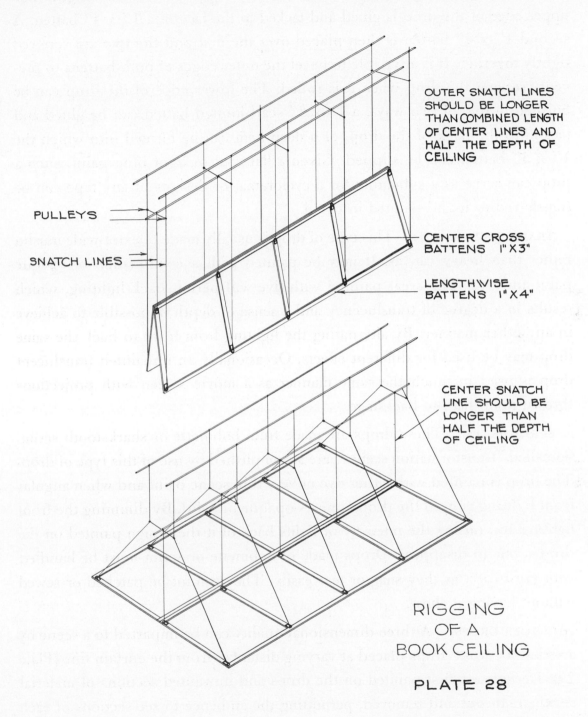

OUTER SNATCH LINES
SHOULD BE LONGER
THAN COMBINED LENGTH
OF CENTER LINES AND
HALF THE DEPTH OF
CEILING

PULLEYS

SNATCH LINES

CENTER CROSS
BATTENS 1"X3"

LENGTHWISE
BATTENS 1"X4"

CENTER SNATCH
LINE SHOULD BE
LONGER THAN
HALF THE DEPTH
OF CEILING

RIGGING
OF A
BOOK CEILING

PLATE 28

velour, with the seaming of the material running parallel to its length. The upper edge of the drop is glued and tacked to the face of a 1″ x 4″ batten. A second 1″ x 4″ batten is then placed over the first and the two are screwed tightly together. It is advisable to bevel the outer edges of both battens to prevent creasing the drop when it is rolled. The lower edge of the drop can be finished in one of two ways: a 1″ x 3″ scarf-jointed batten can be glued and tacked to the back of the drop, or a deep hem can be formed into which the 1″ x 3″ batten can be slipped. Given a flat coat of light blue paint, such a drop can serve as a substitute for a cyclorama, or designs of any type can be transferred to it and painted in detail.

TRANSLUCENT DROPS.   This type of drop is usually made of extra-wide muslin rather than heavy canvas. It may be painted with a combination of opaque paint and dye. The areas painted with dye will permit back lighting, which results in a degree of translucency and a sense of depth impossible to achieve in any other manner. By alternating the lighting from front to back the same drop may be used for different effects. Occasionally an unpainted translucent drop is used in much the same manner as a movie screen with projections thrown upon it from backstage.

SCRIM DROPS.   These drops are made from bobinette or sharkstooth scrim. So-called "transformation scenes" are accomplished by use of this type of drop. The drop is painted with either dye or very thin scene paint and when angular front lighting is used the drop appears opaque or solid. By dimming the front lighting and raising the intensity of lights back of it the design painted on the drop seems to disappear. Drops made of bobinette or scrim must be handled with great care, as they snag or tear easily. They cannot be patched or sewed without having it show.

CUTOUT DROPS.   A three-dimensional quality can be imparted to a scene by a series of cutout drops placed at varying distances from the curtain line (Plate 29). Designs are first painted on the drops and unwanted sections of material are then cut out and removed, permitting the audience to see sections of each drop. Any part of the design not supported by the natural hang of the drop material must be reinforced by netting.

BORDERS.   Borders are vertical masking pieces of cloth suspended over the

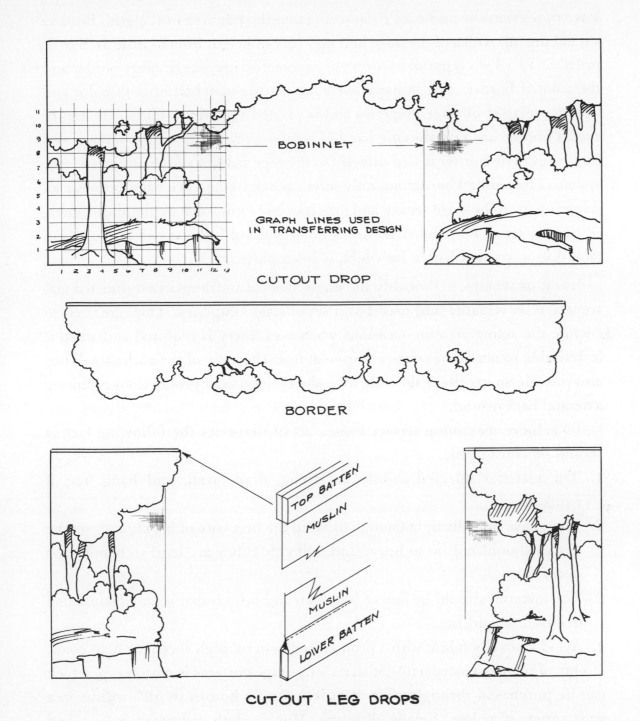

BOBINNET

GRAPH LINES USED
IN TRANSFERRING DESIGN

CUTOUT DROP

BORDER

TOP BATTEN

MUSLIN

MUSLIN

LOWER BATTEN

CUTOUT LEG DROPS

PLATE 29

stage to prevent the audience from seeing into the loft area or the grid. Borders extend the full width of the stage and may vary in height from as little as 2′ or 3′ to 10′ or 12′. Two types of borders are in common use, the drapery border and the painted border. The drapery border is usually matched in both color and material to a set of stage draperies and is pleated to hang in folds. The top of such a border has a reinforcing band of webbing provided with grommets and tie strings. The border is tied directly to the pipe battens of the counterweight system. The painted border not only serves as a masking device but becomes an integral part of the stage setting and may take any form, such as clouds, banners, or tree foliage. The painted border is hung without fullness and is glued and tacked to a wooden batten by which it is supported.

STAGE DRAPERIES.   Probably no single item of unframed two-dimensional scenery is as versatile and useful as a set of stage draperies. They are used to enclose the acting area on occasions when no scenery is required and when it is desirable to mask backstage equipment from the view of the audience. They also provide an excellent alternate for a sky cyclorama in productions requiring a neutral background.

To achieve maximum service from a set of draperies the following factors should be considered:

1. The material selected should be strong, drape well, and hang free of wrinkles.
2. The weave must be tight enough to avoid the necessity of backlining, yet the drapes should not be so heavy and bulky that they are hard to handle and store.
3. The material should be free of both nap and pile so that it may be brushed free of dust and lint.
4. Avoid a novelty fabric with a pronounced pattern, high sheen, or light color.

One of the most satisfactory materials for stage curtains is cotton rep, which can be purchased through most theatrical supply houses in 50″ widths in a wide variety of colors. Velour, duvetyne, Monk's cloth, velveteen, sateen, and cotton flannel are sometimes used for draperies, but in one respect or another they fail to give the satisfaction of rep.

A set of stage draperies will consist of a long back wall, two side walls, and perhaps one or two borders. It is best to have the draperies made up in comparatively small sections, 6'-0", 8'-0", or 10'-0" wide. These widths can be handled more easily than fewer but wider sections and they can be rigged in a greater variety of ways. Each section of curtain should be made with at least 50 percent fullness gathered into pleats and sewed to reinforcing webbing along the upper hem. Through both webbing and curtain material are fitted $\frac{3}{8}$" grommets spaced on 10" centers and supplied with tie lines of $\frac{1}{8}$" diameter cord. The lower hem should contain a chain weight to prevent the curtains from blowing and to help them hang free of wrinkles.

STOCK SCENERY

In an effort to keep down production costs many theatre organizations reuse their scenery many times. Scenery thus saved for possible reuse is called stock scenery; usually it consists of two-dimensional flat framing in the form of jogs, plain flats, and window and door flats. Although the term stock scenery implies a certain standardization of measurements, this applies only to the matter of height, which is determined partly by the sight lines of a given theatre and partly by convenience of shifting and storing. An organization may possess several sets of stock scenery with standardized heights of possibly 18'-0", 14'-0", and 10'-0", or 12'-0", 10'-0", and 8'-0". Since the width of most two-dimensional scenery can be altered with comparative ease, no effort is made to standardize this dimension.

ALTERATION OF STOCK SCENERY

It is possible to alter the size and type of a flat and to repaint it many times before it becomes necessary to wash off excess scene paint or to recover the frame with new material. Scenery can be altered without damaging its value or in any way impairing its expected life. The following suggestions are offered as a guide in the alteration of stock scenery:

1. Risk of damage to the flats can be reduced if the clinched clout nails are withdrawn with a nail puller. When performed with this tool, this operation preserves the corner blocks and keystones for future use and reduces the chances of splitting the framing members.

2. A plain flat can be converted into a window flat by adjusting the position of the toggle bars to form the top and bottom of the window and by inserting two additional vertical stiles to form the window sides. Before removing the old canvas from the window opening, tack along the outside edge of the window-framing members. Run a sharp knife along the inside of the window opening to cut away the canvas. Glue and tack the canvas remaining on the flat to the faces of the window-framing members.

3. The width of a flat can be increased a few inches by nailing or battening strips of 1″ stock of the desired width to the flat stiles. Cover the cracks with strips of canvas or muslin called dutchmen; tack and glue into position.

4. A plain flat or a window flat can be altered into a door flat by the following procedure. Move the toggle bar to correspond to the desired height of the door. Determine the exact location of the door opening; measure and cut two vertical door stiles and nail them into place by using corner blocks and keystones. Remove the part of the lower rail between the inner edges of the door stiles. Reinforce the bottom rail with a sill iron made from $\frac{1}{4}$″ by $\frac{3}{4}$″ strap iron. Remove the canvas from the door opening and tack and glue the canvas remaining on the flat to the door stiles and toggle.

5. A window or door flat can easily be converted into a plain flat. No effort is made to alter the framing assembly of a window flat—a patch is simply placed over the window opening. Care should be taken in selecting the material for the patch to see that it matches the material already on the flat; otherwise the difference in surface texture will be noticeable under the final paint job. If new material must be used as a patch on an old flat, it should be given several coats of paint to reduce the contrast in texture with the surrounding surface. The framing of a door flat can also remain unaltered when it is converted into a plain flat. The patching can be done by inserting a section of lower rail into the space between the door stiles, then applying the patch with glue and tacks. Sometimes it may be advantageous to rebuild the door flat in part by removing the sill iron and door stiles and replacing the lower rail before applying the covering material.

6. Since most stock scenery has been standardized as to height the technician will avoid altering this dimension if at all possible. If he reduces the height of a flat, he also reduces his opportunities to reuse it. If he increases the

height of a unit by battening on an additional frame, he does so at the expense of both weight and strength.

VARIATIONS IN THE USE OF STOCK SCENERY

The rectangular form of two-dimensional scenery lends itself well to a wide range of uses. The technician soon becomes proficient at utilizing stock scenery in any number of ways to reduce building time and production cost. Even such highly irregular forms as a two-dimensional tree cutout, a random board fence, or a series of mountain groundrows each may have as its foundation one or more pieces of stock scenery used in some unusual manner. The drawings on Plate 26 provide several such examples.

Notice that these variations in form were achieved by one of two methods: irregular contours were added to the sides or top of a flat, or the flat was turned to rest upon its stile rather than its rail. The following description of a false proscenium may be taken as another example.

THE TWO-DIMENSIONAL FALSE PROSCENIUM

The false proscenium is a large decorative archway which spans the full width of the stage and is normally placed just upstage of the main curtain and parallel with it (Plate 30). Usually it has a distinctive silhouette that is appropriate for a particular production. Through it the audience views the entire action of the play.

Since the budgets of many community and educational theatres are limited, the management might well consider the construction of such a large unit of scenery too costly. However, it is quite possible to build one at only a fraction of its expected cost by utilizing a series of standard flats that can be taken from the theatre's supply of stock scenery. Five of the seven flats used in the construction of the arch illustrated here were taken from stock. Only the curved sections F and G were newly constructed, and even these were made from lumber salvaged from previous productions and covered with parts of an old drop. The only cost of this archway was that incurred in painting it.

A few moments spent in studying the drawing will reveal that the false proscenium is really nothing but an oversized door flat with contour-forming segments added to the top of the door opening on either side. In this particular

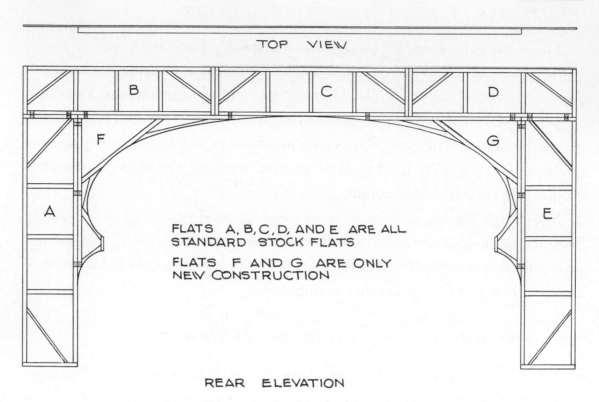

TOP VIEW

B   C   D

F   G

A   E

FLATS A, B, C, D, AND E ARE ALL
STANDARD STOCK FLATS

FLATS F AND G ARE ONLY
NEW CONSTRUCTION

REAR ELEVATION

CONSTRUCTION OF FALSE
PROSCENIUM BY USING STANDARD
FLATS

PLATE 30

case the sides of the arch were formed from two 5'-0" x 18'-0" stock flats. The header across the top was made by hinging three other stock flats end to end. Two of these flats were 14'-0" long, the third was 12'-0" long, and all were a uniform 3'-6" wide.

The problem of transporting such a large unit from the shop to the stage was solved by building the archway in three sections, the header forming one and the two 18'-0" side flats, to which the curved segments had been hinged, the other two. The sections were laid out face up on the stage floor and centered in relation to the regular proscenium arch. The three sections were joined with tight pin hinges that were concealed by gluing and tacking over them a pre-painted dutchman.

The arch was pulled into an upright position and supported by one of the battens of the counterweight system. This batten was lowered to the stage floor and $\frac{3}{8}$" manila snatch lines were tied from it to hanger irons spaced across the rails of the header. To prevent the leg stiles of the arch from breaking as the batten was raised it was necessary to provide support for them by "walking them up."

KEEPING A CARD CATALOGUE

The cost of a production can certainly be materially reduced by altering and reusing stock scenery, but to reuse scenery at all it is first necessary to know how many pieces are available, how many of each type there are, what the exact dimensions are, and what the condition of each piece is. All of this information can be kept in a card catalogue with a number assigned to each piece of scenery. Any convenient method of classification may be used, but one of the simplest is to divide the scenery into types of uniform height, such as 14'-0" jogs, 14'-0" plain flats, etc. Should the theatre possess a second set of stock scenery of a different height, this would be catalogued and filed separately. The catalogue can be extended to cover all items of scenery kept for possible reuse (Plate 31).

Selecting a catalogue number can be simplicity itself. Consecutive numbers from 1 to 200 or 300 are jotted down in a record book. Each piece of scenery is assigned a number which is then painted on the back of the unit in some conspicuous place. In the case of a flat, the number is painted on both stiles

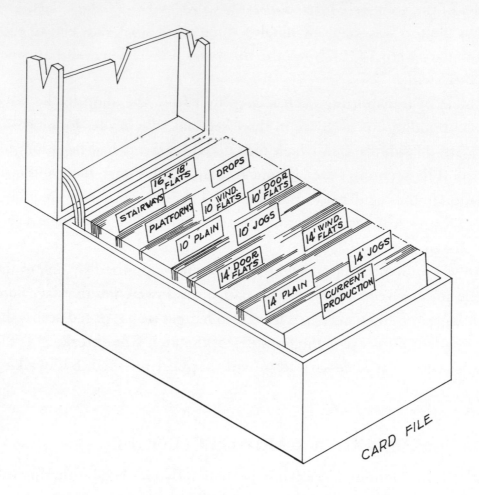

CARD FILE

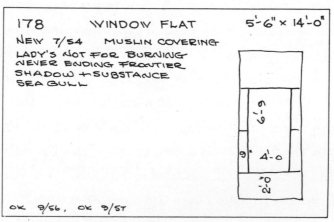

| 178 | WINDOW FLAT | 5'-6" × 14'-0" |

NEW 7/54   MUSLIN COVERING
LADY'S NOT FOR BURNING
NEVER ENDING FRONTIER
SHADOW + SUBSTANCE
SEA GULL

OK 9/56, OK 9/57

SAMPLE CARD

CARD
CATALOGUE

PLATE 31

about 5'-0" from the floor so that no matter which way the flat is stored in the scene dock the number can be readily seen. To indicate in the record book that a particular number has been assigned, a very brief description of the flat follows the catalogue number—for example, No. 124, 2'-6" x 14'-0" jog. A 4" x 6" filing card is used to record the complete description of the unit. Across the top of the card from left to right is the catalogue number, the type of unit, and the overall dimensions. Immediately below and to the left are listed the date of construction, kind of lumber and covering material, color, or special construction details. On the opposite side of the card is a freehand working drawing that gives all key dimensions. Cards representing flats or units of the same type and height are then filed together under their proper index.

As the technician makes his working drawings he will have at his finger tips the complete history and all information he will need concerning each piece of scenery kept in stock. As he makes his selection of units he jots down the name of the production on the card of that unit and files it under a separate "current production" index. This eliminates the possibility of using the same unit of scenery more than once in a production. Should he find it necessary to alter the unit in any way, he makes corresponding changes in the drawing and dimensions on the card. This keeps the catalogue accurate and up to date. With the close of the production, all of the cards are withdrawn from the "current production" index and redistributed into their proper classifications. If a unit of scenery has been so altered, or is in such condition that there is little use in keeping it in stock, it is dismantled for salvageable material and its card destroyed. The corresponding number in the record book is freed for reassignment by simply erasing the unit description.

The time and effort required to establish a card catalogue and to keep it accurate is more than repaid by the advantages it offers:

1. The technician can thumb through a pack of cards rather than a stack of scenery to get the information he needs.
2. There is a great saving of time at the drafting board when units requiring the least alteration can be selected.
3. There is a saving of man hours in the shop where these units are assembled.
4. The cost of the production can be held at a minimum.
5. Unnecessary constructional duplication is avoided.

three-dimensional scenery

Three-DIMENSIONAL scenery includes all architectural features and weight-bearing structures that impart to a setting a sense of solidity or depth. They are constructed separately and are usually handled separately from the two-dimensional scenery against which they may be placed. The factors governing the construction of three-dimensional scenery are identical with those listed for the construction of two-dimensional scenery.

TYPES OF STAGE WINDOWS

The variety of form and size of stage windows is almost limitless; it may range from a slot window in a prison cell to an elaborate stained-glass window in a cathedral. Most stage windows are made from three basic parts—casing, jamb, and sashes. The casing is the practical or decorative framework that overlaps the wall surface and encases the window opening. The jamb, more frequently called the thickness piece in stage terminology, is the frame, which is usually placed at right angles to the casing to simulate the actual thickness of the wall. The sashes are the movable parts of a window—the frames that support the glass. Disregarding the matter of variety of form, stage windows fall into four distinct types: fake, dependent, independent, and practical.

THE FAKE WINDOW

For lack of a better name a simple opening in a flat might be called a fake window (Plate 32). It is an impractical affair that is literally no more than a hole in the flat. The muntins, or crossbars, if any, are likely to be made of twilled tape tacked to the back of the window opening. The casing, and in some cases

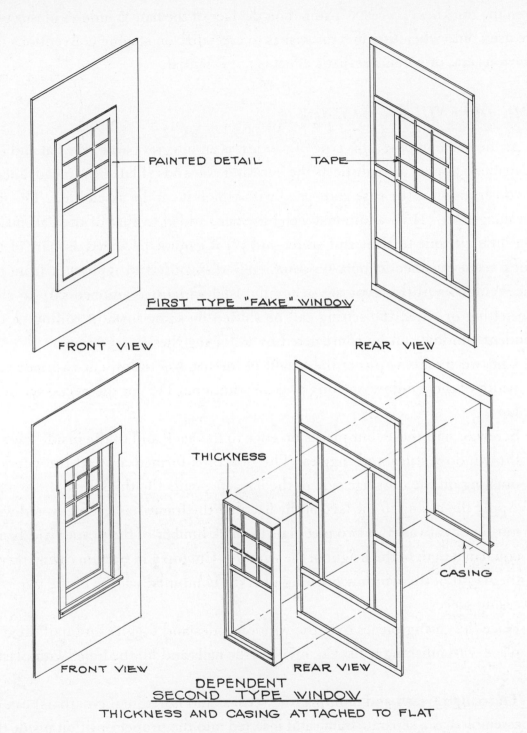

PAINTED DETAIL

TAPE

FIRST TYPE "FAKE" WINDOW

FRONT VIEW

REAR VIEW

THICKNESS

CASING

FRONT VIEW

REAR VIEW

DEPENDENT
SECOND TYPE WINDOW

THICKNESS AND CASING ATTACHED TO FLAT

PLATE 32

even the thickness pieces, is painted on the face of the flat. Windows of this type are used only when the director wishes to capitalize on staging conventions of a previous era, or when a realistic effect is not essential.

THE DEPENDENT WINDOW

As the name implies, this type of window is an integral part of the flat and can be made to appear as realistic as the occasion demands (Plate 32). Its advantage in construction is the ease and speed with which it can be assembled. The disadvantages are (1) its additional weight which, added to that of the flat, makes it a difficult unit to shift and store; and (2) it cannot be saved as part of the stock scenery, since it must be completely dismantled to remove it from the flat. Windows of this type are generally used when it is unnecessary to shift the setting or when the setting can be shifted by some form of rolling. A dependent window can be constructed by following these suggestions:

1. Cut two thickness pieces the height of the window stiles; cut two more the width of the window opening plus an additional $1\frac{1}{2}''$ for the necessary overlap.

2. Screw or nail these four pieces on edge to the back and to the inside faces of the window stiles and toggles. The box thus formed around the window opening on the off-stage side of the flat represents the thickness of the wall.

3. Apply the casing to the face of the flat after the frame has been covered with muslin or canvas. Cut two pieces of $1''$ thick lumber of the proper width and equal in length to the height of the window. Cut top and bottom casing pieces the width of the window opening plus the combined widths of the two side casing pieces.

4. Place the casing pieces over the window stiles and toggles and nail them in place with finishing nails. Countersink the nails and fill the holes with plastic wood.

5. The window sash and muntins (the vertical and horizontal crossbars) can be assembled as a separate frame and inserted into the proper position inside the thickness piece. If the design of the sash is simple, it may be easier to assemble the various parts and join them directly to the thickness piece than to construct them as a separate frame.

THE INDEPENDENT WINDOW

This window is made as a separate unit which can be inserted or removed from a window flat with both speed and ease (Plate 33). Windows constructed and shifted in this manner require that adequate clearance be provided in the size of the opening cut in the window flat. This type of window and window flat is not difficult to construct if the suggestions given below are followed:

1. Make the opening in the window flat 3″ wider and $2\frac{1}{4}$″ higher than the specified inside dimensions of the window. This allows for the thickness of the lumber from which the window is made and for the necessary clearance required for easy insertion and removal of the window unit.

2. Cut and assemble the four thickness pieces into a box with inside dimensions corresponding to those specified by the designer's plans.

3. Assemble the window sash as a separate frame, or build it as an integral part of the thickness frame as previously described.

4. Join the casing directly to the edge of the thickness piece with $1\frac{1}{2}$″ No. 9 flat-head screws with the heads countersunk and covered with plastic wood. (Putty cannot be used, as the oil in it will discolor the water-soluble scene paint.)

5. With large angle irons reinforce the back of the butt joints formed by the casing.

6. Decorative trim and molding can be applied directly over the face of the casing. Glue and brad these into position.

7. The casing overlapping the window stiles and toggles on the face of the flat prevents the window unit from falling through the flat, while strap hinges mounted on the back of the window thickness and locking in back of the window stiles hold it solidly in place.

THE PRACTICAL WINDOW

The practical window differs from the dependent and independent types only in having a practical sash that may be raised or lowered. Even with the practical window there is usually just one part of the sash that is capable of movement. The frame of the movable sash is made slightly less in width than the distance between the two side thickness pieces. This provides the neces-

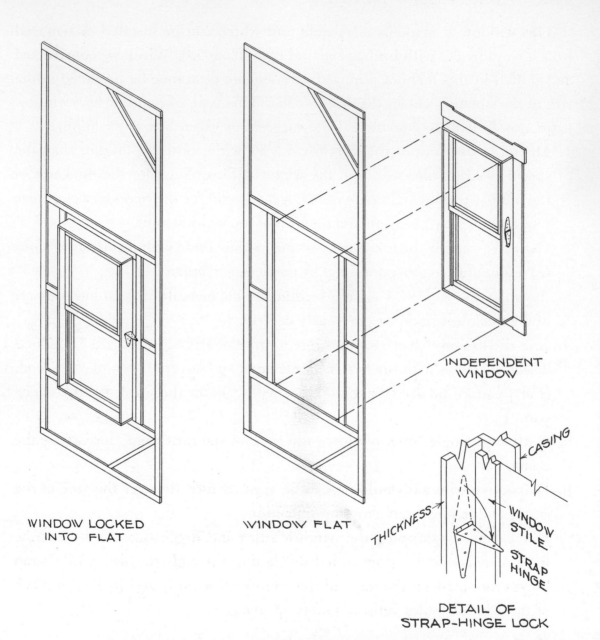

WINDOW LOCKED
INTO FLAT

WINDOW FLAT

INDEPENDENT
WINDOW

CASING

THICKNESS

WINDOW
STILE

STRAP
HINGE

DETAIL OF
STRAP-HINGE LOCK

WINDOW FLAT AND INDEPENDENT WINDOW

PLATE 33

sary clearance so that the frame can be easily moved. Strips of $\frac{3}{8}''$ x $\frac{3}{8}''$ wood are placed on either side of the sash frame to hold it in place and to serve as guides. Since it is impossible to use conventional counterweight balances or tension lifts on a stage window to hold the sash in a raised position, one of the following alternatives can be used:

1. Place the guide strips tightly against either side of the sash, thus creating enough friction to hold the sash at the desired level.
2. Fit metal plungers into holes drilled through the width of the sash frame that will engage holes drilled into the thickness pieces.
3. Drill $\frac{7}{16}''$ holes about $\frac{7}{8}''$ deep into the outer edges of the sash frame. Insert into each hole $\frac{3}{8}''$ x $1''$ compression springs fitted with hardwood caps. Compress the springs and insert the sash into the window frame. Attach the guide strips. The force of the springs shoving the hardwood caps against the thickness pieces will hold the window sash in place. The amount of tension exerted by the springs can be regulated by varying the depth of the holes into which the springs fit.

TYPES OF STAGE DOORS

Doorways are among the architectural features that the designer will use to help establish the period and character of a setting. As such, they are subject to great variety in shape and detail, as dictated by the period from which they are taken and by the circumstances of the play. The materials used, manner of construction, and method of attaching hardware to a stage door have been tested and found practical by years of stage use. Interior doors (door leading from one room to another) are hinged on the off-stage side of the thickness pieces; when located in a side wall, they are mounted so that they will swing off-stage and upstage. This arrangement provides the following advantages:

1. Having the door swing off-stage makes it easier for an actor to make a fast exit or entrance.
2. Valuable on-stage floor space is reserved for the movement of actors or the placement of props or furniture.
3. The door itself serves as a partial backing.
4. It permits the audience to see the thickness pieces of the doorway when the door is closed.

5. The door is finished on only one side, thus permitting the use of lighter weight lumber and giving a faster method of joining.

The method of building doors and door frames falls into the same pattern of types as that used in building windows.

FAKE DOOR

This type of door is completely artificial in appearance and is the counterpart of the fake window previously discussed. The door is made as a simple canvas-covered flat hinged flush with the face of the door flat. The casing and thickness are usually painted on the flat; frequently even the lower rail of the flat is left in place, forcing the actors either to step or trip over it.

DEPENDENT DOORWAY

Doorways of this type are built as an integral part of the door flat (Plate 34). These doors can be easily and quickly built, but their additional weight makes the door flat difficult to shift and store. The door is the only part of the doorway that can be saved for possible reuse, as the thickness pieces and casing must be dismantled to remove them from the flat. The thickness pieces and the casing for the door are assembled in the same manner as those for the dependent window. (See steps 1 through 4 on page 110.) Follow the steps listed below in building an unpaneled or flush door:

1. From 1″ x 4″ lumber cut two rails 1½″ longer than the width of the door opening. Cut the door stiles the same length as the height of the door opening minus the combined width of the two rails. Cut the center toggle to fit between the stiles.
2. Assemble the various parts of the door in their proper positions. Test the accuracy of all right angles and join the parts by fastening with corner blocks and keystones.
3. Cover the face of the door with a single sheet of beaverboard or ¼″ fir plywood. Use 1″ wire brads to fasten covering to frame.
4. Hinge the door to the back of the thickness piece with 6″ or 8″ strap hinges. See Plate 34 for method of bending the hinges and attaching them.
5. Use a rim knob lock latching assembly attached to the back of the door. The catch is mounted on the end of a short length of 1″ x 4″ attached to the outside face of the thickness (Plate 34).

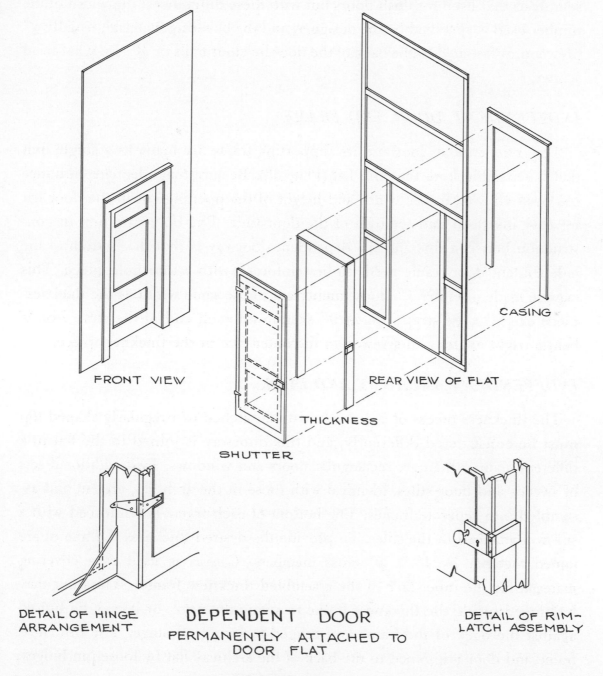

FRONT VIEW

CASING

REAR VIEW OF FLAT

THICKNESS

SHUTTER

DETAIL OF HINGE
ARRANGEMENT

DETAIL OF RIM-
LATCH ASSEMBLY

DEPENDENT DOOR
PERMANENTLY ATTACHED TO
DOOR FLAT

PLATE 34

To build doors with recessed panels, follow the same general method of assembly as that used for flush doors but with these differences: the width of the lumber used is specified by the designer, and the covering material, usually $\frac{1}{4}''$ plywood, is fastened to the back of the door by clout nails or $\frac{7}{8}''$ No. 9 flat-head screws.

INDEPENDENT DOOR AND FRAME

The independent door and its supporting frame are made as a single unit that is separable from the door flat (Plate 35). Be sure that adequate clearance has been allowed in the width and height of the opening cut in the door flat for easy insertion and removal of the door unit. The only variation in construction between this and the dependent doorway is that the bottom of the independent door frame needs to be reinforced with a threshold piece. This may be made of either 1″ stock lumber cut to the same width as the thickness piece or $\frac{3}{16}''$ x $\frac{3}{4}''$ strap iron. A 9″ section on each end of the strap iron is bent at right angles and screwed to the outer face of the thickness piece.

INDEPENDENT ARCHWAY AND DOOR

The thickness pieces of a doorway with an arched or irregularly shaped top must be constructed differently, and this doorway is joined to the flat in a different manner than are rectangular doors and windows. Two additional sets of sweeps and door stiles, identical with those in the arch flat, are cut and assembled into separate frames. The bottom of each frame is reinforced with a sill iron attached to the stiles. To provide the desired thickness the frames are joined together by 1″ x 3″ cross members. Canvas is used as a covering material for the inner face of the assembled thickness frames. The door may be hinged inside the thickness frame to swing on stage, or it may be butted against the back of the frame and hinged to swing off stage. The thickness frame and door are joined to the back of the archway flat by loose-pin hinges.

EXTERIOR DOOR AND FRAME

An exterior door differs from a conventional stage door in that it is designed to swing into the setting, thereby exposing both of its faces. A door of this type may be used with either a dependent or an independent frame. The

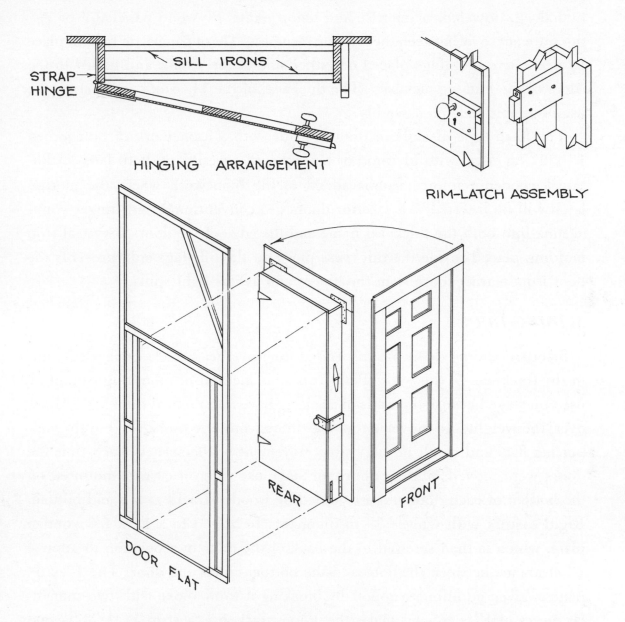

STRAP HINGE

SILL IRONS

HINGING ARRANGEMENT

RIM-LATCH ASSEMBLY

DOOR FLAT

REAR

FRONT

DOOR FLAT AND INDEPENDENT DOOR UNIT

PLATE 35

parts of the exterior door can be made from $1\frac{1}{4}''$ stock that has been joined by halved, doweled, or mortise and tenon joints. Plywood panels $\frac{1}{8}''$ or $\frac{3}{16}''$ thick are cut to fit between the framing members. These panels are held in place by decorative moldings placed on either side of the panels and nailed to the edges of the framing members. The thickness of the $1\frac{1}{4}''$ stock will permit the use of a mortise latch assembly.

The flush type of exterior door is made with a framework of butt-joined $1'' \times 2''$ on edge, with plywood or beaverboard covering on both faces. Additional wooden reinforcement is added to the framework where the mortise latch will be inserted. All exterior doors use conventional butt hinges countersunk into both the thickness frame and the edge of the door. A special stop molding placed inside the thickness piece on the off-stage side prevents the door from tearing loose from the hinges and avoids light spills.

SLIDING DOORS

Standard sliding doors are suspended from overhead tracks concealed within the thickness of the walls (Plate 36). This method of mounting cannot be used on stage because the walls of a setting have no practical thickness. Moreover, the weight and movement of the doors would be transferred to the supporting flats and result in the visible movement of the scenery each time the doors were moved. Sliding doors for stage use ride on castors mounted on the bottom of each door and are guided by wooden tracks at top and bottom. Rigid castors with wheels $3''$ in diameter are bolted to a $1'' \times 6''$ wooden plate, which is then screwed to the back of the door in a position to allow a $\frac{3}{4}''$ clearance between the floor and the bottom rail of the door. The $1'' \times 6''$ plate is given additional support by blocking it from above with two triangular pieces of $1'' \times 6''$. To make the lower track use a strip of $\frac{1}{4}''$ plywood twice the length of the combined width of the two doors. Bevel strips of $1'' \times 2''$ and nail them to the plywood to form a groove slightly wider than the width of the castor wheel. The top track is made from lengths of standard $1'' \times 3''$ and $1'' \times 2''$ assembled as illustrated. The upper track is attached to the top of the thickness piece; the lower track can be screwed to the stage floor. Retaining strips are screwed to the off-stage edge of each door to engage the thickness pieces and to prevent the doors from rolling beyond the halfway point of the door opening.

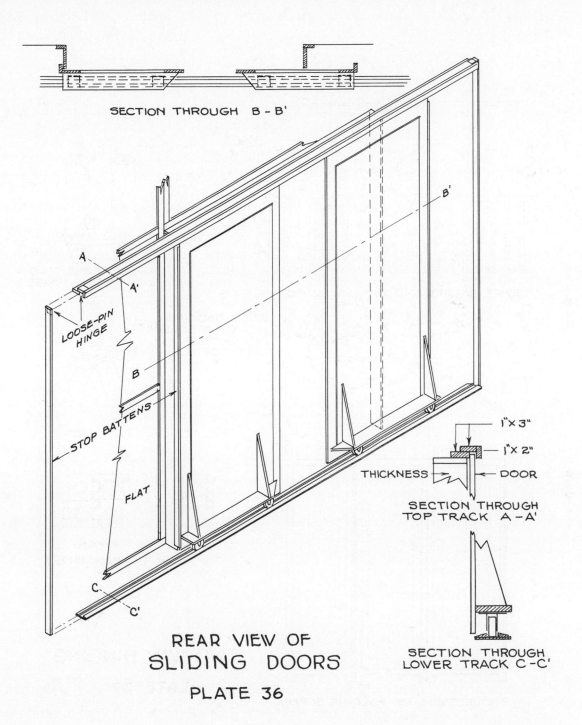

SECTION THROUGH B - B'

LOOSE-PIN
HINGE

STOP BATTENS

FLAT

1"x 3"

1"x 2"

THICKNESS   DOOR

SECTION THROUGH
TOP TRACK A - A'

SECTION THROUGH
LOWER TRACK C -C'

REAR VIEW OF
SLIDING DOORS
PLATE 36

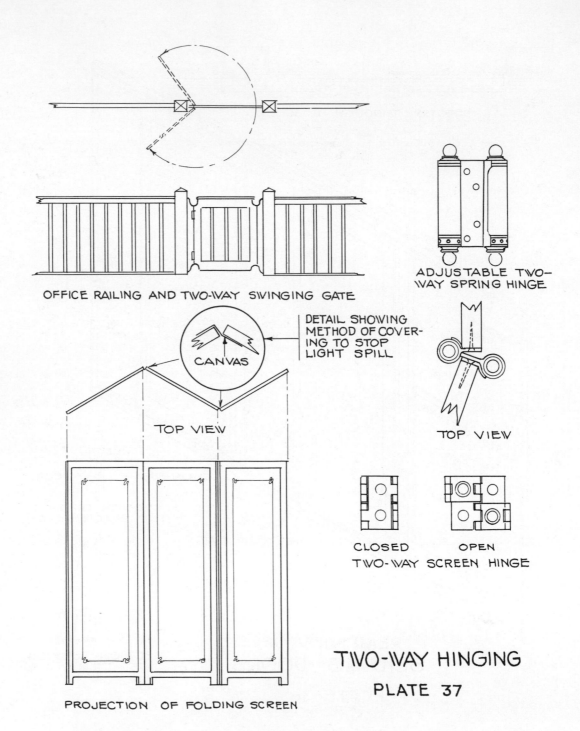

OFFICE RAILING AND TWO-WAY SWINGING GATE

ADJUSTABLE TWO-WAY SPRING HINGE

DETAIL SHOWING METHOD OF COVERING TO STOP LIGHT SPILL

CANVAS

TOP VIEW

TOP VIEW

CLOSED   OPEN
TWO-WAY SCREEN HINGE

PROJECTION OF FOLDING SCREEN

TWO-WAY HINGING
PLATE 37

TWO-WAY SWINGING DOORS

Barroom doors, waist-high office doors, and old-fashioned swinging doors like those sometimes found between kitchen and dining room are no more difficult to build than double-faced exterior doors (Plate 37). The special two-way spring hinges required for mounting this type of door can be obtained from any well-stocked hardware store. Be sure to get the type of hinge that has an adjustment for the spring so that the rate of swing can be controlled. The swinging door is hinged from the center of the thickness piece and is free to travel in an arc of 180 degrees before the door strikes the face of the thickness. A greater arc can be provided by mounting a vertical batten in the center of the thickness piece and hinging the door from this. The wider the batten, the farther the door will swing before striking the edges of the thickness pieces.

ARCHITECTURAL TRIM

A conventional realistic interior makes extensive use of three-dimensional architectural trim. Such trim includes baseboards, chair rails, panels, plate rails, picture molds, pilasters, columns, and cornices (Plate 38). The designer makes use of these in two ways: (1) they help him establish the period and nationality on which the setting was patterned; and (2) with the exception of the vertical pilaster and column, the horizontal lines offered by the remaining trim serve as a means of counteracting the exaggerated height of most stage settings. For the same reason that the height and width of a room is exaggerated for stage use, the width and depth of all architectural trim is proportionally increased. This permits the audience to see and appreciate the detail of the trim from all parts of the house.

In the not-too-distant past such architectural trim was achieved by painting on the face of the scenery, but this practice has given way to the building of actual three-dimensional facsimiles that are applied to the face of the scenery. Unquestionably the latter method produces a much more convincing realistic effect.

The problem associated with the use of three-dimensional trim is not one of construction but one affecting the cost, method of rigging, and manner of shifting. Assuming that the budget is liberal, the single-set production can be

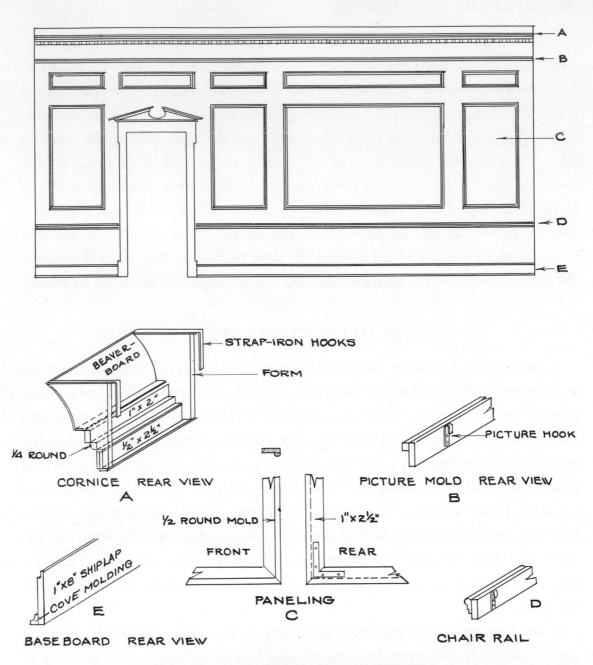

A

B

C

D

E

STRAP-IRON HOOKS

BEAVER-BOARD

FORM

1" x 2"

¼ ROUND

½" x 2½"

CORNICE   REAR VIEW

A

PICTURE HOOK

PICTURE MOLD   REAR VIEW

B

½ ROUND MOLD

1" x 2½"

FRONT

REAR

PANELING

C

1"x8" SHIPLAP

COVE MOLDING

E

BASEBOARD   REAR VIEW

CHAIR RAIL

D

THREE-DIMENSIONAL ARCHITECTURAL
TRIM

PLATE 38

dressed with as much trim as the design and the work schedule will allow. When the setting is to be shifted, attention must be given to the manner of rigging the trim. Hinged flat scenery with three-dimensional trim mounted across its face cannot be folded unless the trim is temporarily removed. If trim remains in place, the scenery must be moved by either flying it or rolling it.

BASEBOARD

The baseboard, sometimes called the mopboard, is a projecting board or wide molding which is placed against the wall at its junction with the floor and extends completely around the room. An inexpensive baseboard can be made from 6″, 8″, or 10″ carsiding or shiplap. Additional molding or strips of wood can be nailed to the face of the baseboard if a more elaborate pattern is required. The baseboard can be permanently attached by screwing or nailing it to the face of the scenery. If it must be removed during a scene shift, it should be attached by picture hooks and eyes. A single hook and eye near the end of each section of baseboard is all that is required to hold it in place.

CHAIR RAIL

The chair rail is a projecting rail or decorative molding extending around the walls of a room to protect them from damage from the backs of chairs. It is usually placed at a height of 2′-4″ to 2′-10″ from the floor. An effective but inexpensive chair rail can be made from 1″ x 3″ and 1″ x 2″ stock joined at right angles to each other, with the face of the 1″ x 2″ nailed to the edge of the 1″ x 3″; this forms an overhanging lip of 1″. If a more decorative rail is desired, additional molding, dentils, or even strips of varying widths of beaverboard can be nailed to the face of the 1″ x 3″ beneath the projecting lip. The completed chair rail can be attached to the scenery by picture hooks and eyes or permanently attached by screws or nails.

PANELS

The paneling of a room is the division of various parts of the walls into areas, usually rectangular in shape, with their centers recessed or outlined with decorative molding. The recessed panel can be made in one of two ways: (1) The panels can be formed within the framework of a flat with additional horizontal and vertical members. The covering material is mounted on the back of the panel section and the rest of the covering is placed on the face of the flat. This method of construction necessitates major alterations of all stock scenery used for this purpose and results in an increased cost and weight of each unit. However (2) a recessed panel can be faked by fastening rectangular frames of decorative molding to the face of a flat and painting the enclosed area a little darker than the rest of the surrounding surface. At points where the panel frames cannot be fastened to the stiles or toggles of the flat, additional battens are added to the back of the flat for support of the frames. If the setting must be shifted, the panels can either be attached by picture hooks and eyes and so removed, or they must be so placed that they will not interfere with the folding of any hinged units. The insertion of a tumbler between two hinged flats will provide adequate clearance for the panel frames when the flats are folded face to face.

PLATE RAILS AND PICTURE MOLDING

Trim of this type is constructed and mounted in much the same manner as chair rails. Every possible effort should be made to avoid removing this type of trim from scenery during a shift, as it is usually mounted so high that it cannot be conveniently reached without a ladder. When such trim is essential and it is necessary to shift the scenery, the trim is permanently mounted in place and the wall sections are shifted by flying them or rolling them on tip jacks, outriggers, or wagons.

CEILING BEAMS

In a setting where period and circumstances justify their use, there is probably no more distinctive architectural trim than ceiling beams (Plate 39). A one-set show, of course, offers no major problem concerning either the construction or the manner of rigging the beams—they are simply attached to the cross battens of the ceiling. However, when the same ceiling must be used for several settings in a production, or when the production is to be taken on the road, some other method of construction and shifting must be devised. Plate 39 illustrates one possible solution to these problems.

The beaming of this particular setting, a Midwestern farmhouse, consisted

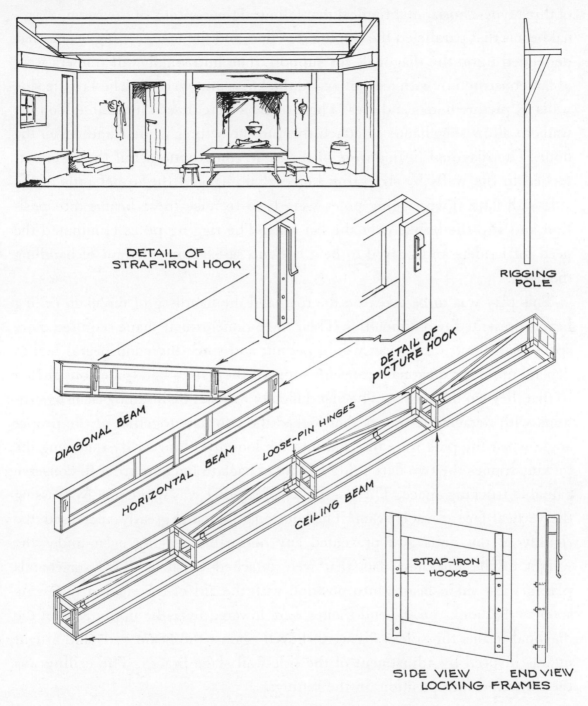

DETAIL OF
STRAP-IRON HOOK

RIGGING
POLE

DIAGONAL BEAM

HORIZONTAL BEAM

LOOSE-PIN HINGES

DETAIL OF
PICTURE HOOK

CEILING BEAM

STRAP-IRON
HOOKS

SIDE VIEW   END VIEW
LOCKING FRAMES

DETACHABLE CEILING BEAMS

PLATE 39

of three types: horizontal timbers that followed the contour of the room, diagonal beams that paralleled the sloping roof line, and the main ceiling beams that depended upon the diagonals for support. The horizontal wall timbers were of flat construction with a 4″ plywood thickness and were attached to the side walls by picture hooks and eyes. These timbers were placed low enough on the walls to allow stagehands to attach them to the setting while standing on the floor. The diagonal beams were of the same construction, but they were attached to the walls by strap-iron hooks that engaged the upper rails of the side-wall flats. Two rigging poles were used to raise these beams into position and slip the hooks over the flat rails. The rigging poles eliminated the need for ladders and proved to be a fast and satisfactory method of handling the units.

This play was to be taken on the road and the handling of the main ceiling beams presented two difficulties: Their three-dimensional shape required more space than the trucking van would permit; and since the main beams had to depend upon the diagonal beams for support, the frames had to be constructed so that they would not sag. The first difficulty was met by building them as two-folds with detachable frames that locked the two flats together at the proper angle when the pins were inserted into the loose-pin hinges. By removing the locking frames the two flats could be folded back to back in order to conserve valuable trucking space. The possibility of sagging was overcome by trussing the vertical face of each beam. This diagonal bracing greatly increased the rigidity of the units and prevented any noticeable sagging even under the weight of the thickness flats that were attached to them. Two stagehands placed these main beams into position with the aid of the rigging poles. As soon as the hooks on the end frames were lowered over the upper rails of the diagonal beams the side walls were shoved against the beam ends and a tight fit was insured by adjustment of the side-wall stage braces. The ceiling was then lowered into position on the setting.

PILASTERS

Vertical beams or pilasters are frequently used in conjunction with heavy horizontal beaming such as that just described. Pilasters (Plate 40) are rectangular in shape; they are structurally a part of the wall but project out from it

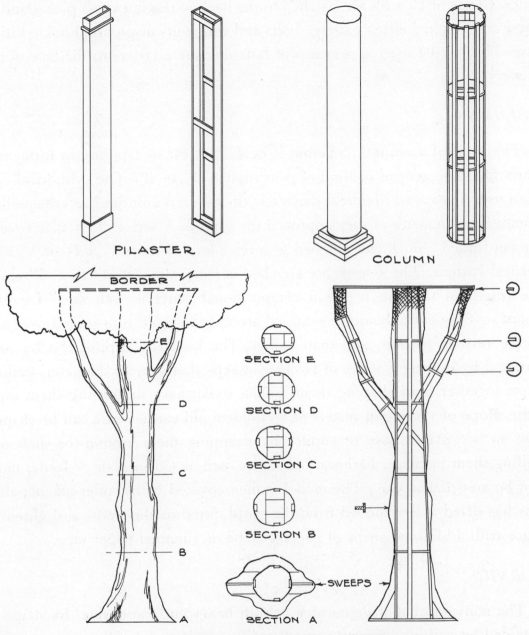

PILASTER   COLUMN

BORDER

E

D

C

B

A

SECTION E

SECTION D

SECTION C

SECTION B

SWEEPS

SECTION A

THREE-DIMENSIONAL TREE

PLATE 40

about one-third of the width of the pilaster. They are made of plain flat construction with thickness pieces of either 1″ stock or ¼″ plywood attached to both stiles. Cleats of 1″ x 3″ are fastened to the back of the thickness pieces and to these are attached either carriage bolts and wing nuts or picture hooks. Either assembly may be used as a means of fastening the pilasters to the face of the scenery.

COLUMNS

The shaft of a column, whether it be cylindrical or tapering in form, employs the same general method of construction (Plate 40). The cylindrical column uses sweeps of identical diameter; the tapered column has sweeps that diminish in diameter as they approach the capitol. A series of circular sweeps are cut from 1″ stock and notched to receive four or more 1″ x 2″ or 1″ x 3″ vertical battens. The sweeps are attached at intervals of 2′-0″ to 2′-6″ along the length of the battens. Thin compositional material such as ⅛″ Lacquer board or Easy-curve board is wrapped around the shaft, butt-joined over one of the vertical battens, and then nailed. The base and capitol can be constructed by cutting a series of circular sweeps that vary in diameter, nailing them together, and shaping them with a spokeshave or turning them on a lathe. Rope of varying diameters or sections of old garden hose can be shaped into an acceptable base or capitol by wrapping them around the shaft and nailing them in place. Elaborate capitols, such as Corinthian or Ionic, must first be modeled in clay. The model is then covered with papier-mâché; after this has dried it is removed from the mold, fitted to the shaft, and glued in place with additional strips of papier-mâché or gummed paper tape.

CORNICE

The conventional stage cornice is both heavy and expensive. Its shape is obtained by nailing different sizes of molding and stock lumber to supporting forms that give the cornice its desired shape (Plate 41). The finished cornice is attached to the scenery by inserting a batten on the back of the cornice through a slot cut in the scenery and locking it in place on the back with loose-pin hinges or turn buttons. This method of construction and rigging is too expensive for the low budgets of most educational and community theatres.

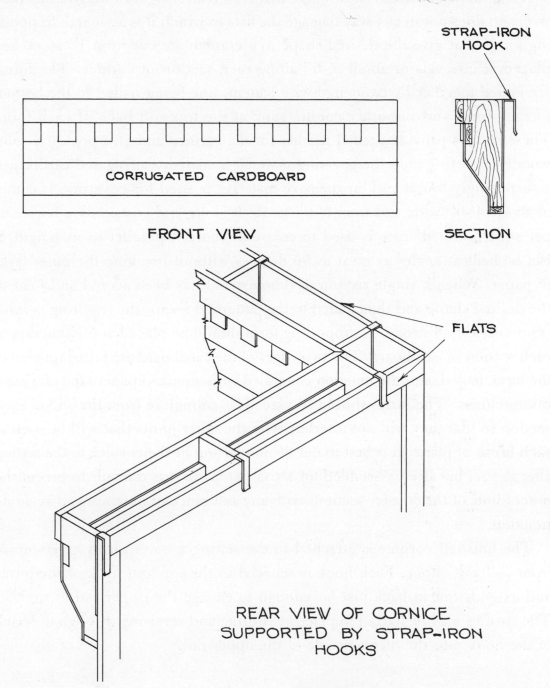

STRAP-IRON
HOOK

CORRUGATED CARDBOARD

FRONT VIEW

SECTION

FLATS

REAR VIEW OF CORNICE
SUPPORTED BY STRAP-IRON
HOOKS

PLATE 41

A simplified cornice is shown here that is extremely light in weight, inexpensive, and does not in any way damage the flats to which it is attached. Supporting forms that give the desired shape to a cornice are cut from 1″ stock and placed at intervals of about 3′-6″ along each section of cornice. The forms are joined together by two lengthwise battens, one being nailed to the bottom of each form and the other countersunk at the top and back of each form. These battens provide needed rigidity for the cornice and also present a solid wooden face to which the covering material is nailed. Corrugated cardboard, a surprisingly tough and inexpensive material, is used for covering. It comes in sheets 4′-0″ wide and from 6′-0″ to 10′-0″ long and costs only a few cents per square foot. If care is used to crease or score it parallel to its length, it can be bent at angles as great as 90 degrees without breaking the outer layer of paper. When a single section of this material has been scored and bent to the desired shape and then nailed to the patterned forms, the resulting cornice is both rigid and strong. A supporting form should be placed at the junction of each section of cardboard. The two edges of the cardboard are butt-joined over the form, nailed, and the junction concealed with gummed paper tape or a muslin dutchman. The forms should be placed far enough in from the end of each section so that they will not interfere with the miter joints that will be used at each break of plane. It is best to cut the miters and fit the cornice to the setting after the set has been assembled for a trial setup, as it is difficult to precut the miter joints of the cornice sections with any assurance of obtaining an accurate junction.

The finished cornice is attached to the setting by strap-iron hooks made from $\frac{3}{16}″$ x $\frac{3}{4}″$ stock. Each hook is screwed to the top and back of the forms and extends out in back just far enough to engage the upper rail of the flat. The cornice may be locked in place by drilling and screwing through the back of the hook into the off-stage side of the upper rail.

STAGE PLATFORMS

Few features of a stage setting delight both the director and the actors more than the extensive use of varied acting levels. These make possible variety in stage movement and grouping not otherwise possible.

There are three types of platforms normally used for this purpose; two are folding platforms of different types, and the third is a rigid platform. The latter is preferred by most technicians.

THE RIGID PLATFORM

The rigid platform has many advantages: it is easier and much faster to build, it is less expensive, it may be easily varied in height, it can be made much stronger by the addition of extra legs, it may be readily converted into a wagon, and two or more may be bolted together in numerous ways (Plate 42). The only serious disadvantage of the rigid platform is that it is heavier, and when it is legged up and ready for use, it is both bulkier and more space-consuming than a parallel or folding platform.

The supporting frame of the rigid platform can be built of either 1″ x 4″ or 1″ x 6″ white pine or 2″ x 4″ or 2″ x 6″ fir. If economy is the first consideration, it would be well to consider the use of 2″ fir, for, while it is somewhat heavier than white pine, it is about half as expensive. Assemble the outside frame first, placing the framing member on edge for greater strength and butt-joining them with common 12-penny nails. The inside supporting members should run parallel with the length of the platform and should not be spaced farther apart than 2′-0″. The platform top can be made of white pine tongue and groove flooring, either nailed or screwed to the supporting frame. A much stronger platform top is made by flooring the frame with $\frac{3}{4}$″ 5-ply fir. The top of the platform should be padded with either felt or jute; if the budget it limited, an old rug or even several layers of folded newspapers can be used, tacked in place to prevent their shifting under the covering material. Heavyweight muslin, or preferably canvas, is used as covering for the padding, allowing sufficient width and length so that it may be carried down and glued and tacked to the sides of the frame. There is little chance of snagging or tearing the covering when it is attached in this manner.

The height of a platform can be varied by bolting 2″ x 4″ legs to the inside corners of the frame with $\frac{3}{8}$″ x $3\frac{1}{2}$″ carriage bolts. Sets of legs of different heights can be kept for future use, provided some method is found to identify them with their position on the platform. Any platform over one foot in height should have the legs diagonally braced by lengths of 1″ x 3″ against the inner face of the platform sides and ends.

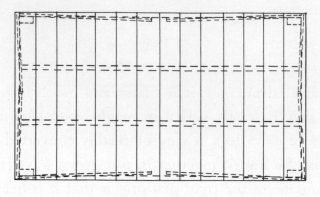

TOP VIEW

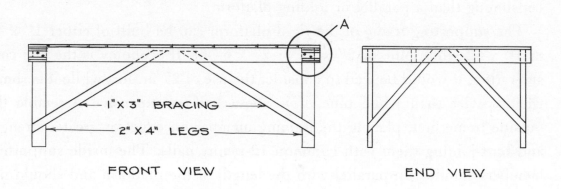

1" X 3" BRACING

2" X 4" LEGS

FRONT VIEW

END VIEW

A

RIGID PLATFORM

PLATE 42

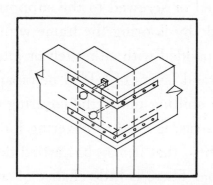

DETAIL A
PERFORATED STRAP-IRON
REINFORCEMENT FOR CORNER

THE CONTINENTAL PARALLEL

The two types of folding platforms just mentioned are the Continental parallel and the Standard parallel. Both have removable tops and supporting frames that can be folded. The general pattern of construction is similar in both; the principal difference lies in the fact that the center supports of the Continental parallel are removable and it has a different hinging arrangement (Plate 43). These factors give it three major advantages over the Standard: (1) Since the center supporting frames are detachable, they do not interfere with the folding of the outside frames. This permits the center frames to be placed closer together, thus providing greater strength and support for the platform top. (2) The hinging arrangement permits the supporting frames to be folded into a compact unit no longer than the platform, thus requiring less storage space. (3) It is possible to build these parallels to larger dimensions than is practical with the Standard parallel.

The supporting frames for a Continental parallel are made of 1″ x 3″ white pine stock assembled by mortise and tenon joints, halved joints, or butt joints reinforced by corner blocks and keystones. It will be noticed in the illustration that the outside end frames are each made in two sections and hinged to fold inside the side frames. The center frames are slipped into place between two pairs of 1″ x 1½″ vertical battens that are screwed to the inner face of the outside side frames. The center frames are equipped with strap-iron hooks countersunk at each end of the top rail. The hooks engage the top of the side frame, which should be notched to accommodate the $\frac{3}{16}$″ thickness of the hooks. This permits the top to rest solidly against the supporting frames. The hooks are essential for two reasons: they prevent the center frames from slipping out of their grooves when the assembled parallel is picked up and moved, and they serve to hold the side frames equidistant from each other.

The removable tops of these platforms are made from either tongue and groove white pine flooring or from a single sheet of $\frac{3}{4}$″ fir plywood. Battens of 1″ x 4″ are screwed into place on the underside of the top $\frac{7}{8}$″ or 1″ in from its outer edges. When the top is placed in position, the 1″ x 4″ battens fit down inside and against the faces of the supporting frames. This holds the top in place and prevents the frames from folding. The parallel top is padded and covered in

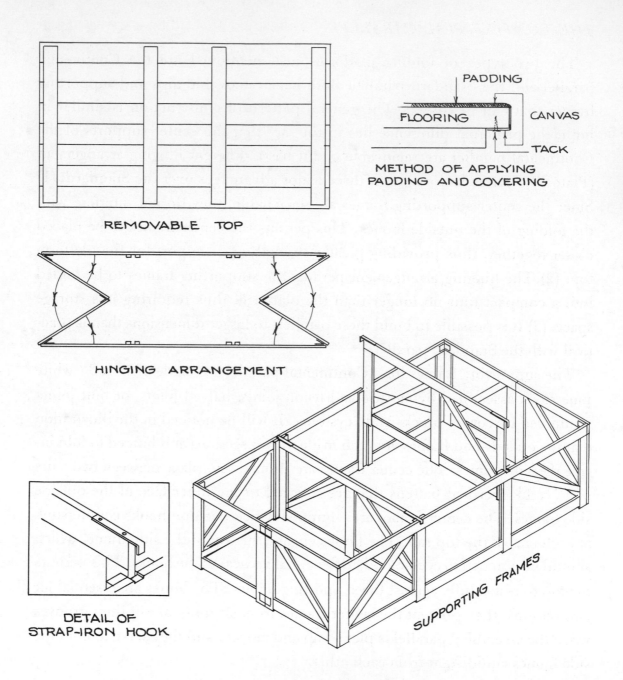

PADDING

FLOORING

CANVAS

TACK

METHOD OF APPLYING
PADDING AND COVERING

REMOVABLE TOP

HINGING ARRANGEMENT

DETAIL OF
STRAP-IRON HOOK

SUPPORTING FRAMES

THE CONTINENTAL PARALLEL

PLATE 43

much the same manner as the rigid platform, allowing a sufficient overhang of the covering material so that it can be pulled over the edges and tacked to the underside of the platform top.

THE STANDARD PARALLEL

As already noted, the similarity between the Standard and Continental parallel is great: both are folding platforms, both have removable tops, and both have hinged supporting frames. It is evident from Plate 44 that the length of the Standard parallel is increased by its width when the frames are folded together. It is equally evident that when more than one inner supporting frame is used, they will bind against each other to such a degree that it is impossible to fold the side frames into a compact unit. These two facts limit both the size and the strength of this type of parallel. However, it possesses one advantage: it can be more quickly shifted, since all of the supporting frames are hinged into a single unit.

The cost of building materials and the time required to construct either the Standard or Continental parallel make this a relatively expensive unit of scenery. For this reason the dimensions of a single parallel, or a set of them, should be determined more by the possibility of future reuse than by the dictates of a specific production. One method of achieving this standardization is to establish the height of the parallels in multiples of the average step riser, either 6″ or 7″. The width and length might be standardized by dimensions that best combine with each other and with the overall dimensions of the stage where they will be used.

STAIRWAYS

Stairways for stage use are generally classified as dependent, independent, and curved. Such details as the pitch of the stairs, height of the risers, and depth of the treads are determined by the designer; the manner of construction and method of shifting are the responsibility of the technician. Any type of stairway consists of risers, treads, and carriages. The treads are the horizontal planes, the risers are the vertical faces of the steps, and the carriages are the supporting frames to which treads and risers are attached (Plate 45).

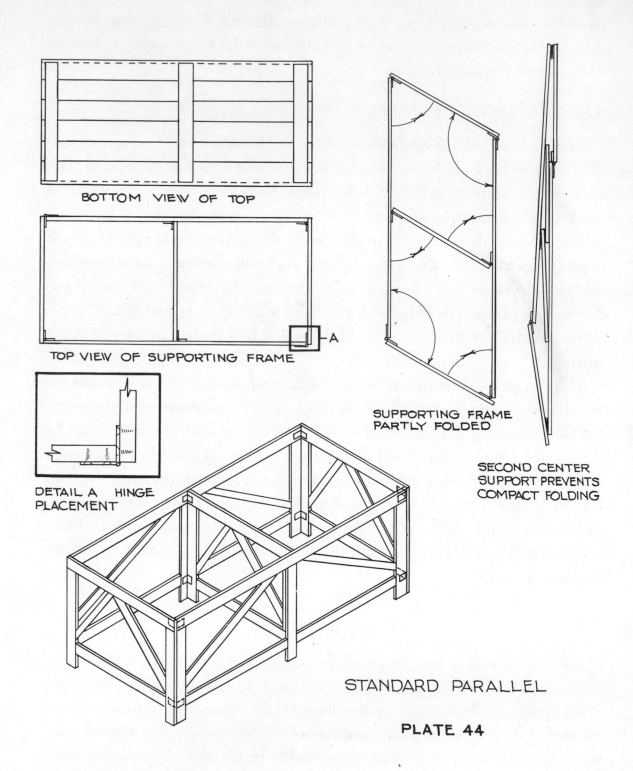

BOTTOM VIEW OF TOP

TOP VIEW OF SUPPORTING FRAME

A

DETAIL A HINGE
PLACEMENT

SUPPORTING FRAME
PARTLY FOLDED

SECOND CENTER
SUPPORT PREVENTS
COMPACT FOLDING

STANDARD PARALLEL

PLATE 44

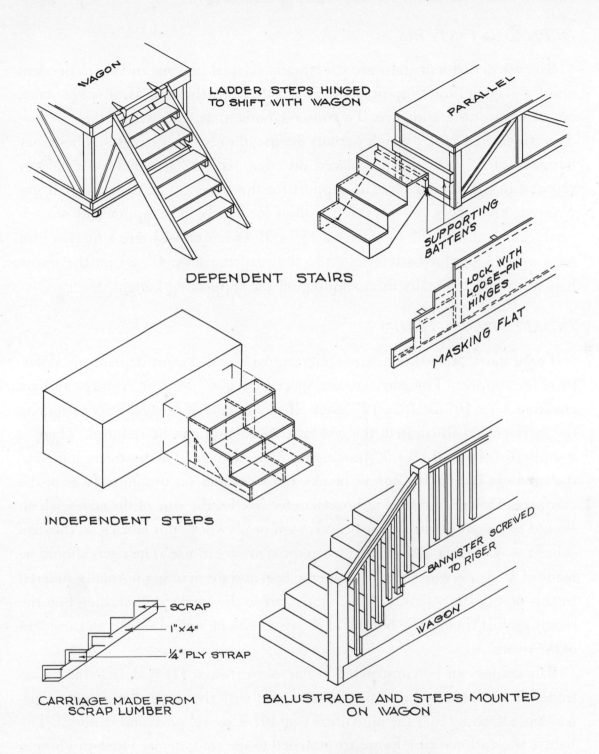

WAGON

LADDER STEPS HINGED
TO SHIFT WITH WAGON

PARALLEL

DEPENDENT STAIRS

SUPPORTING
BATTENS

LOCK WITH
LOOSE-PIN
HINGES

MASKING FLAT

INDEPENDENT STEPS

SCRAP

1" x 4"

¼" PLY STRAP

CARRIAGE MADE FROM
SCRAP LUMBER

BANNISTER SCREWED
TO RISER

WAGON

BALUSTRADE AND STEPS MOUNTED
ON WAGON

PLATE 45

DEPENDENT STAIRS

Because dependent stairs are structurally skeletal in form and are dependent upon a platform for support, they are most frequently used as off-stage stairs, out of sight of the audience. To conserve both space and weight they are seldom wider than 2'-0", which permits the use of only two carriages. These may be made of 2" x 6" boards placed on edge, with 2" x 4" cleats nailed or screwed to their inner faces as support for the treads. The risers are left uncovered. Five-ply $\frac{3}{4}$" fir plywood is used for treads. The upper end of each carriage is countersunk to receive a $1\frac{1}{4}$" x 3" horizontal batten, which in turn rests upon a similar batten bolted to the platform legs. Cleats on the upper batten prevent the stairs from slipping off the supporting batten.

INDEPENDENT STAIRS

These stairs carry their own supporting base and do not depend up a platform for support. The carriages are spaced on 1'-6" to 2'-0" centers and are cut from 1" x 10" or 1" x 12" stock. If scrap material is used in constructing the carriages, as illustrated, the cost of construction can be reduced. There is a supporting base of 1" x 3" framing for each carriage. The bases are joined to the carriages by placing corner blocks and keystones on the inner faces of the carriages. This provides an unbroken outer face for the side of the stairs, which should be covered with either beaverboard or plywood, not fabrics, as they are subject to wrinkling and shaking when the stairs are in use. The risers should be made of $\frac{1}{4}$" fir plywood to withstand the heel and toe scuffing normally suffered by this part of the stairway. Attach the risers to the carriages first; then butt the treads against them. The bottom of the risers can be nailed solidly to the edges of the treads.

Balustrades can be constructed in one of two ways: (1) A detachable balustrade can be made by building a masking flat with the same shape as the stairway and attaching to it the individual bannisters, newel post, and handrail. The balustrade and masking frame are attached to the stairway by loose-pin hinges screwed to the back of the frame and to the treads of the stairs. Although this balustrade has the advantage of being removable, it is difficult to join it to the stairs rigidly enough to prevent it from shaking when in use. (2) A much stronger balustrade can be made by attaching the bannisters permanently to the step unit. Each alternate bannister is moved into a position on the step where one face of its base is flush against the riser. In this position it can be nailed to the step from both the bottom and side. The other alternate bannisters are attached by doweling or nailing them through their base to the face of the treads. Such a stairway assembly is heavy and difficult to shift unless it has been mounted on a wagon or a set of lift jacks.

THE CURVED STAIRWAY

The curved stairway adds a distinctly decorative element to settings in which its use can be logically justified. However, directors and designers should recognize the fact that there are certain disadvantages associated with the use of such a stairway, and unless some extensive use can be made of it as an additional acting area, it might be well to consider some other type of stairway. A curved stairway requires an exceptional amount of stage floor space in order to reach a given elevation, and occupies just as much off-stage storage space when it is necessary to shift it. While such stairways are not difficult to build, their irregular shape makes it difficult to store them as stock scenery, or even to reuse them in other productions without extensive alterations. Under these conditions they may well become luxury units that many theatres can ill afford.

Plate 46 illustrates the principle of construction used in building a curved stairway. It also shows how the unit can be shifted by mounting it on a wagon. The wagon was made from rigid platforms that had been kept as stock scenery, and they were used as wagons without altering their dimensions. One platform was used to form the stairway landing. Two others were bolted together and converted into a single wagon 7″ high on which were mounted both the landing platform and the curved steps. Wagon B actually formed the first step of the unit. The radial carriages were constructed as independent frames. They were made of 1″ x 3″ stock cut to the desired width and height, and were placed in position to coincide with the risers. The step treads rested upon the top of one riser frame and were supported by a batten placed at the same height on the face of the adjacent frame.

A solid curved balustrade was used on both sides of the step unit. These were made of beaverboard sheets temporarily nailed into position, marked to the desired shape and height, then removed and cut. They were permanently

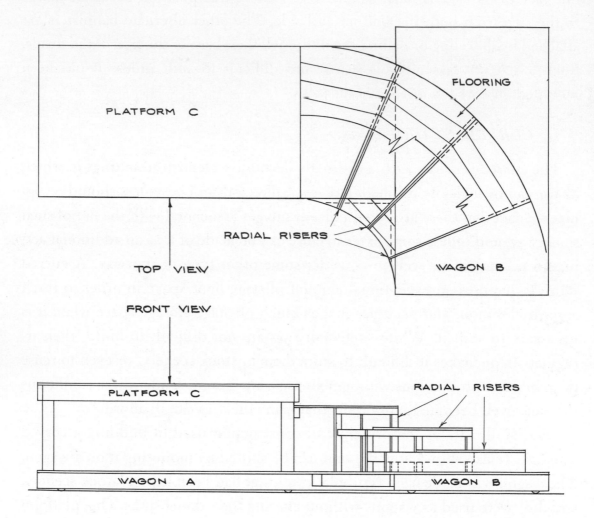

FRAMING AND ASSEMBLY FOR A
CURVED STAIRWAY

PLATE 46

nailed into place and reinforced on the upstage sides by vertical 1″ x 3″ battens screwed to the face of the riser frames. The 4″-wide handrail that formed the horizontal top of the balustrade was made of strips of $\frac{1}{4}$″ plywood that were first bent into position, marked, and then cut to shape and nailed to the tops of the vertical reinforcing battens. The junction between the handrails and the wall faces was covered with strips of muslin glued into place.

FIREPLACES

Designers often use fireplaces as a means of giving additional interest and distinctive detail to their settings. Although fireplaces may appear radically different from each other in design, an analysis of their structural form reveals that they generally fall into one of two categories. They may be built as an integral part of the wall or they may be constructed as independent free-standing units. An example of each type of fireplace is illustrated on Plate 47.

DEPENDENT FIREPLACE

A dependent fireplace is much the easiest and fastest to build. The flat used in building the firebox opening, such as that illustrated, is basically nothing but a door flat, and the construction is identical with it. The mantel is constructed separately and attached to the flat by bolting it to the stiles or to a special supporting toggle. Should the mantel interfere with shifting or storing the flats, it can be attached to them by picture hooks and eyes or with carriage bolts and wing nuts, and removed for the shift. The backing of the firebox opening is made of three small flats hinged together and locked to the back of the fireplace flat with loose-pin hinges. The remaining details, such as cupboard doors and planked facing, can either be built into or painted on the face of the flats.

INDEPENDENT FIREPLACE

In the illustration given of this type of fireplace, the lower section consists of a small wagon, an arched flat, two small flats, and a practical mantel. Supported by the mantel is the overmantel assembly, consisting of a plain flat flanked by two solid lengths of 1″ x 8″, and a decorative shield made from Celotex, a fibrous composition material. Three-dimensional trim in the form

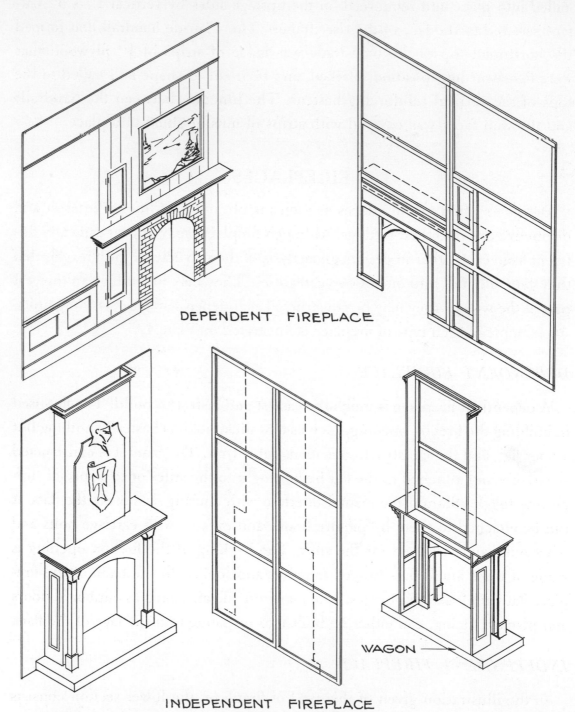

DEPENDENT FIREPLACE

WAGON

INDEPENDENT FIREPLACE

PLATE 47

of molding and decorative pilasters is applied over the face of the flat frames. The whole assembly is permanently joined into a single unit and shifted by rolling. It may be locked to the wall flats against which it is placed by one or two carriage bolts that project through any conveniently placed toggle or stile and fastened by wing nuts.

TREES

Three-dimensional trees, either half-round or completely circular, can be made by following rather closely the procedure outlined for the construction of columns and shown on Plate 40. A series of sweeps duplicating the shape and dimensions of sections taken through the tree at given heights, are constructed from 1″ stock and notched to receive 1″ x 3″ vertical battens. The flaring roots at the base of the tree or irregularities in the contour of the trunk can be added by cutting 1″ stock to the desired shapes and attaching them to the outer faces of the vertical battens. Large branches are constructed in the same manner as the trunk of the tree. The vertical battens of the branches are interlocked with those of the tree by extending them from one side of the tree trunk to the other and fastening them in place with bolts, screws, nails, or even wire.

The final shape of the tree is determined by 1″ mesh chicken wire molded, shaped, and stapled to the wooden framework. Over the chicken wire is placed three or four layers of papier-mâché. This can best be done by tearing newspapers into strips about 4″ or 5″ wide, covering one side of them with a 25 to 75 percent mixture of hot amber glue and cold water paste, and applying the strips to the chicken wire. If difficulty is encountered in making the first layer of paper adhere to the oily surface of the wire, the paper may be broken or torn occasionally and the resulting tabs folded around individual strands of the chicken wire. This procedure makes sure that the papier-mâché will follow the molded contours of the wire. Allow each layer of paper to dry before applying the next. Since the papier-mâché is brittle and easily damaged after it has dried, it should be protected by strips of muslin applied in the same manner as the layers of paper. Bark texture can be worked into the muslin by pinching the material into the desired shape after it has been applied to the papier-mâché.

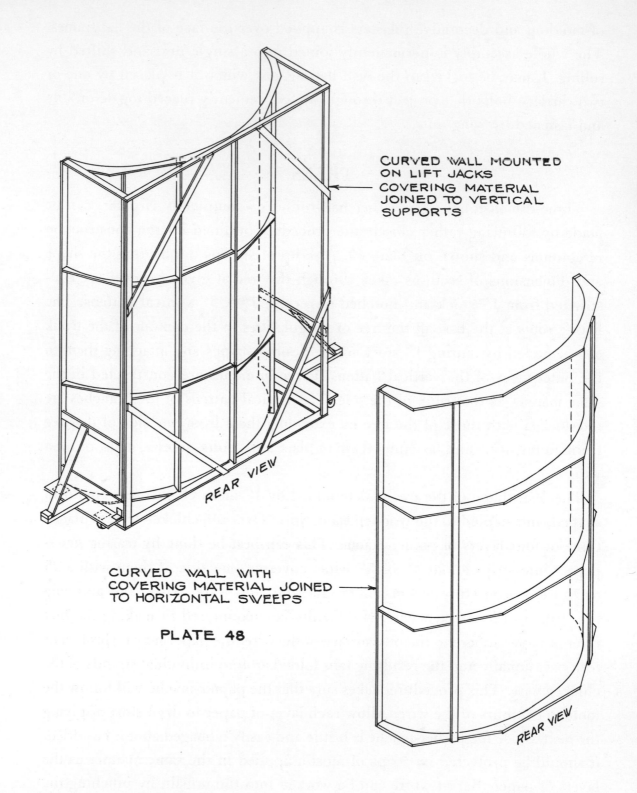

CURVED WALL MOUNTED
ON LIFT JACKS
COVERING MATERIAL
JOINED TO VERTICAL
SUPPORTS

REAR VIEW

CURVED WALL WITH
COVERING MATERIAL JOINED
TO HORIZONTAL SWEEPS

PLATE 48

REAR VIEW

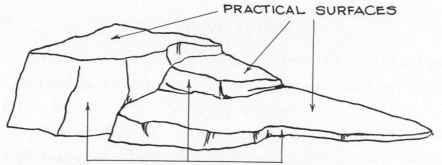

PRACTICAL SURFACES

NEAR VERTICAL FACES COVERED WITH
PAPIER-MÂCHÉ OVER SHAPED CHICKEN WIRE

PLATFORM TOPS MADE OF
¾" 5-PLY OR TONGUE AND
GROOVE FLOORING

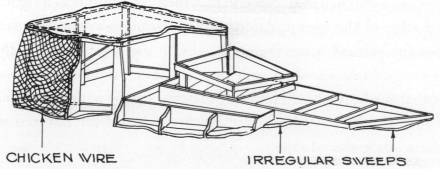

CHICKEN WIRE

IRREGULAR SWEEPS

IRREGULAR FRAMING USED IN BUILDING
A PRACTICAL (WEIGHT-BEARING)
STAGE ROCK

PLATE 49

If the shape of the branches is highly irregular, the width of the paper and muslin strips should be reduced. The narrower the strips, the more easily and smoothly they can be applied to an irregular shape.

CURVED WALLS

A setting designed with curved walls is undoubtedly an esthetic pleasure, but the technical problems associated with the construction and shifting of convex or concave wall sections make their use questionable. Curved wall sections are not difficult to build, but they are expensive, too bulky to be kept as stock scenery, and too heavy to shift easily unless it is possible to mount them on an outrigger or wagon. Plate 48 shows the general method of assembly. Reinforced sweeps are made for the top and bottom of the curved section. If the arc is wide, it may be necessary to form each sweep from a series of segments battened together. Vertical 1″ x 3″ battens are spaced on 2′-0″ centers along the circumference of the sweep and nailed in place so that their 3″ width is at a right angle to the curved edge of the sweep. Additional horizontal sweeps are made by fitting between the vertical battens segments cut on the same radius as the top and bottom sweeps. Make sure that both vertical battens and horizontal sweeps are so placed that the beaverboard covering material can be nailed to them. The junctions formed by the butted edges of the beaverboard are covered with a muslin dutchman or gummed tape.

ROCKS

Stage rocks may be used only for decorative purposes, or they may have to withstand the movement and weight of actors. Decorative rocks are made of a lightweight wooden frame that approximates the desired shape and covered with chicken wire and papier-mâché (Plate 49). Practical rocks usually have a series of slanting platform surfaces supported by a solid frame that form the practical or weight-bearing surfaces. Vertical faces and planes that are not practical are covered and shaped by chicken wire and papier-mâché. A practical rock, such as the one illustrated, could be shifted in one of two ways: it could be constructed as three separate units and moved manually, or it could be built as a single unit on an irregularly shaped wagon and rolled.

chapter VII

the stage and its equipment

THE educational theatre is a fabulous creation. Its life began only within the present century, yet in that brief time it has succeeded in bringing live drama to countless audiences in every state of the union. Considering the speed of its growth it is not too surprising that the educational theatre should have made mistakes in planning the stages that were to house its productions, or that some of these mistakes and limitations should be perpetuated in yet other theatres by architects and building committees unfamiliar with the requirements of a stage or of the productions to be presented there.

THE DEVELOPMENT OF THE EDUCATIONAL THEATRE PLANT

When drama was finding its place in the curriculum of our educational system it had first to prove its worth to the administration and to a skeptical public. Men with vision and determination, who were convinced that drama should be a fully accredited part of our educational system, set about the gigantic task of finding a home for it. There was no idea of constructing a theatre building—there were simply no funds available for such a purpose. It became a problem of finding an unused space in some existing building, of convincing the administration that it could be put to good use, and then of converting it into something that resembled an auditorium and a stage. It was only natural that such makeshift theatres abounded in limitations of every conceivable nature. Two such theatres, both in Iowa, will serve as examples. The first of these was on the third floor of the natural science building, which housed a 65'-0" square auditorium seating 1200. Appended to one of its four walls was a speaker's platform bounded by a semicircular plaster wall with a radius of just 18'-0". This platform became the so-called stage. Two doors of conventional size lead from either side of the stage into the backstage space. This backstage area consisted of a semicircular passageway 6'-0" wide, whose outer wall was pierced by a continuous row of windows. On the floor directly above the passageway were the dressing rooms, without windows and without toilets. The scene shop was in an old wooden two-car garage located in an alley a block away and three floors down from the stage. The scene dock and storage room was in the basement of an old building across the river, a mile and a half from the shop! In spite of these limitations over 180 full-length plays were presented on this stage before the late Professor E. C. Mabie's dreams were realized with the construction of the University Theatre at Iowa in 1936.

The second theatre, in a basement under the library, possessed a modest auditorium seating about 220, with folding chairs placed on graduated levels. The proscenium opening was approximately 24'-0" wide. The depth of the stage was 25'-0" and there was perhaps 10'-0" of wing space on each side of the arch. But the grid, formed by the floor of the library above, was 9'-0" from the stage floor, and a supporting steel column was located slightly to one side of center stage not more than 10'-0" from the curtain line! This column was an indispensable part of every setting, now disguised as a lamp post, now a tree, again as a newel post or a sewer pipe, but always there in some form. Somehow this organization managed to incorporate their supporting column into forty productions before Coe College built their new auditorium and stage in 1950.

These are not isolated examples, carefully selected to prove a point, but quite typical of the type of stage that most dramatic departments were forced to use until they had proved their right to better facilities. It was not until the late 1920's that the first theatre buildings were constructed for educational purposes. After the need for work in dramatics became evident and the pattern for building had been established, first one institution and then another followed the lead, until many of our colleges and universities are now either at work on the plans for, or possess, excellent theatre plants. This pattern of building has not been confined to the universities and colleges alone; it has been extended to many of our larger high schools, where both thought and money are being spent to provide stages for dramatic productions.

There is little similarity between these new theatres except that all possess an auditorium and a stage of some kind. This diversity in plan and form is a healthy condition, indicative of a vital and imaginative theatre, a theatre that is not wedded to a standardize method of production. The newer theatres fall roughly into three general classifications: the conventional stage with a proscenium arch separating the auditorium from the stage, the modified stage with some unusual treatment of the proscenium arch, and finally the arena stage. Iowa, Indiana, and Wisconsin all have new theatres of the conventional type. Baylor University in Texas has a modified stage with three proscenium arches and an auditorium equipped with swivel seats—a theatre capable of a remarkable degree of flexibility in production methods. The Ring Theatre at the University of Miami and the Penthouse Theatre at the University of Washington are good examples of the arena type.

It is not the intention of the author to discuss the production methods that have led to variations in the form of theatre buildings, or to take up the problems of planning theatre buildings in general. This chapter will be devoted to a discussion of the various parts of the stage and to the equipment required to fit it for production work (Plate 50).

THE STRUCTURAL PARTS OF A STAGE

THE ORCHESTRA PIT

Traditionally the orchestra pit has been a characteristic feature of the American theatre, but for the sake of a closer relationship between audience and actor some of the newer theatres have eliminated the pit entirely. The immediate goal of the actor-spectator relationship was achieved, but at the expense of productions requiring the services of an orchestra.

The old-fashioned brass-bordered moat that separates the audience from the stage apron is not necessary. A much more flexible and practical use of the space required for a pit can be made by following one of two schemes. The installation of an elevator that will lower a section of the auditorium floor to form a pit

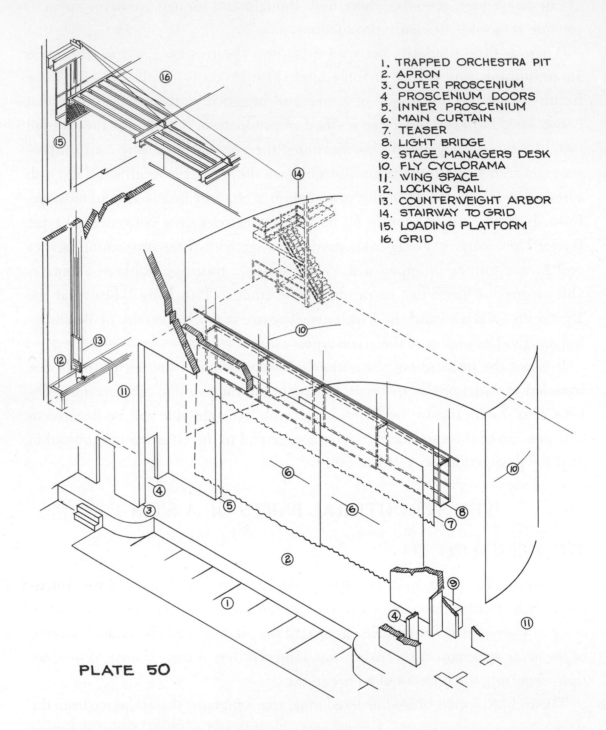

1. TRAPPED ORCHESTRA PIT
2. APRON
3. OUTER PROSCENIUM
4. PROSCENIUM DOORS
5. INNER PROSCENIUM
6. MAIN CURTAIN
7. TEASER
8. LIGHT BRIDGE
9. STAGE MANAGERS DESK
10. FLY CYCLORAMA
11. WING SPACE
12. LOCKING RAIL
13. COUNTERWEIGHT ARBOR
14. STAIRWAY TO GRID
15. LOADING PLATFORM
16. GRID

PLATE 50

is quite successful. When there is no need for the orchestra pit, the elevator is raised to the auditorium floor level and fitted with additional rows of seats. By removing the temporary seats and raising the elevator to the level of the stage floor, additional playing space is added to the depth of the stage. An alternate scheme eliminates the considerable cost of the elevator. A pit is constructed to the depth of 3'-6" to 4'-0" below the level of the auditorium floor and its top is fitted with sections of flooring that slide out of the way under the apron of the stage. A temporary guard rail is erected around the edges of the pit, from which masking drapes are hung to shield the audience from the glare of the music-rack lights. When the services of the orchestra are not required the pit is covered, providing space for additional rows of temporary seats.

THE FORESTAGE

The forestage, or the apron as it is more commonly called, is that part of the stage floor extending beyond the curtain line into the auditorium. Whether or not the apron should be incorporated into the plans for new legitimate or community theatres has been the subject of many a heated debate. There are those who maintain that the forestage, like the orchestra pit, creates an unnecessary barrier between the audience and the actors, that it is nothing but a heritage from a bygone period and has long since lost its usefulness. The climax of the argument is usually reached by some such statement as, "Move the proscenium to the downstage side of the apron and gain that much more valuable space backstage where it is really needed." Others will argue just as heatedly in favor of the forestage, and they will point out its value as space for entr'act entertainment, for announcements, for certain types of productions, and for helping to establish esthetic distance. As far as the commercial and the community theatre is concerned, there seems to be no indication that the argument will be solved to everyone's satisfaction.

There is no argument between those responsible for planning educational theatres as to the desirability of the forestage. There seems to be universal agreement as to its usefulness. Extensive use can be made of the auditorium for large classes when the stage is equipped with an apron that can serve as a speaker's platform. Readings, recitals, lectures, and similar activities can be held on the forestage against a background provided by the closed main curtain, without the necessity of dismantling or striking any scenery that might be in position on stage. With both the asbestos curtain and the main curtain closed, classroom exercises in acting and directing can be held on the apron while crew assignments are carried out on stage. Without the apron, certain types of period plays, so frequently found in the play programs of the educational theatre, cannot be done without incorporating a simulated forestage into the set design and taking the space for it from the valuable backstage area.

The forestage need not be an elaborate or extensive affair; if it has no more depth than 6'-0" to 8'-0", it will meet the needs listed above. Some means of access to and from the apron should be provided other than that afforded by parting the front curtain. Unobtrusive doorways placed on either side of the apron, and connecting passageways leading from them to the backstage area and to the front of the house provide a flexible and desirable arrangement.

THE PROSCENIUM ARCH

In spite of its name, the proscenium arch is generally rectangular is shape. In theatres that possess an opening with an arched or rounded top in the proscenium wall, it is usually necessary to alter the opening into a rectangular shape by hanging expensive velour draperies just upstage of the proscenium opening. The reason for this is simple: most conventional stage settings are rectangular in shape and unless the audience is to see the rigging that supports all of the flown scenery and stage lights the top of the setting must be masked.

Although the proscenium arch can hardly be classified as a piece of stage equipment, its importance as it affects other stage equipment or the sight lines is so great that some mention of it here cannot be avoided. The size and shape of the arch is determined for a specific theatre by a study of its relation to the form and dimensions of the auditorium, and to the amount and distribution of available backstage space. The dimensions of the proscenium arch should not be selected at random; nor should it be assumed that because certain dimensions are satisfactory in one theatre they will be equally suitable in another theatre with an entirely different plan and arrangement. A few moments spent in a study of the plans for a proposed theatre will reveal that sight lines drawn from any position in the auditorium to the stage are governed by the limits of the proscenium arch. By testing the sight lines from the extreme seats in the auditorium—that is, from the highest seats in the balcony, from the extreme side seats in the orchestra, and from the seats closest to the proscenium—it is possible to determine how much or how little a spectator seated at those positions can see of the stage.

The desire of certain civic groups to possess the biggest and the best of everything has been carried over into the field of theatre architecture, and has occasionally resulted in the construction of a theatre that is literally too large for dramatic productions. Auditoriums seating 2, 3, or 4000 people, with proscenium arches 60'-0", 70'-0" or even 85'-0" wide, are not uncommon. These stages may be beautifully suited for spectacles, extravaganzas, and opera; but they are just too large for dramatic productions. The same fault could occur in the educational theatre should an administration decide that an all-purpose auditorium should be built to house the concert and lecture series as well as dramatic productions. Such an auditorium would of necessity be large enough to house most of the student body, and the stage would be fitted with a proscenium correspondingly wide.

For dramatic productions the acceptable width of the proscenium arch is from 32'-0" to possibly 36'-0" or 38'-0". When the arch is made much wider than this, there is an immediate increase in the problems affecting the movement of actors, the design of scenery, and the cost of production. The timing and pacing of actors' movements, without objectional delays, increases in difficulty in direct proportion to the width of the stage. The action of most plays is laid in interior settings of some type, such as a living room, a den, a kitchen, or a bedroom. When the designer attempts to adapt the normal dimensions of such rooms to a stage that may be 45'-0" in width, he does so at the expense of any sense of reality. The wall areas have been so exaggerated and extended that the stage furniture and properties seem out of scale and isolated against them. More decorative properties and furniture are then added, in an effort to make the setting seem more habitable. As the setting is extended in size, and as additional furniture is required to dress it, the cost of building scenery and renting properties increases.

STAGE EQUIPMENT

THE ASBESTOS CURTAIN

State or city laws may require the installation of an asbestos fire curtain as part of the safety equipment of a theatre. Should a fire occur an asbestos curtain can be lowered to prevent the spread of fire from one part of the theatre to another. The composition of asbestos material is such that it cannot be pleated or folded and it must be rigged so that it hangs as a two-dimensional plane (Plate 51). The width of the asbestos must be greater than that of the proscenium opening, to provide at least a 1'-0" or 1'-6" overlap on each side of the arch. The outer edges of the asbestos are fitted with metal rings through which steel cables are stretched between the stage floor and the grid. This rigging prevents the asbestos from being sucked out of position by a heavy draft, and insures a tight junction between the curtain and the proscenium wall. Just beyond the edges of the asbestos on each side are steel smoke pockets—vertical steel troughs bolted to the proscenium wall. They extend out and around the sides of the asbestos to form a protective shield. The asbestos is raised and lowered by a variation in the rigging of a conventional counterweight unit. The arbor, in this case, is mounted on the back of the proscenium wall in such a position that the operating line and its floor block are within a few feet of the asbestos. A special safety feature in the rigging of the asbestos is the cut-line that makes it possible to lower the curtain either automatically or manually from positions on either side of the arch. To achieve this, the balance between the asbestos and the counterweight is deliberately kept uneven so that the curtain is a little heavier than the weights in the arbor. This requires the use of a special $\frac{3}{8}''$ rope, called the cut-line, to hold the curtain in position after it has been raised. At one side of the arch an end of the cut-line is attached to the floor. From this point it extends to the grid, over a block, across the grid to a second block, and then down to the stage floor and through a third block. The free end of the line is then tied to the operating line of the asbestos to hold it in place. At 10'-0" or 15'-0" intervals along the full length of the cut-line are inserted fusible links that are designed to separate when the temperature reaches a given degree. The curtain would be lowered automatically by the separation of any of

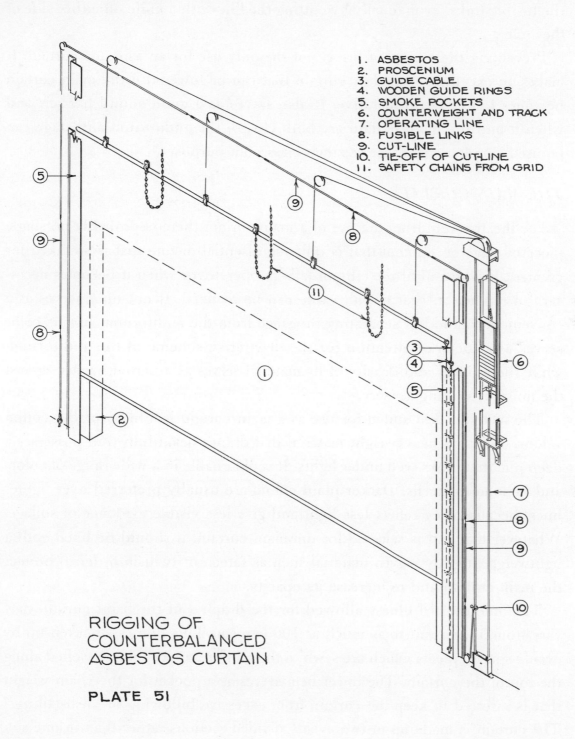

1. ASBESTOS
2. PROSCENIUM
3. GUIDE CABLE
4. WOODEN GUIDE RINGS
5. SMOKE POCKETS
6. COUNTERWEIGHT AND TRACK
7. OPERATING LINE
8. FUSIBLE LINKS
9. CUT-LINE
10. TIE-OFF OF CUT-LINE
11. SAFETY CHAINS FROM GRID

RIGGING OF
COUNTERBALANCED
ASBESTOS CURTAIN

PLATE 51

the fusible links, or manually by cutting the line with a knife on either side of the arch.

Preventing the spread of fire is not the only use for an asbestos curtain. It makes an excellent secondary curtain that can be lowered if the main curtain becomes fouled or inoperative. It also serves as a good sound barrier; and when it and the main curtain are both closed, the auditorium and stage can be used simultaneously for separate classroom purposes.

THE MAIN CURTAIN

For theatres requiring the use of a main curtain there is probably no single piece of stage equipment that is quite so essential or one that is so taken for granted. It is not until the curtain fails to operate, or when it becomes necessary to replace it, that its full value can be realized. It not only serves as a convenient method of separating the stage from the auditorium, but its color serves as a focus of attention for the decorative scheme of the auditorium, while the fullness and density of its material serves as a partial barrier against the noise of shifting scenery.

The material best suited for use as a main curtain is a high-quality cotton velour. This is a heavyweight material that drapes beautifully and possesses a deep pile that looks well under lights. It is obtainable in a wide range of colors and in some patterns. Darker plain colors are usually preferred over lighter hues, because they reflect less light and give less visible evidence of soilage. Whatever material is selected for the main curtain, it should be lined with a lightweight, tightly woven material such as sateen or twill in order to protect the main curtain and to increase its opacity.

The amount of fullness allowed for the draping of the front curtain may vary from 50 percent to as much as 100 percent. This fullness is taken up by evenly spaced pleats which are sewn to the reinforcing webbing attached along the top of the curtain. The lower hem serves as a pocket for the chain weight that is inserted to keep the curtain from excessive billowing or "fish-tailing." The curtain is made up in two evenly divided sections rather than in one single continuous piece. This provides several advantages: the center opening provides access to the apron from the back stage area, the two sections are easier to handle than one large one when rigging or having it cleaned, and the

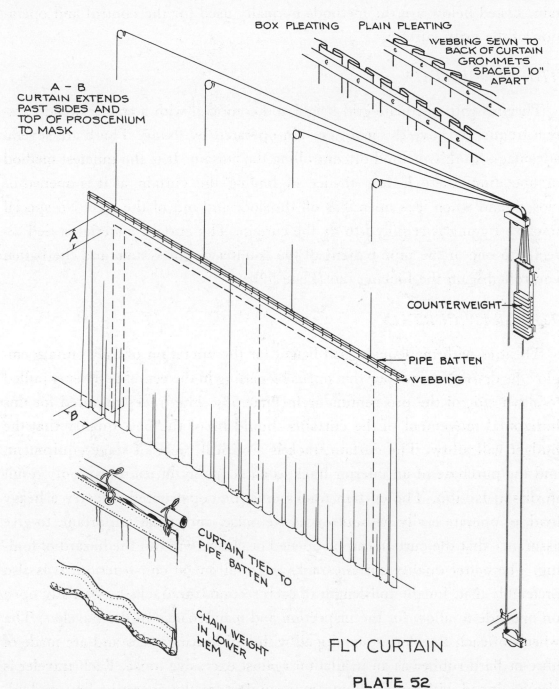

BOX PLEATING   PLAIN PLEATING

WEBBING SEWN TO
BACK OF CURTAIN
GROMMETS
SPACED 10"
APART

A – B
CURTAIN EXTENDS
PAST SIDES AND
TOP OF PROSCENIUM
TO MASK

A

COUNTERWEIGHT

B

PIPE BATTEN

WEBBING

CURTAIN TIED TO
PIPE BATTEN

CHAIN WEIGHT
IN LOWER
HEM

FLY CURTAIN

PLATE 52

curtain must be divided if it is to be operated as either a draw or a tab curtain. Listed below are the methods normally used for the control and operation of the main curtain.

THE FLY CURTAIN

Theatres with adequate grid height and equipped with a counterweight system frequently have the main curtain operated by flying. There are several advantages to this method of controlling the curtain. It is the quietest method of operation, there is less chance of fouling the curtain as it is opened or closed; and when it is open it is off the floor and out of the way. No special track or rigging is required to fly the curtain. The curtain material is tied directly to one of the pipe battens of the counterweight system and the batten controlled from the locking rail (Plate 52).

THE DRAW CURTAIN

Theatres with inadequate grid height for the operation of a fly curtain employ the draw curtain—one that opens by parting in the center and being pulled to either side of the proscenium arch (Plate 53). The tracks required for this horizontal movement of the curtains should be of the best quality that the budget will allow. The curtain track is a critical piece of stage equipment, and the purchase of an inferior track as an economy measure can only result in dissatisfaction. The curtain tracks must be constructed to carry a heavy load, to operate easily without excessive noise, and, most important, to give assurance that the curtain can be opened or closed without the hazard of fouling. The better-quality curtain tracks are of all-metal construction. It is also preferable that, for the full length of each section, the tracks be partially open on one side to allow for the inspection and maintenance of the travelers. The wheels of each traveler are equipped with ball-bearing races and are made of fibre or hard rubber as an insulation against excessive noise. Each traveler is also equipped with rubber bumpers, a support for the operating line, and adjustable tie chains.

The draw-curtain track is formed by two separate sections, each extending 1'-6" past the center line of the stage in order to provide a 3'-0" overlap for the curtain material. If the full width of the arch is to be utilized, it is essential that the curtain tracks extend off stage past the edges of the arch far

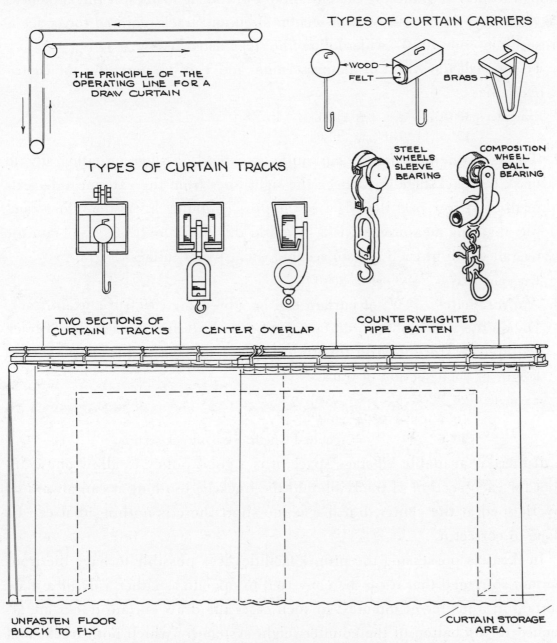

THE PRINCIPLE OF THE
OPERATING LINE FOR A
DRAW CURTAIN

TYPES OF CURTAIN CARRIERS

WOOD

FELT

BRASS

STEEL
WHEELS
SLEEVE
BEARING

COMPOSITION
WHEEL
BALL
BEARING

TYPES OF CURTAIN TRACKS

TWO SECTIONS OF
CURTAIN TRACKS

CENTER OVERLAP

COUNTERWEIGHTED
PIPE BATTEN

UNFASTEN FLOOR
BLOCK TO FLY

CURTAIN STORAGE
AREA

COMBINED FLY AND DRAW CURTAIN

PLATE 53

enough to permit gathering the curtain out of the sight lines of the audience. To determine the length of each section of curtain track required to service a proscenium arch 30'-0'' wide, follow the steps listed below:

1. To one-half the width of the proscenium add 1'-6'' required for the center overlap.

    Example: 30'-0'' ÷ 2   = 15'-0''
              15'-0'' + 1'-6'' = 16'-6''

2. To determine how far the curtain must extend off stage on either side to mask the backstage area check the sight lines from the extreme side seats in the first row past the edges of the proscenium arch. Assume, for example, that this measurement is 3'-6''. Add this 3'-6'' to 16'-6'' to obtain the overall width of each curtain section, exclusive of fullness.

    Example: 16'-6'' + 3'-6'' = 20'-0''

3. Approximately 5'-0'' of curtain can be stored on 1'-0'' of curtain track. Divide the width of each curtain section by 5 to find the amount of track required to store it. Add this to the 16'-6'' measurement for the correct length of each section of track.

    Example: 20'-0'' ÷ 5   =   4'-0''
              16'-6'' + 4'-0'' = 20'-6''
              20'-6''   = required length of each track section.

If there is available off-stage space, it is a good policy to allow one extra foot for each section of track. Should the track be too long it can always be overlapped at the center, but if it is too short there is nothing that can be done to correct it.

In theatres possessing the proper facilities it is possible to have the front curtain so rigged that it can be converted to operate as either a fly or a draw curtain in a matter of minutes. In such cases the draw curtain tracks are attached to the batten of the counterweight system by which both tracks and curtains can be raised and lowered. The only necessary alteration of the rigging required to change from draw to fly operation is unfastening the floor block of the draw-curtain lines and serving them around the end of the track.

THE TAB CURTAIN

The tab curtain is operated by two lines that run through a series of rings attached to a webbing sewn diagonally across the back of each curtain sec-

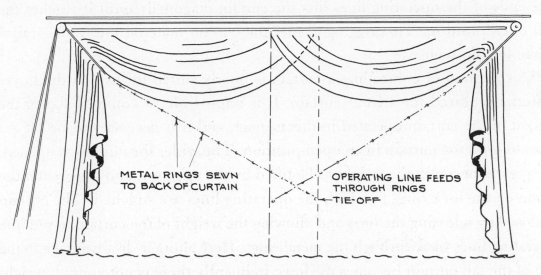

METAL RINGS SEWN
TO BACK OF CURTAIN

OPERATING LINE FEEDS
THROUGH RINGS

TIE-OFF

TAB CURTAIN

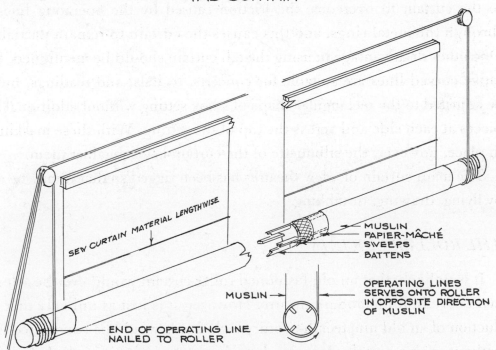

SEW CURTAIN MATERIAL LENGTHWISE

MUSLIN
PAPIER-MÂCHÉ
SWEEPS
BATTENS

MUSLIN

OPERATING LINES
SERVES ONTO ROLLER
IN OPPOSITE DIRECTION
OF MUSLIN

END OF OPERATING LINE
NAILED TO ROLLER

ROLLER CURTAIN

PLATE 54

tion (Plate 54). Each line is tied off to the last and lowest ring. Pulling the free ends of the operating lines lifts the curtain diagonally until it reaches the full open position. This rigging drapes the curtain material into a decorative frame for the stage.

This method of controlling a curtain is poorly suited for use on the heavy material required for a front curtain. It is impossible to counterbalance the weight of the curtain operated in this manner, and it is necessary to tie off the lines to hold the curtain in an open position. The wider the curtain is opened, the greater becomes the weight to be lifted by the operator, and the greater the strain on the lock rings to which the operating lines are attached. The curtain is closed by releasing the lines and allowing the weight of the curtain to pull the operating lines back through the metal rings. Here another disadvantage to the use of the tab curtain becomes obvious: frequently there is not enough weight to the curtain to overcome the friction caused by the operating lines sliding through the metal rings, and this causes the curtain to remain partially open. One other disadvantage in using the tab curtain should be mentioned. Its decorative curved lines are suitable for concerts, recitals, and readings, but cannot be adjusted to the rectangular shape of a box setting without additional masking pieces at each side and across the top of the setting. With these masking pieces in place, however, the silhouette of the curtain is lost against them.

The main curtain of a few theatres has been rigged so that it may be operated by flying, drawing, or tabbing.

THE ROLLER CURTAIN

It is unlikely that an old-fashioned roller curtain would ever be selected as a main curtain for a modern theatre. However, it is just as unlikely that the production of an old nineteenth-century melodrama would be considered complete without such a curtain. It is simple to operate, requires very little building material, and can be used when lack of space prevents the use of any other type of curtain (Plate 54). Unlike other front curtains, the roller curtain is made from inexpensive muslin or canvas, assembled without fullness of any kind, and then painted with some kind of a decorative scene, usually bordered by advertisements of local merchants. The curtain material is supported by wooden battens in the same manner as for a regular drop. The lower hem is attached to a

wooden cylinder or roller 8″ in diameter and about 3′-0″ longer than the required width of the curtain. The framework of the roller is made from a series
of wooden discs 8″ in diameter and four to six lengthwise battens. The discs
are cut from $\frac{3}{4}$″ 5-ply and the battens from 1″ x 3″ lumber. It is usually
necessary to scarf-joint two pieces of 1″ x 3″ end to end to make one lengthwise batten. The discs are spaced at 3′-0″ to 4′-0″ intervals along the length
of the roller and are notched to receive the 1″ x 3″ battens. The wooden frame
is covered with chicken wire, then papier-mâché, and finally strips of muslin
glued over the dried papier-mâché.

The roller curtain is operated by two ropes that run from the floor through
two overhead pulleys, then down to the points where they are attached at either
end of the roller. The ropes are wrapped around the ends of the roller enough
times to equal the vertical distance to be traveled by the roller. By pulling on the
free ends of the rope, the roller is both turned and raised at the same time, which
winds the curtain material around the roller. The operating lines must be tied
off to a cleat to hold the curtain in the open position.

TEASER AND TORMENTORS

Within certain limits the size of any proscenium arch can be altered by
using a teaser and tormentors. The teaser is a horizontal masking border, usually made of the same material as the front curtain. It is attached to a batten
of the counterweight system and suspended just upstage of the main curtain
(Plate 55). The exposed area above settings of different heights can be masked
by raising or lowering the teaser. The tormentors are vertical masking pieces,
usually of plain flat construction, placed on either side of the proscenium
opening just upstage of the teaser. They may be hinged together or arranged
as a series of overlapping shutters that can either be shoved on stage to reduce the width of the arch or withdrawn to reveal its full width. Tormentor
flats are usually covered with black velour or regular scene canvas painted
black to avoid reflecting light.

THE LIGHT BRIDGE

Immediately upstage of the teaser is the light bridge. This is a metal framework about 2′-0″ wide extending a few feet past the limits of the proscenium

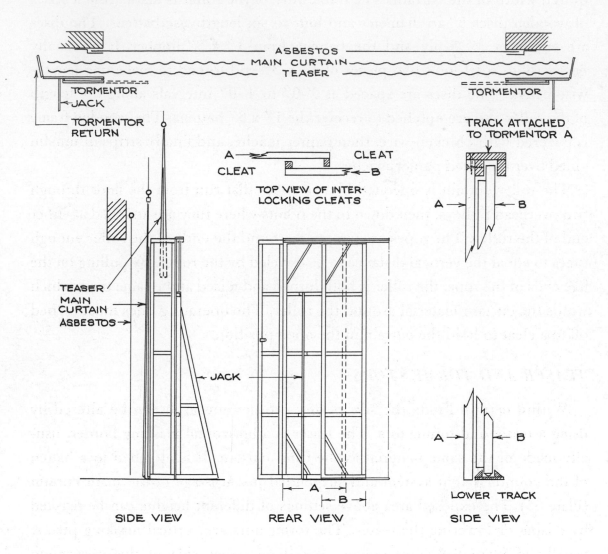

ASBESTOS
MAIN CURTAIN
TEASER

TORMENTOR
JACK

TORMENTOR
RETURN

TORMENTOR

TRACK ATTACHED
TO TORMENTOR A

CLEAT

CLEAT

A

B

TOP VIEW OF INTER-
LOCKING CLEATS

A → ← B

TEASER
MAIN
CURTAIN
ASBESTOS →

← JACK →

A → ← B

LOWER TRACK

A

B

SIDE VIEW

REAR VIEW

SIDE VIEW

ADJUSTABLE TEASER AND TORMENTORS

PLATE 55

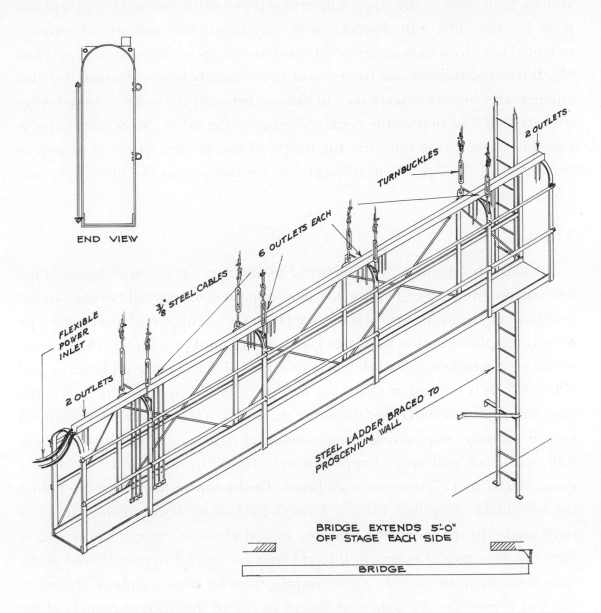

END VIEW

2 OUTLETS

TURNBUCKLES

6 OUTLETS EACH

3/8 STEEL CABLES

FLEXIBLE
POWER
INLET

2 OUTLETS

STEEL LADDER BRACED TO
PROSCENIUM WALL

BRIDGE EXTENDS 5'-0"
OFF STAGE EACH SIDE

BRIDGE

COUNTERWEIGHTED LIGHT BRIDGE

PLATE 56

arch on both sides of the stage. The bridge is an improvement of, and replacement for, the "first light border." It is suspended from two sets of counterweighted lines by which it may be adjusted to settings of different heights (Plate 56). It is raised and lowered by means of an electrically powered winch that also compensates for any discrepancy in balance between the weight of the bridge with its load and that of the counterweights in the arbor. Since the bridge is constructed so that it can carry the weight of one or two operators as well as the weight of the lighting instruments, its advantage over the older light batten is obvious.

THE GRIDIRON

No matter what type of flying system a theatre may have—sandbags and rope line rigging, counterweight system, multiple-speed counterweight system, or the new Izenour electronic grid—it is essential that it be supported from some type of working platform that possesses great strength and provides a safe place on which crew members can work. Such a working platform is the gridiron, or grid (Plate 57). It is located at a distance of 5'-0" to 8'-0" beneath the roof of the stage house and extends over the entire stage area. The modern grid is formed by pairs of heavy supporting beams running at right angles to the proscenium wall, with each pair spaced approximately 10'-0" from the next. There is a space of 10" to 12" between each beam. To the top of the beams are bolted the loft blocks. A grilled floor is formed by bolting light channel irons at right angles to the supporting beams, spaced about 3" apart. These spaces form the necessary openings in the grid floor for special rigging effects; at the same time the irons provide a safe working floor for crew members. Access to the grid is provided by a stairway placed in one of the upstage corners of the stage house where it will be as much out of the way as possible. Open ladders to the grid are a senseless hazard in an educational theatre.

SANDBAGS AND ROPE-LINE RIGGING

The simplest and one of the oldest methods of flying scenery is lifting it by a series of ropes. If the load is too heavy for one man to handle easily, a sandbag can be added to the free end of the lines as counterbalance. Many of our older theatres are still so equipped. The ropes or lines run from a batten to

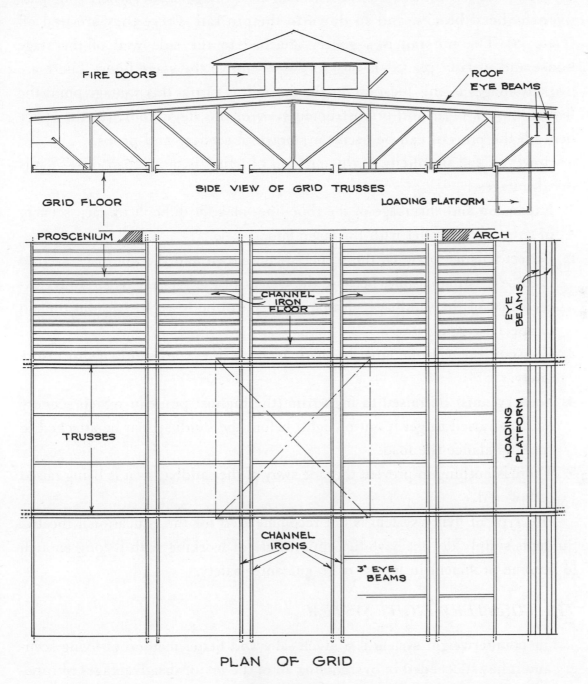

FIRE DOORS

ROOF
EYE BEAMS

SIDE VIEW OF GRID TRUSSES

GRID FLOOR

LOADING PLATFORM

PROSCENIUM   ARCH

CHANNEL
IRON
FLOOR

EYE
BEAMS

TRUSSES

LOADING
PLATFORM

CHANNEL
IRONS

3" EYE
BEAMS

PLAN OF GRID

PLATE 57

the grid, over loft blocks, then to one side of the stage house, where they pass over the head blocks, and so down to the pin rail where they are tied off (Plate 58). The pin rail is a gallery attached to the side wall of the stage house and usually placed 15'-0" to 20'-0" above the stage floor. There are two advantages to this location for the pin rail: (1) from this vantage point the flymen have a clear and unobstructed view of the stage floor; (2) the space beneath the pin rail can be used for storage of scenery and props.

However, the simplicity of this method of flying is more than offset by its disadvantages.

1. Expansion and shrinkage of the rope lines make it difficult to keep scenery in trim, i.e., parallel with the stage floor.

2. Perfect balance between the scenery being flown and the sandbags used to balance it is impossible, because the weight of the scenery must always exceed that of the sandbags, so that scenery can be lowered without the aid of special rigging lines.

3. Constant inspections must be made of rope lines and sandbags to insure safety.

4. Scenery must be raised to high trim (the highest point to which scenery must be raised to get it out of sight) before the sandbag can be attached to counterbalance the load.

5. There is nothing to prevent the side sway of the sandbag as it is being raised or lowered.

This type of flying system is not recommended for the educational theatre. Students simply do not have the opportunity of working with it long enough to become proficient in its use or to guarantee safety.

THE COUNTERWEIGHT SYSTEM

The counterweight system is a much safer and better method of flying scenery and it has succeeded in overcoming all of the major disadvantages of rope-line rigging. In this system the rope lines have been replaced by steel cables, which run from a pipe batten to the grid, over the loft blocks to one side of the stage where they pass over the lead block, and are fastened off to a movable metal frame called the arbor (Plate 58). The cables are of such length that when the batten can be reached from the floor, the arbor is at the top of the stage house opposite the grid. Attached to the grid is the loading platform,

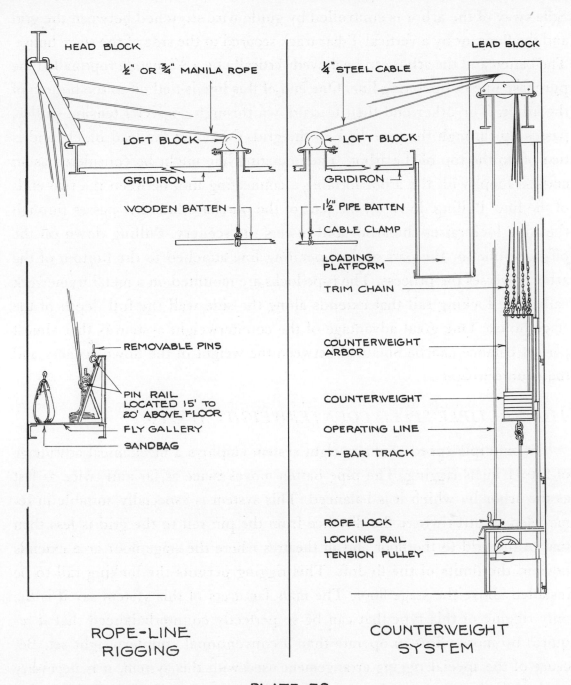

HEAD BLOCK

½" OR ¾" MANILA ROPE

LOFT BLOCK

GRIDIRON

WOODEN BATTEN

LEAD BLOCK

¼" STEEL CABLE

LOFT BLOCK

GRIDIRON

1½" PIPE BATTEN

CABLE CLAMP

LOADING PLATFORM

TRIM CHAIN

COUNTERWEIGHT ARBOR

COUNTERWEIGHT

OPERATING LINE

T-BAR TRACK

ROPE LOCK

LOCKING RAIL

TENSION PULLEY

REMOVABLE PINS

PIN RAIL
LOCATED 15' TO
20' ABOVE FLOOR

FLY GALLERY

SANDBAG

ROPE-LINE
RIGGING

COUNTERWEIGHT
SYSTEM

PLATE 58

from which the counterweights can be loaded into or removed from the arbor. Side sway of the arbor is controlled by guide wire stretched between the grid and the floor, or by a vertical T-bar track secured to the side of the stage house. The batten and the arbor can be moved vertically by a $\frac{3}{4}''$ manila rope called the purchase line or operating line. One end of this line is tied off to the bottom of the arbor. The other end then feeds down through a special tension pulley, passes up through the rope lock to the grid, then over the lead block, and is tied off to the top of the arbor. The operating line might be considered as an endless loop, with the arbor forming a connecting link between the two ends of the line. Pulling down on the part of the purchase line that passes through the rope lock raises the arbor and lowers the scenery. Pulling down on the off-stage line, or the part of the operating line attached to the bottom of the arbor, reverses the process. The rope locks are mounted on a metal framework called the locking rail that extends along the side wall the full depth of the stage house. One great advantage of the counterweight system is that almost perfect balance can be obtained between the weight of the flown scenery and the counterweights.

THE MULTIPLE-SPEED COUNTERWEIGHT SYSTEM

The multiple-speed counterweight system employs a mechanical advantage of 2 to 1 in its rigging. The pipe batten moves twice as far and twice as fast as the arbor by which it is balanced. This system is especially suitable in re-modeled theatres where the distance from the pin rail to the grid is less than that of the grid to the floor and in theatres where the stage floor area extends beyond the limits of the fly loft. This rigging permits the locking rail to be installed above the stage floor. The manufacturers of this system say it is the only rigging of this type that can be so perfectly counterbalanced that it requires no more effort to operate than a conventional counterweight set. Because of the special rigging arrangement used with this system, it is necessary to double the amount of counterweight normally required to balance the weight of scenery.

THE IZENOUR SYNCHRONOUS WINCH SYSTEM

The most recent development in equipment for flying scenery is the new Izenour synchronous winch system. At the time of this writing the first installation of this system is being made at Hofstra College, Long Island. Here all forms of counterbalance weights have been replaced by a series of electronically controlled winches, each one trunion-mounted on the front and rear of the stage house. Hoisting cables run from the winches to dollies that may be shifted to any position on the grid. The cables can be lowered to where they may be attached directly to the scenery or, in conjunction with cables from other units, attached to battens. The hoisting units can be controlled separately or in combination from a control board backstage. The advantages of this system are the added safety afforded by the elimination of all sandbags and counterweights and the added flexibility provided by the movable hoists.

CYCLORAMAS

The problem of providing the bit of sky seen through the windows of a setting is easily solved with a conventional backing, but the need for a wide expanse of sky required in many exterior settings has plagued dozens of designers. The problem has been solved in various ways. Where the budget is limited and the back wall of the stage house is unadorned by radiators, pipes and other permanent equipment, a coat of plaster and sky-blue paint has often sufficed. The dependable though old-fashioned sky drop is also still used extensively. But these devices provide only a partial solution—the problem of masking the sides of the stage still remains. A step forward from the use of the sky drop was the introduction of the arm cyclorama. This was literally three sky drops—one across the back of the stage and one on each side extending obliquely toward offstage left and right. However, this arrangement presented an angular junction at the point where the side arms met the rear drop, a junction both unsightly and difficult to light. Continued experimentation has led to the development of the various types of cloth cycloramas that have proved highly satisfactory.

THE FLY CYC

The modern cyclorama is an unbroken expanse of canvas, either dyed or painted a sky blue, suspended from a U-shaped pipe batten, and enclosing the acting area on three sides. A second pipe batten is laced to the bottom of the cyc to hold the material free of wrinkles and prevent it from blowing. The cyc is raised and lowered by means of the counterweight system. Eight steel cables, from two arbors bolted together, are passed around muling blocks (blocks mounted in a horizontal position on the grid to change the direction of the cables), over special loft blocks, and then down to the top curved pipe batten, where they are clamped off. When the cyc is in its lowered position on stage there must be 18'-0" to 24'-0" of loft space above the top batten to permit the cyc to be raised above the stage floor by this distance. This provides the necessary clearance for the movement of scenery and reduces the likelihood of damage to the cyc.

The size of the cyc is determined by testing the horizontal and vertical sight lines from the extreme side seats in the front row against both the height and depth of the cyc. For example, when the proscenium arch is used at its full height and width, a person seated in one of these front seats should not be able to see the top of the cyc, or beyond the downstage limits of the side arms.

The placement of the cyc on stage in relation to the acting area and to the off-stage area is very important. The side arms must be placed far enough off stage to allow adequate clearance for free movement of the counterweight battens, and enough floor space beyond the normal wall limits of a setting for placing backings. But, if the side arms are placed too far off stage, this could seriously reduce the space saved for storage of scenery and properties. Enough space should be left upstage of the cyc (3'-0" or 4'-0") for a crossover for actors and crew members.

THE TRIP CYC

A variation of the fly cyc is the trip, or folding, cyc, which can be used in theatres with too little grid height for a regular fly cyc (Plate 59). The size and shape of a trip cyc may be identical with that of a regular fly cyc, but it differs in three respects: (1) the top batten of the trip cyc is permanently chained to the grid; (2) this cyc is fitted with a third curved pipe batten (the trip batten) which is laced to the back of the cyc material at a distance of 20'-0" or 24'-0" above the bottom batten. The third difference lies in the rigging. The cables of the counterweight sets are attached to the trip batten, and as these are raised the lower section of the cyc is lifted vertically while the upper section is folded to half its height by the same movement.

The trip cyc has two minor disadvantages: (1) Only the part of the cyc be-

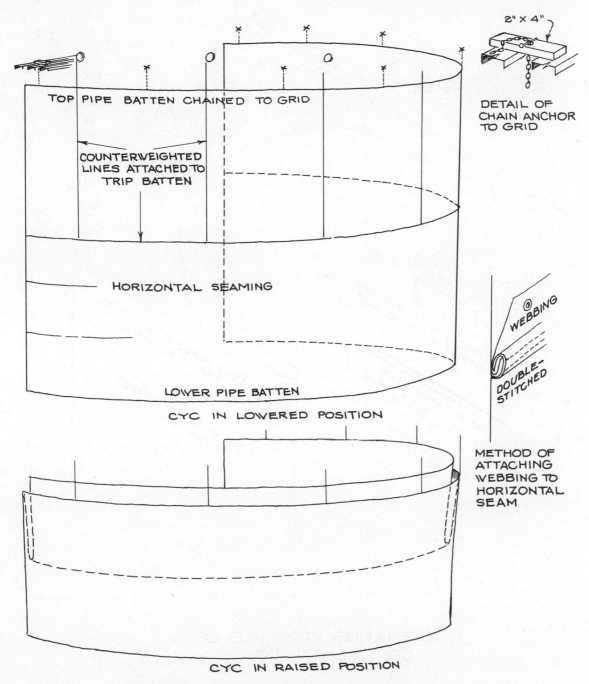

2" X 4"

DETAIL OF
CHAIN ANCHOR
TO GRID

TOP PIPE BATTEN CHAINED TO GRID

COUNTERWEIGHTED
LINES ATTACHED TO
TRIP BATTEN

HORIZONTAL SEAMING

WEBBING

DOUBLE-
STITCHED

LOWER PIPE BATTEN

CYC IN LOWERED POSITION

METHOD OF
ATTACHING
WEBBING TO
HORIZONTAL
SEAM

CYC IN RAISED POSITION

DIAGRAM OF TRIP CYC RIGGING

PLATE 59

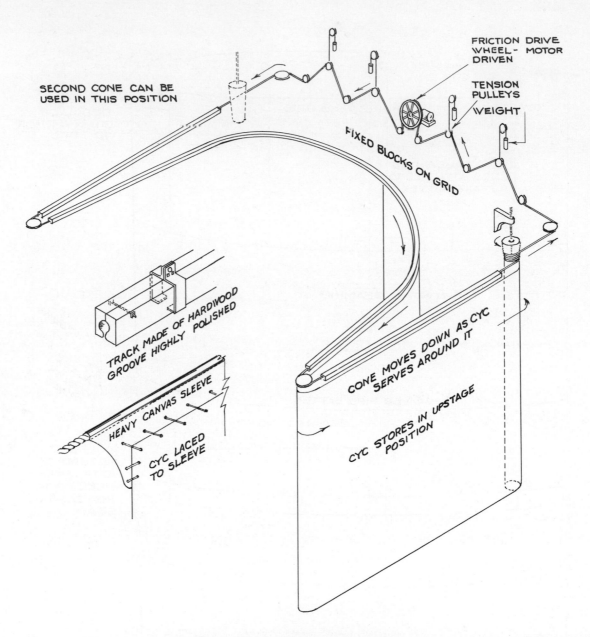

SECOND CONE CAN BE
USED IN THIS POSITION

FRICTION DRIVE
WHEEL- MOTOR
DRIVEN

TENSION
PULLEYS

WEIGHT

FIXED BLOCKS ON GRID

TRACK MADE OF HARDWOOD
GROOVE HIGHLY POLISHED

HEAVY CANVAS SLEEVE

CYC LACED
TO SLEEVE

CONE MOVES DOWN AS CYC
SERVES AROUND IT

CYC STORES IN UPSTAGE
POSITION

OPERATING PRINCIPLE OF
CONTINENTAL CYC

PLATE 60

neath the trip batten can be perfectly counterbalanced; as the cyc is raised the batten also lifts some of the weight of the material of the upper section. This increases the weight that must be manually lifted by the lineman operating the cyc. This is not too serious, as the weight does not become too great for one stagehand to lift it. (2) Wrinkles may appear around the trip batten after the cyc material has stretched. This can be easily corrected by retrimming the top batten through adjustment of the anchor chains holding it to the grid.

THE LINNEBACH CYC

Adolph Linnebach of Munich perfected a cloth cyclorama that operates on an entirely new principle. Like the trip cyc, it is suitable for theatres with insufficient grid height to permit the use of the conventional fly cyclorama. In shape the Linnebach cyc is similar to that of the fly cyc, but instead of being lifted vertically it moves horizontally and is stored by serving around a cone. The cyc is suspended from a hollow curved track which has an open slot on the bottom extending its full length. Feeding through the track is a rope of large diameter to which is attached a heavy canvas sleeve that drops through the slot in the track. The main body of the cyc is laced to the sleeve. Plate 60 illustrates this method of operation.

THE PLASTER DOME

A few theatres are equipped with plaster domes instead of cloth cycloramas. The back and sides of the dome are similar in shape to those of the cyclorama, but the dome also has an enclosing top that curves in overhead toward the proscenium arch. About the only advantage offered by this dome is its superior reflecting surface and the durability of the plaster, but its disadvantages are numerous. Its initial cost far exceeds the cost of a cloth cyclorama; the curved overhead extension precludes the possibility of using any extensive system of flying scenery; and, probably most serious of all, the permanent side walls force the movement of all actors, crew members, scenery, and props through restricted channels between the ends of the side arms and the proscenium wall, resulting in time-consuming traffic jams during scene shifts. In an effort to overcome the disadvantage of a dome built in a fixed position, the Germans developed a dome that could be rolled backward from the proscenium arch to clear the stage area.

This scheme, while eliminating one disadvantage, introduces two others: it requires an almost prohibitive amount of floor space to store it, and its construction cost is beyond the limit of most educational theatre budgets.

THE FLOOR CLOTH

The principal acting areas of the stage are covered with a heavy canvas cloth stretched over felt or jute padding. This floor cloth is usually dark brown, tan, or gray-green. It is laid with its downstage edge even with the curtain line. It extends about 4'-0" or 5'-0" beyond the proscenium arch on each side and upstage to a point beyond the average depth of a setting. It is usually tacked directly to the stage floor. Holding the floor cloth in place by fastening grommets over projecting screw heads driven into the floor is unsatisfactory. The heads of the projecting screws are hard to see and easy to trip over and they are soon bent and battered by rolling scenery.

The floor cloth not only improves the appearance of settings that cannot make use of carpeting, but it also serves to muffle the noise created by shifting scenery and props and to deaden the sound of the footsteps of actors and crews.

handling, joining, and shifting scenery

As we have seen in Chapters V and VI, a set of scenery consists of a series of individual parts or units made separately and joined together by various methods to form the finished setting. Since these individual pieces of scenery will be handled many times during the process of shifting, whatever methods are used in joining them together on stage must be governed by the ease and quietness of assembly and by the degree of compactness and portability. This chapter is concerned with how individual pieces of scenery can be handled, joined, and shifted.

HANDLING SCENERY

Two-dimensional framed scenery is comparatively light in weight, but its width and height can make it very awkward for an inexperienced person to move (Plate 61). Furthermore, time spent in building and painting scenery can be lost and the scenery damaged seriously in any number of ways by improper handling. Careless stacking or handling methods can result in ruined paint jobs, stretched or snagged or torn covering material and in extreme cases even warped or broken framing members. Damage of this type can usually be avoided by following the suggestions for handling scenery listed below.

RAISING A FLAT

All but the largest and heaviest flats can be raised to a vertical position by a single person. Move to the center of the flat and lift it so that it rests on one stile. Balance it in this position and move toward its base. Place one foot against the

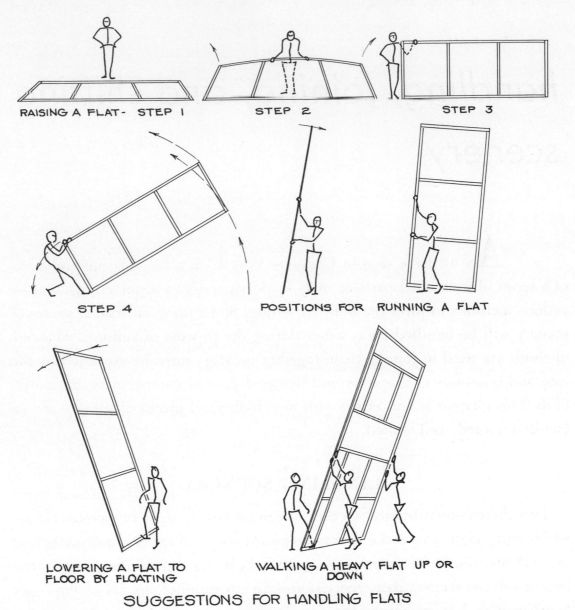

RAISING A FLAT— STEP 1   STEP 2   STEP 3

STEP 4   POSITIONS FOR RUNNING A FLAT

LOWERING A FLAT TO FLOOR BY FLOATING   WALKING A HEAVY FLAT UP OR DOWN

SUGGESTIONS FOR HANDLING FLATS

PLATE 61

lower corner and with both hands gripping the upper corner pull sharply downward and out. As the flat reaches the vertical position move to one side of it and grasp the stile with one hand placed a little above head level. The other arm crosses the body at the waist with the hand gripping the stile from this level. The lower arm is kept rigidly in this position while the upper arm is used to balance the flat. A few moments spent experimenting with this grip and balancing the flat will reveal how easily is can be controlled.

WALKING OR RUNNING A FLAT

The above method of gripping a flat forces the stagehand to face in the direction he proposes to move. The flat is at one side of him and in such a position that it will not interfere with his view. Lifting the leading edge of the flat a few inches from the floor, and with the top of the flat leaning in slightly over him, the stagehand moves rapidly in the desired direction. The trailing corner of the flat skids along on the floor and serves as a partial stabilizer. The more rapidly a flat is moved, the greater is the air pressure exerted against its side surfaces—a fact that can be used to good advantage in helping to balance any wide flat that is being moved.

RAISING A HEAVY FLAT OR A SERIES OF HINGED FLATS

Oversized flats or several flats that have been joined together require two or more stagehands to raise them. The lower rails must be blocked to prevent their slipping; the upper rails are lifted until the stagehands can reach the stiles. They then raise the unit to a vertical position by "walking" hand over hand along the stiles. Care must be taken not to push against the unsupported canvas during this process or the covering material will be badly stretched. Large flats and folded flats are best moved by two crew members. The lead man grips the flat in the same manner as if he were handling it alone, while the second man grips the trailing edge and pushes as well as helping to balance it. The second man must not lift the trailing corner from the floor, as this makes the unit extremely difficult to balance.

LOWERING FLATS FROM A VERTICAL POSITION

Single-plane flats or a series of plane flats that are not folded into a compact stack can be "floated" to the floor by blocking the lower rails and allowing the flats to fall face down; the air cushion caught under the flat surfaces will prevent their falling rapidly enough to be damaged. However, care must be taken to release both sides of the unit to fall at the same time; otherwise the air cushion will escape and one side of the unit may strike the floor with sufficient force to damage it. Extremely heavy flats, narrow flats, and flats with extensive door or window openings in them are best lowered to the floor by "walking them down."

STACKING SCENERY

Units of scenery will be moved and stored temporarily any number of times in the process of building and during the run of a production. A little care in stacking can avoid possible damage.

1. The more nearly vertical the scenery can be stacked, the less risk there will be of warping the stiles and the less floor space will be required.
2. On the back of each unit should be painted act and scene identification numbers. Stack the units in the order in which they will be used.
3. Stack the scenery on stage as close to the position where it will be used as possible.
4. Protect the paint job by stacking with painted surfaces placed face to face.

JOINING SCENERY

The fact that scenery must be portable and easily joined is one of the conditions governing its construction and shifting. The technician will have determined by his analysis of the production how the individual parts of the setting will be made, how they are to be joined to form units, and how these units will be assembled into the completed setting. His decisions on these matters are governed by two considerations: the ease and convenience of handling the part during construction, and the rapidity and quietness of assembling it during a scene shift. Scenery is assembled by being permanently joined, by hinging, or by lashing.

PERMANENT JOINING

Within the limits of portability, any part of the setting that can be handled as a unit is permanently joined by means of bolts, screws, or nails. The various parts of such units as a fireplace, a door, or a window will be so assembled. A stairway and its backings may be permanently joined by mounting them on a wagon and shifting them by rolling. Individual flats may be permanently joined to each other by hinging. Permanent joining is used except when it will interfere with the fast and easy assembly of units during a scene shift.

HINGING

Hinging scenery can provide either a permanent or a temporary method of joining (Plate 62). Permanent junctions are formed by the use of tight-pin back-flap hinges, temporary junctions by pin hinges with removable pins. By using a loose-pin hinge any two units can be quietly and quickly locked together or taken apart.

It is an unusual setting that does not have a wall area greater than the maximum width of any individual flat. Such expanses of wall are usually formed by permanently hinging a series of flats edge to edge and covering both the junction and the hinges with a strip of canvas called a dutchman. For flats that are to fold face to face one hinge is placed on the face of the flat a foot down from the top, the second a foot up from the bottom and the third midway between. Hinges should not be separated by a greater distance than 4'-0" or 5'-0", as this may result in irregularities in alignment of the stiles that will in turn cause the dutchman to buckle or wrinkle. Only when the scenery is too light in color and subjected to strong side lighting is it necessary to countersink the hinges, since the shadow of hinges may then prove objectionable. The diagrams in Plate 62 illustrate some of the problems that must be met in hinging two or more flats together. Two flats of any widths can be hinged together and will fold without complications. Three flats of varying widths can be hinged together, provided that the widest flat can be placed in the center. This permits the two outer flats to fold over each other without binding. Three flats of almost identical widths cannot be folded together without the stile of one binding against that of another. This problem can be overcome by inserting a vertical 1" x 3", called a tumbler, between two of the flats and hinging it to both. This will provide the necessary clearance for folding the flats into a compact unit.

If a hinged unit is to be shifted by running, it is well to avoid joining more than three large flats or four small ones together. A standard plain flat 5'-9" x

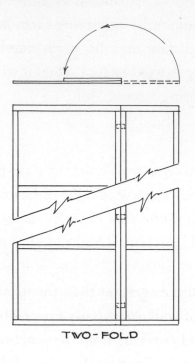

TWO-FOLD

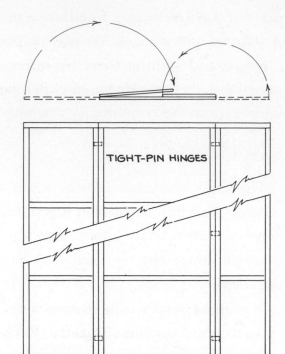

TIGHT-PIN HINGES

THREE-FOLD PLACE WIDE FLAT IN
THE CENTER

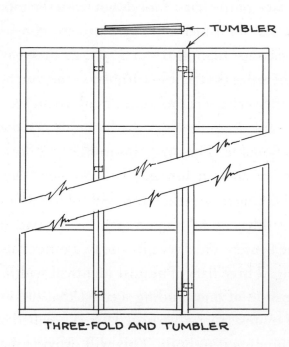

TUMBLER

THREE-FOLD AND TUMBLER

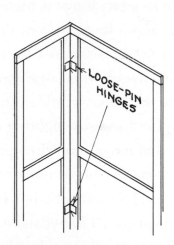

LOOSE-PIN
HINGES

FLATS HINGED ON BACK

JOINING FLATS BY HINGING

PLATE 62

14'-0" that has been painted two or three times will weigh about 35 to 40 pounds; four such flats would make a top heavy unit of 160 pounds! Hinging flats together has the following advantages:

1. It reduces the number of individual flats to be handled.
2. It reduces the number of required lashings.
3. It reduces the time required for shifting.
4. It eliminates the visible junction between flats that are joined edge to edge.
5. It holds flats more rigidly in place than lashing does.
6. The paint job is automatically protected when flats fold face to face.

JOINING SCENERY BY LASHING

Even when a setting does not have to be shifted it is rare to find one that does not have some of its units joined by lashing. If for no other reason than convenience in assembling and striking, it is worth the little time required to fit the units with lashing hardware. There is a strong possibility too, if the various parts of the setting have been permanently joined by nails or screws, that some will be damaged during the process of dismantling. Student crews seem to work much harder and with more abandon in striking a set than at any other time. One or two misdirected blows with a hammer, or an energetic yank on the lower part of a stile that is still nailed to another unit at the top can result in damaged stock.

Lashing is the process of joining two flats by lacing them together with $\frac{1}{4}''$ cotton sash cord that engages cleats placed alternately at graduated heights on both flats. As one faces the rear of two flats that are to be joined by this method, the lash line is always attached to the upper right-hand corner of the left flat. It can be attached to a conventional lash-line eye that is screwed in place on the inner edge of the stile just beneath the upper corner block; or a $\frac{3}{8}''$ hole drilled through the corner block can be substituted for a lash-line eye. In either case the lash line is inserted in the hole, knotted, drawn tight, and trimmed so that the free end will just touch the floor. This leaves an adequate length for the tie-off knot, and yet is not long enough to be stepped on when the flat is being shifted, or to get caught under a stack of scenery.

PLACEMENT OF LASHING HARDWARE (PLATE 63). There are three standard measurements governing the placing of lash cleats. The highest cleat should be

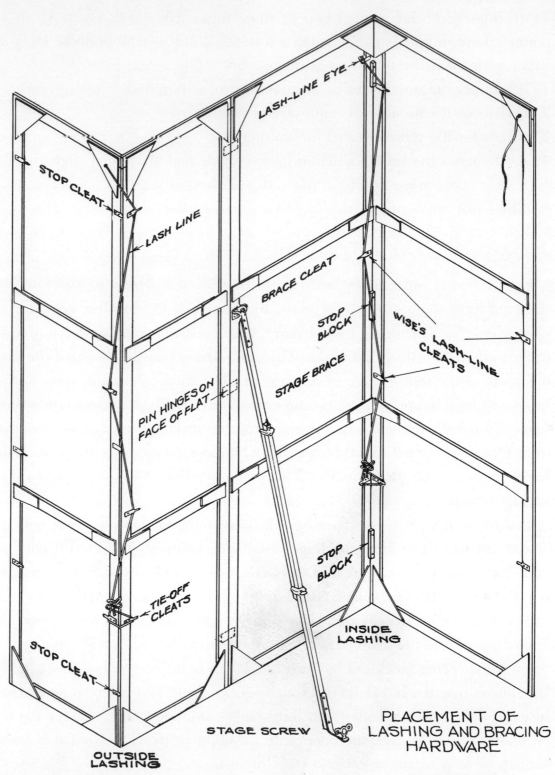

STOP CLEAT

LASH-LINE EYE

LASH LINE

BRACE CLEAT

STOP BLOCK

WISE'S LASH-LINE CLEATS

STAGE BRACE

PIN HINGES ON FACE OF FLAT

TIE-OFF CLEATS

STOP BLOCK

INSIDE LASHING

STOP CLEAT

STAGE SCREW

OUTSIDE LASHING

PLACEMENT OF LASHING AND BRACING HARDWARE

PLATE 63

placed about 1'-6" below the top of the flat. If it is placed closer to the anchor point of the lash line, it is hard to throw the lash line around it. For the same reason no lash cleat should be placed closer to a toggle bar than 6" or 8" unless the cleat can be reached from the floor. The third fixed measurement is the height of the two tie-off cleats. These should be placed exactly opposite each other 3'-0" from the floor. If they are placed lower than this, they are awkward for the stagehand to reach while tieing off the lash line. Furthermore, unless the lash line is left longer than the flat, there is not enough of it below the cleats with which to make a tie-off knot, and the disadvantage of having the lash line longer than the flat has already been mentioned. The number of lash cleats in addition to the highest and tie-off cleats is determined by the height of the flat. These cleats are placed alternately on the two flats about 3'-0" apart.

THROWING THE LASH LINE.   Throwing the lash line around the cleats requires a little skill and a great deal of practice. An experienced stagehand can do it with great speed and practically no noise. A novice, on the other hand, may add several long minutes to a scene shift, and sound as though he were beating a rug while he was at it. Lashing two flats together is accomplished in the following manner: First place the two edges of the flats in position, align them, and hold them in place with the left hand. Grasp the lash line with the right hand, pull it taut, and hold it a second or two in this position until it has stopped all movement. Now make a sharp semicircular movement to the right which will give a partial loop to the line. At the same instant allow a little slack in the line by raising the right arm so that the loop can travel the full length of the lash line. Since the uppermost cleat is on the right-hand flat, the right-handed loop has a good chance of engaging it. The next lower cleat will be on the left-hand flat so that a loop thrown to the left will engage it. This process is repeated with each cleat until the two tie-off cleats are reached. Pass the line under both these cleats, form a loop with the end of the line, and pass it under that part of the line just above the cleats. Pull down sharply on the loop; this will draw the lash line tight and insure a close junction between the flats. Complete the tie-off knot by passing a second loop through the first and pulling it tight. This knot is illustrated on Plate 63 and Plate 74, Fig. 99. The sound effect of beating a rug is usually caused by holding the lash line too tight and snapping it violently against the back of the canvas. This is not only an objectionable noise but there is an excellent chance of chipping the paint off the face of the flat.

TYPES OF LASHING JOINTS.   There are three types of possible lashings: outside lashing, edge-to-edge or 180-degree lashing, and inside lashing. If the technician has any choice in the matter, he will select units that can be joined by using the outside lashing, as this is by far the easiest to make. Any junction formed by two flats whose backs are separated by an angle greater than 180 degrees is considered an outside lashing. The edge-to-edge lashing is used only when the junction between the flats can be concealed by architectural trim placed over the face of the flats, or when the junction will be out of sight of the audience. It is practically impossible to lash the edges of two flats tightly enough together to keep the junction from being visible or to keep a backstage light from spilling through. The inside lashing is formed when the backs of the flats are placed at an angle of less than 180 degrees. This type of lashing is avoided whenever possible, because the more acute the angle between the flats becomes the less room there is for handling the lash line. Furthermore, because of the change in the direction of the lash line's pull on the cleats, there is a risk that the cleats will be torn loose from the stiles when the line is pulled tight.

The butt joints formed by the edges of flats joined by lashing should be placed as nearly parallel to the proscenium opening as is possible. This makes the junction a little less obvious; more important, it destroys the possibility of seeing a backstage light from out front.

THE USE OF STOP CLEATS AND STOP BLOCKS.   A set of either stop cleats or stop blocks is placed on one of any two flats that are to be joined by lashing. Stop cleats are an aid in aligning the edges of the flats and are used only on outside and edge-to-edge lashings. The stop cleat is a $3''$ length of strap iron $\frac{3}{4}''$ wide, with one end drilled to receive two screws. The cleat is attached to the stile with its free end projecting $\frac{3}{4}''$ beyond the outer edge of the stile. Three cleats usually make up the set employed on each lashing—one placed near the top of the flat, one near the bottom, and the third midway between the two.

An inside lashing requires the use of stop blocks to prevent one flat from slipping past the edge of the other. These stop blocks are made from scrap lumber by cutting strips of wood $1''$ wide and $6''$ to $8''$ long and drilling each strip to receive two No. 9 1½″ screws. The blocks are screwed to the back of the stile ¾″ from the outer edge in approximately the same positions as the stop cleats: one near the top, one near the bottom, and the other halfway between these two.

SUBSTITUTE LASHING HARDWARE.   If the budget will not permit the purchase of conventional lashing hardware, it is possible to make acceptable substitute lash cleats and stop cleats. Probably the best lash cleat is made from ¼″ plywood, 2″ wide by 4½″ long. Shape one end of the cleat into a rounded point and attach the other end to the flat by screws or clout nails. A stronger lash cleat can be made from strap iron ⅛″ thick by ¾″ wide. Cut this into 4½″ lengths, drill one end to receive two round-headed screws, and round off the other end with an emery wheel. Still another and less expensive lash cleat can be made from a 6″ length of 1″ x 3″. This block is nailed or screwed to the back of the stile and a heavy round-headed screw is driven into its inner edge and left projecting by 1″ or so. The line can be lashed around this projecting screw. Projecting nails or screws driven directly into the inner edges of stiles are not satisfactory, since the lack of clearance between them and the canvas makes them hard to engage with the lash line. Use of the block as just described gives an added ¾″ in clearance.

An unorthodox, but highly effective, method of joining scenery is the use of either C-clamps or adjustable wooden clamps. Occasionally two or more wagons (platforms mounted on castors) may be joined into a single unit while on stage and locked by clamps fitted around adjoining framing members. Sometimes the clamps can be used to good advantage for joining edge to edge two flats that cannot be drawn tightly enough together by lashing.

BRACING SCENERY

There are few things quite so shattering to the illusion created by a well-constructed and well-painted setting as to have the setting shake and wobble when an actor touches it or a door is closed. Since scenery must necessarily be light in weight, it must also be solidly braced to eliminate this possibility of shaking. At the same time, the bracing of scenery must be governed by the same factors that dictate its construction, namely, that the bracing be light and portable, strong, and capable of fast and quiet joining and disassembly.

The temporary bracing of scenery is normally accomplished by one of several methods: (1) by use of a standard adjustable stage brace, cleat, and stage screw; (2) by use of rigid or folding jacks; (3) by use of stiffening battens; and (4) by bracing one unit against another that can be placed at an angle to it. When a setting does not have to be shifted, the bracing can be of a permanent type—supported by diagonal braces, jacks, or guy wires that may be nailed, screwed, or bolted into place.

THE STAGE BRACE

The most common method of bracing scenery is by the use of a standard adjustable stage brace. This brace consists of two overlapping lengths of hardwood that can be extended or contracted and held at the desired length by tightening a thumbscrew. One end of the brace is equipped with a double-pronged curved hook that is designed to engage the eye of a brace cleat. The lower end of the brace is equipped with either an angular or a curved rigid footiron through which a stage screw can be driven into the floor to lock the brace into position. The cleat is attached to the rear of the stile at a point a little above half the height of the flat. Scenery, of course, can be braced at any point where there is need for it, but under normal circumstances it is usually braced on the back of flats that have been joined by hinging. There is usually little need of bracing at a point where two flats are joined by lashing. Those flats are generally at an angle to each other and so brace themselves.

There are exceptional cases where, for one reason or another, stage screws cannot be driven into the stage floor—floors of linoleum-covered concrete or highly polished hardwood are examples. In such situations one of the following alternatives can be used: (1) rigid or folding jacks can be attached to the scenery with their bases weighted down by sandbags; (2) regular stage braces can be used, provided special wooden bases are constructed to receive the stage screws. A base of this type is made of 2″ stock; it is about 20″ square, with a rubber bathmat glued to its under surface to prevent its slipping. Additional stability can be given to the bases by weighting them down with sandbags.

RIGID AND FOLDING JACKS

In situations where the shape or size of scenery prevents the use of standard stage braces, or when the scenery is subjected to violent action, bracing is

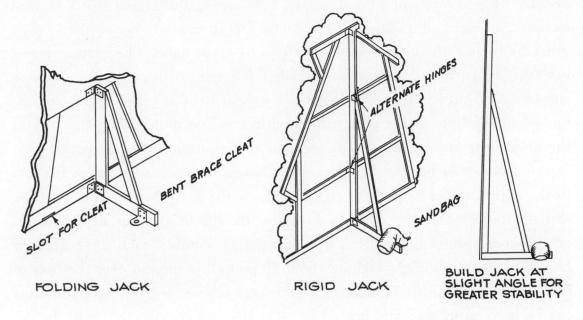

FOLDING JACK

SLOT FOR CLEAT

BENT BRACE CLEAT

RIGID JACK

ALTERNATE HINGES

SANDBAG

BUILD JACK AT
SLIGHT ANGLE FOR
GREATER STABILITY

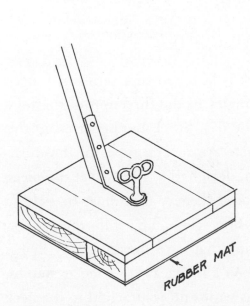

PROTECTIVE FLOOR BLOCK

RUBBER MAT

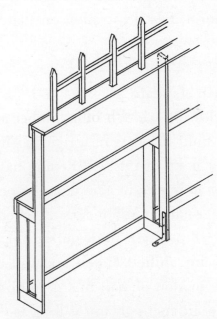

RIGID JACK ADAPTED TO
IRREGULAR SHAPE

PLATE 64

usually accomplished by a homemade brace called a jack. The jack is a three-cornered frame made of 1″ x 3″ or 1″ x 4″ stock, and consists of a vertical member, a base, and a diagonal (Plate 64). The three parts are joined to each other by corner blocks and keystones held by clout nails. The vertical member must be extended at least two-thirds the height of the unit for adequate support. A rigid footiron or a stage-brace cleat bent at right angles and attached to the base of the jack will provide a means of screwing the jack to the floor. The jack is fastened to the flat by hinging it either to a stile or to two or more cross battens. By placing the hinges on alternate sides of the vertical the jack is held rigidly at right angles to the flat. On flats that must be shifted the jack can be folded flush against the flat by placing all the hinges on the same side of the vertical. For lightweight cutouts such as bushes or hedges, a small sandbag weighing about 10 pounds is thrown over the base of the jack as a substitute for footirons and stage screws. Irregular shaped units can be both supported and braced by jacks that are constructed to fit the desired form. See illustration on Plate 64.

STIFFENING BATTENS

When standard 1″ x 3″ or 1″ x 4″ stock is fastened to a series of hinged flats with the width of the lumber at right angles to the direction of the fold, it will hold the flats in a rigid position (Plate 65). Stock lumber used in this manner is known as a stiffening batten. There are several types of these battens, or stiffeners, in common use: permanent, detachable, and swivel stiffeners.

1. A permanent stiffener is attached to units of scenery that must be held in a rigid position both during the playing of a scene and while the scenery is being shifted. The back wall of a setting that is to be shifted by flying, or a section of wall that is to be handled on a tip jack, are good examples. The stiffener is made as long as the unit is wide and is attached to the back of the flats by hinging it on alternate sides to the stiles. Usually one stiffener placed at a height about two-thirds that of the flats is adequate. On exceptionally tall flats (18′-0″ or over) it may be necessary to use two. The stiffener, like the jack, may be shaped to conform with any irregular formed unit and can be used in a vertical as well as horizontal position.

2. The detachable stiffener is used on units that require additional bracing

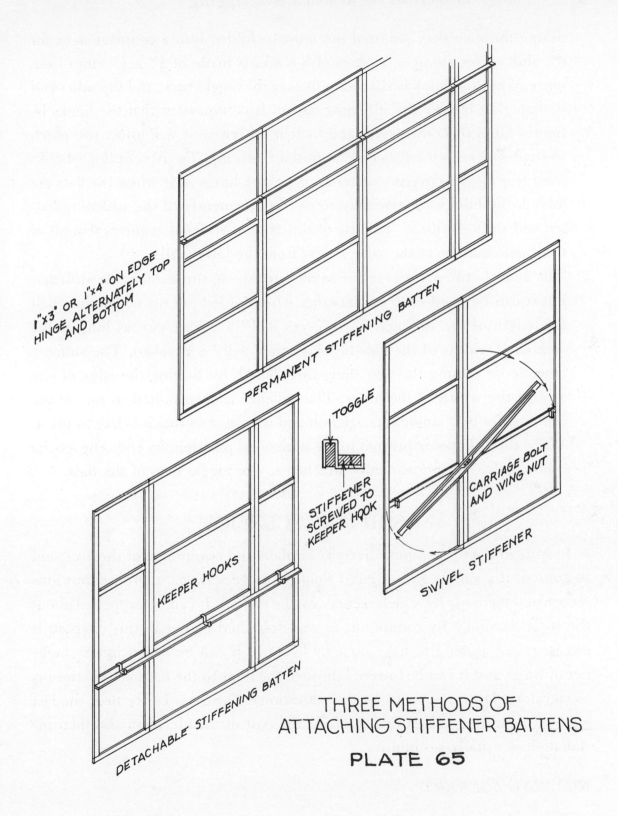

1"x3" OR 1"x4" ON EDGE
HINGE ALTERNATELY TOP
AND BOTTOM

PERMANENT STIFFENING BATTEN

TOGGLE

STIFFENER
SCREWED TO
KEEPER HOOK

KEEPER HOOKS

CARRIAGE BOLT
AND WING NUT

SWIVEL STIFFENER

DETACHABLE STIFFENING BATTEN

THREE METHODS OF
ATTACHING STIFFENER BATTENS

PLATE 65

during the time they are used but must be folded into a compact stack for the shift or for storage. A series of S-hooks is made of $\frac{1}{4}''$ x $\frac{3}{4}''$ strap iron; one end of each hook is shaped to fit over the toggle bars, and the other end is shaped to receive the stiffening batten. It is important that the hooks be tightly fitted to both toggles and batten; otherwise it will allow too much free movement to the flats it is supposedly bracing. To prevent the S-hooks from tearing the covering material or poking holes in it when the flats are folded, the hooks are generally screwed permanently to the stiffening batten and shifted with it. The use of this type of stiffener requires that all of the toggle bars be at the same height from the lower rails.

3. The swivel stiffener serves the same purpose as the detachable stiffener, but it can be used only on flats that when folded are no wider than half the length of the stiffener. Two pieces of 1″ x 3″ are cut, as long as the combined widths of the flats to which they will be attached. The stiffener is made by joining the two along their length by butting the edge of one against the width of the other. The stiffener is then bolted to one of the center stiles by a single carriage bolt and wing nut so that it is free to pivot. When the stiffener is pivoted to the horizontal position, its ends engage the S-hooks that are permanently attached to the toggle bars of the flats.

SHIFTING SCENERY

In spite of the tremendous diversity in plans and equipment of theatres, and in spite of the variety in form and shape of stage settings, there are but four recognized methods by which scenery can be shifted. It can be propelled about the stage manually by running it, as was described earlier in this chapter; it can be raised above the stage floor by flying it; it can be rolled in any number of ways; and it can be lowered through the floor to the basement by means of elevators. However, as far as the educational theatre is concerned, the last method of shifting is best disregarded—the cost of the elevators and their installation is usually prohibitive.

RUNNING SCENERY

This is the simplest and the most commonly used method of shifting scenery. It requires no special equipment and on very small stages is frequently the only way that it can be shifted at all. No matter how elaborately a stage may be equipped or how much floor space there may be, some parts of each setting are usually shifted by running.

FLYING SCENERY

Flying is the fastest and quietest method of shifting. Moreover, it has the advantage of keeping scenery off the stage floor and out of the way when not in use, and it automatically stores it where there is little likelihood of its being damaged. It has already been pointed out that there are four systems used in flying scenery: rope-line rigging and sandbag balance, counterweight system, multiple-speed counterweight system, and the new Izenour electronic grid. Of these the counterweight system is most frequently found in educational theatres, and hence a detailed account of its use is given here. To suspend a unit of scenery from a counterweight batten proceed as follows:

1. Select and lower to within a few feet of the floor a batten that is at the desired distance from the arch.
2. Establish the correct position for the flown unit in respect to the center line of the stage and mark it on the stage floor.
3. Place the unit face down on these marks with the upper rails or batten directly beneath the pipe batten from which it will be suspended.
4. Attach the scenery to the batten with chain, rope, wire, or batten clamps. (The permanent hardware, such as hanger irons, hook hanger irons, ceiling plates, etc., was bolted to the scenery while it was still in the shop.)
5. Balance the weight of the scenery with counterweights placed in the arbor.
6. Raise the scenery to a vertical position and make final adjustments in both counterbalance and snatch lines to obtain perfect balance and trim.
7. Place identification card on the locking rail to identify the unit with the operating line controlling its movement.
8. Reverse the procedure to remove scenery from a counterbalanced batten.

SAFETY PRECAUTIONS FOR USE WITH THE COUNTERWEIGHT SYSTEM.   There is nothing complicated about the use of the counterweight system. By exercising a little common sense, and by following the precautions listed below, it is possible to avoid unnecessary risks.

1. Clear the stage of all personnel when crew members are working on the

grid. Clear the area under the loading platform when counterweights are being loaded or unloaded.

2. When crew members are working on the grid or loading platform, do not permit them to carry extra tools or objects that might fall from their pockets to the floor below.

3. Do not stack counterweights above the lip of the loading platform where they might be knocked off.

4. In the process of rigging scenery to fly, attach the scenery to the batten first and then add the counterweights to the arbor.

5. In striking scenery (dismantling the production), unload the counterweights from the arbor first and then unfasten the scenery.

6. Heavy units of scenery should be flown with the snatch lines attached to the bottom member of the piece, to place all joints under compression.

7. Inspect and eliminate all faulty materials used in attaching scenery to the batten.

8. All hardware used in supporting a flown unit should be bolted in place. Screws used alone may pull loose from soft wood if subjected to a sudden strain.

9. Do not attempt to lower unbalanced scenery or counterweights by pressure of the rope lock on the operating line.

ROLLING SCENERY

Three-dimensional, heavy, or irregular shaped scenery is most easily shifted by mounting it on castors and rolling it. This method of shifting is not only the easiest, but also one of the most adaptable techniques for moving scenery. It can be employed for moving the smaller individual parts of a setting or adapted to handle whole wall sections; or it can be used to shift an entire setting, including all of the decorative and practical properties. Rolling units can be powered by one of three methods: they can be moved manually by being pulled or shoved, they can be moved mechanically by the aid of winches or tackle rigging, or they can be so rigged that they are driven electrically.

WAGON STAGES.   One of the advantages of the rigid over the parallel platform is the ease with which it can be converted into a small wagon. Plate 66 illustrates the method of attaching castors to the underside of the plaform tops

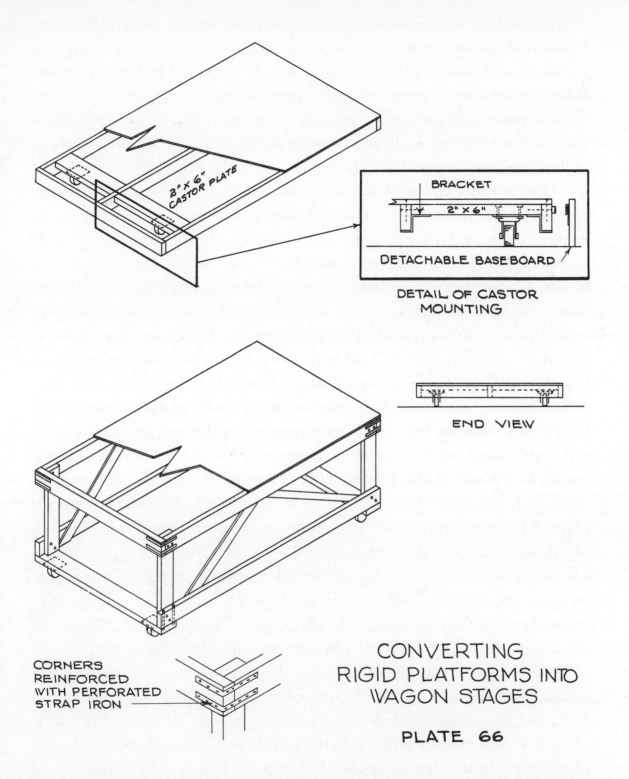

2" X 6"
CASTOR PLATE

BRACKET

2" X 6"

DETACHABLE BASEBOARD

DETAIL OF CASTOR
MOUNTING

END VIEW

CORNERS
REINFORCED
WITH PERFORATED
STRAP IRON

CONVERTING
RIGID PLATFORMS INTO
WAGON STAGES

PLATE 66

to convert them into either single-step wagons or wagons of greater height. Probably the most commonly used wagon height is the single-step unit with an elevation of about 7″ from the stage floor. This size can be used in a raised alcove, at the base of a stairway, or in a raised entranceway. Wagons of this height must be equipped with castors of the proper size and capacity. Those illustrated are rubber-tired swivel castors that measure $4\frac{1}{2}$″ from the bottom of the wheel to the top of the plate; they are fitted with wheels 3″ in diameter. These castors are rated as a medium-heavy-duty type with a maximum capacity of 400 pounds. Castors of this height can be so mounted that the finished wagon is only $6\frac{3}{4}$″ high. To attach them, turn the platform upside down and measure the distance between the 2″ x 4″ supporting members. Cut four lengths of 2″ x 6″ and test-fit them into the four corners of the platform. These will form the plates to which the castors will be bolted. Since they will remain permanently attached to the platforms after the castors have been removed, be sure that they are held back 4 or 5 inches from the end frames so that they will not take up the space required for bolting legs to the same platform. Mark the position of the castors on the 2″ x 6″ plates and drill holes for $\frac{3}{8}$″ x $2\frac{1}{2}$″ carriage bolts. Be sure to countersink the bolt heads so that the top of the plates will fit flush against the underside of the flooring. Bolt the castors into place, fit the 2″ x 6″ plates into position on the platform, and drive 12-penny nails through the 2″ x 4″ framework into the ends of each plate. Additional support can be given to the assembly by screwing the floor boards directly above the castors to the 2″ x 4″ framing. This type of assembly has proved satisfactory for all normal wagon loads. Under exceptional weight loads, brackets made from $\frac{1}{4}$″ or $\frac{5}{16}$″ x $2\frac{1}{2}$″ strap iron are made to fit under the 2″ x 4″ frames and to the underside of the castor plate. Bolting the brackets to the 2″ x 6″s greatly increases the strength of the wagon.

Attaching castors to platforms higher than a single step is comparatively simple. In this case the 2″ x 6″ castor plate is cut as long as the platform is wide, and the castors are bolted to its face 3″ in from each end. Legs made of 2″ x 4″ are used in addition to the castors and castor plates to raise the platform top to the desired height; these legs are bolted to the framework of the platform. Fastened to the side of the legs and flush with their bottoms are additional 2″ x 4″ frames, to which the castor plates are bolted. This assembly eliminates any danger of the castor plates twisting off, which can happen if the plates are joined to the frame by nailing.

It is necessary to lock wagon stages in place on-stage to stop any tendency they may have to roll as a result of the movements of the actors. This is done by forcing wedges between the floor and the underside of the wagon, so that the weight of the wagon rests on the wedges rather than on the castors. This locking method is successful only when the wedges can be placed on opposite sides of the platform; otherwise the wagons may slip off the wedges. Another and more reliable job of locking is done by bolting hinged foot irons to the sides of a wagon and stage screwing them into place. Before the wagon is moved be sure that the free end of the footiron is folded up out of the way so that it will not gouge into the floor or tear the floor cloth. A turn button can be used to hold it out of the way, or the axle of the hinge can be tightened by a few blows of a hammer to increase the friction and eliminate the free movement of the hinge.

Heavily loaded wagons are best moved manually by pull ropes or pull bars on each corner. Pull ropes are tied to ceiling plates or hanger irons that are bolted to the sides or top of the wagon. The free ends of the ropes are knotted to provide a hand hold to pull and guide the wagon. Pull bars are detachable and are made of $\frac{3}{8}''$ iron rods with a handle shaped at one end and a sharp right-angle hook at the other. By engaging the hooks into holes drilled in the platform tops, the movement of the wagon can be easily controlled.

SLIP STAGES.   The only difference between a wagon stage and a slip stage is that the latter is much larger and rolls on rigid castors or flanged wheels and a track (Plate 67). Small wagons are mounted on four or six swivel castors and so may be moved about in any direction with ease, because the castors will pivot to follow the direction of pull. A large wagon requires many castors to support it, and this increases the difficulty of getting all of them properly aligned. Unless the castors are all pivoted to approximately the same angle it becomes almost impossible to move the wagon without much pulling and prying. For this reason the large slip stage is mounted on rigid castors or on flanged wheels that will limit its movement to two directions. When the off-stage space left and right is equal in length to the width of the proscenium arch, two slip stages can be employed. Slip stages large enough to carry a full setting are

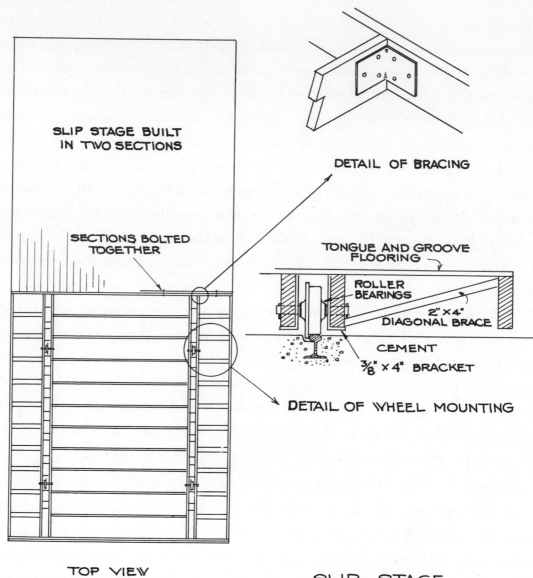

SLIP STAGE BUILT
IN TWO SECTIONS

SECTIONS BOLTED
TOGETHER

DETAIL OF BRACING

TONGUE AND GROOVE
FLOORING

ROLLER
BEARINGS

2" X 4"
DIAGONAL BRACE

CEMENT

3/8" X 4" BRACKET

DETAIL OF WHEEL MOUNTING

TOP VIEW

SLIP STAGE
PLATE 67

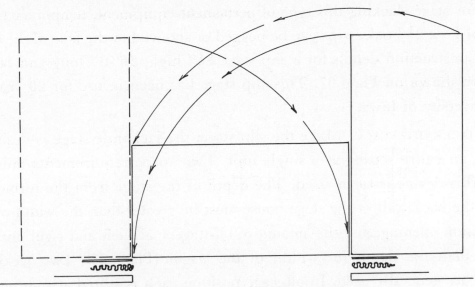

PLAN OF JACKKNIFE STAGE

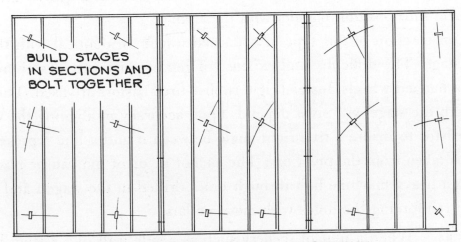

BUILD STAGES
IN SECTIONS AND
BOLT TOGETHER

PLAN SHOWING WHEEL ALIGNMENT

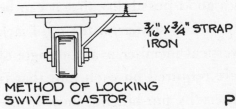

3/16" X 3/4" STRAP
IRON

METHOD OF LOCKING
SWIVEL CASTOR

PLATE 68

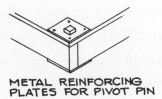

METAL REINFORCING
PLATES FOR PIVOT PIN

generally mounted on flanged wheels that roll on tracks embedded in the stage floor. For stages lacking this type of permanent equipment, temporary tracks made of 1″ x 2½″ oak strips can be pegged or screwed to the face of the stage floor. Construction details for a slip stage 8½″ high, 36′-0″ long and 16′-0″ wide are shown on Plate 67. This slip stage has been in use for 20 years at the University of Iowa.

THE JACKKNIFE STAGE.   Like the slip stage, the jackknife stage is designed to shift an entire setting as a single unit. Two space requirements must be met if this device is to be used. The depth of the stage from the tormentor line to the back wall of the stage house must be greater than the width of the proscenium opening; and the amount of off-stage space left and right must be greater than the depth (or width) of the wagon (Plate 68). Two jackknife wagons are generally used. In off-stage position each is stored at right angles to the proscenium arch, with the corner nearest the arch anchored by a pivot pin. The stages are brought into service by rolling them in a quarter arc; this brings them into position parallel with the arch.

The construction of this type of oversized wagon is identical with that of the slip stage. The difficulty and expense of getting curved tracks eliminates the use of flanged wheels. Instead rigid rubber-tired castors are used. The ease with which the stage will pivot depends upon accuracy in aligning the wheel of each castor to insure a true right angle between it and a line representing the radius taken from the pivot pin. The anchor or pivot pin can be made by dropping a heavy machine bolt through holes drilled in the wagon and stage floor and reinforcing the holes with metal collars.

TIP JACKS.   When a unit of scenery such as a side wall of a setting is too heavy to run, cannot be folded or cannot be flown—in short, when it seems impossible to shift it by any means—there is a good possibility that it can be fitted with tip jacks and moved easily. The tip jack is similar to the rigid jack except that it is fitted with castors and the vertical member is at an angle of less than 90 degrees to its base. Two jacks are required on each unit that is to be so shifted. They are attached to the scenery by pin-hinging them to the cross members of the flats and to the stiffening battens, as illustrated on Plate 69. Note that when the scenery is in an upright position none of its weight

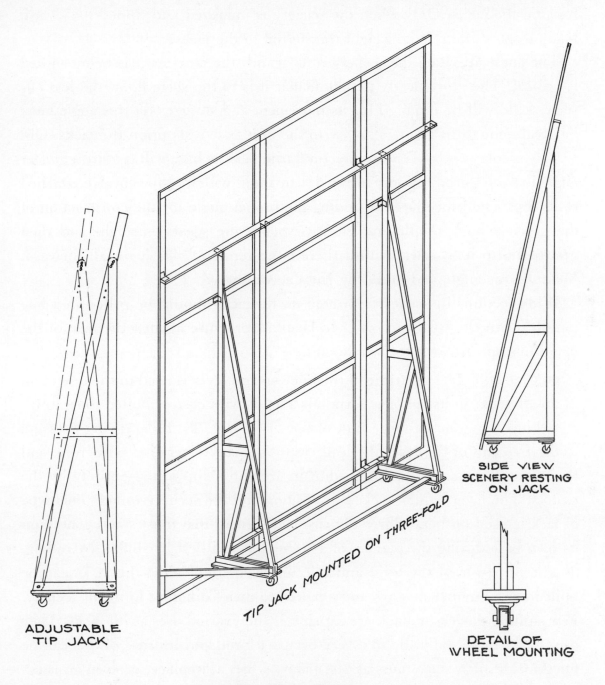

ADJUSTABLE
TIP JACK

TIP JACK MOUNTED ON THREE-FOLD

SIDE VIEW
SCENERY RESTING
ON JACK

DETAIL OF
WHEEL MOUNTING

THE TIP JACK

PLATE 69

rests on the jacks. Only when the scenery is unlashed and tipped backward, ready to be shifted, is its weight transferred to the jacks.

The angle at which the scenery rests against the jacks as it is being shifted is critical. The more nearly perpendicular it is to the stage floor, the less off-stage space will be required for its movement and storage; yet this angle must be great enough to insure stability to the unit as it rests upon the jacks. Obviously scenery with heavy architectural trim near its base will require a greater angle to keep it from tipping forward than a unit with a heavy cornice attached to its top. The procedure for finding the proper angle for the construction of the jacks is both simple and effective. Stand the scenery upright and then gradually tip it backward until there is no tendency for it to fall forward. Measure this angle and build the jacks accordingly.

Wide sections of scenery mounted on tip jacks should be rolled in a line parallel with the width in order to keep air pressure against the face of the flats from tipping over the whole unit.

LIFT JACKS.   The principle of the fulcrum and lever is used in the operation of the lift jack. In its simplest form it is a lever, with castors bolted to its lower face, hinged by one end to a unit of scenery (Plate 70). By applying pressure to the free end of the lever the lead castor is made to serve as a fulcrum, and the scenery can easily be lifted until its weight is supported entirely by the castors. The lever is then locked in position and the scenery rolled. This type of jack is used on heavy three-dimensional scenery that must stand solidly on its own base during the playing of a scene, but can best be shifted by rolling.

The principle of the lever and fulcrum is so simple that the jacks can be built in any number of ways and adapted to many different forms of scenery. Few shifting devices, in fact, are capable of such varied uses as lift jacks. They can, for instance, be made in a very compact form, and because of this can be fitted inside such stage units as a stairway, a bar, a fireplace, or even an irregular shaped practical rock. Plate 70 illustrates how lift jacks were attached to shift a small setting. Several other examples, including a detachable lift jack, are illustrated on Plates 87, 88, and 89.

OUTRIGGERS.   Occasionally a piece of scenery is of such an odd shape or size that it seems to defy all methods of shifting. For example, a semicircular concave window alcove would certainly be too heavy to run, its shape would

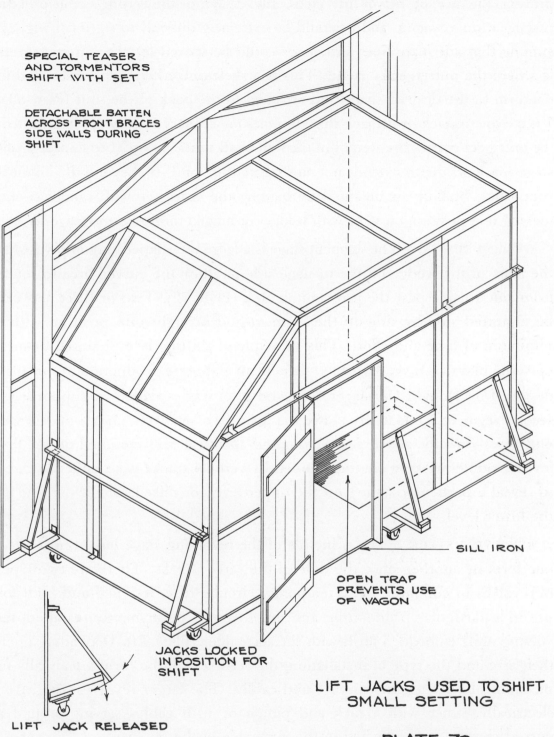

SPECIAL TEASER
AND TORMENTORS
SHIFT WITH SET

DETACHABLE BATTEN
ACROSS FRONT BRACES
SIDE WALLS DURING
SHIFT

SILL IRON

OPEN TRAP
PREVENTS USE
OF WAGON

JACKS LOCKED
IN POSITION FOR
SHIFT

LIFT JACK RELEASED

LIFT JACKS USED TO SHIFT
SMALL SETTING

PLATE 70

prevent the use of tip or lift jacks, the design of the setting could prevent placing it on a wagon, and it would be extremely difficult to rig for flying, assuming that adequate lines and space could be spared for the purpose. Here is where the outrigger is useful. This is a skeletonized wagon constructed to conform to the desired shape and attached to the back of the unit (Plate 71). Unlike the tip jack or lift jack that supports the scenery only when it is shifted, the outrigger carries the weight of the unit at all times. In order to conserve offstage space, its depth extends not more than 3′-0″ or 3′-6″ beyond the unit it is supporting. Stability is obtained by loading the outrigger with sandbags and locking it in position on stage with wedges or hinged footirons and stage screws.

SEGMENT STAGES. The segment stage is a large pie-shaped wagon pivoted at the apex of the wedge on the upstage side to allow the curved area to rotate from side to side past the proscenium arch (Plate 72). Two or three sets can be mounted side by side on the segment and brought into position with a minimum of time and effort. This principle of shifting is well suited to such episodic plays as *Sweet Mystery of Life*. In an elaborate production of this play designed by Donald Oenslager, a second level was provided by supporting a second segment immediately above the first. Two sets were placed on the second level directly above two settings of identical size mounted on the first level. Double-masking shutters guided by vertical tracks were either lowered to reveal a particular setting on the upper level, or raised to disclose one on the lower level.

REVOLVING STAGE. The principle of the revolving stage has been used in one form or another since the time of the early Greeks. There are two types of revolves in common use: a temporary circular disc designed and built for use in a particular production; and much larger, permanently installed, revolving units embedded flush with the stage floor (Plate 73). Depending upon their size and the type of installation, the revolves can be turned manually or mechanically by use of winches and cables. The larger revolves are driven electrically, either with a rack and pinion or with cables serving around a curved channel iron attached to the underside of the revolve.

When used for shifting realistic settings, the revolve is not without its disadvantages. Its very shape restricts the form of settings placed on it to some variation of a segment; its circular shape makes it impossible to have side walls

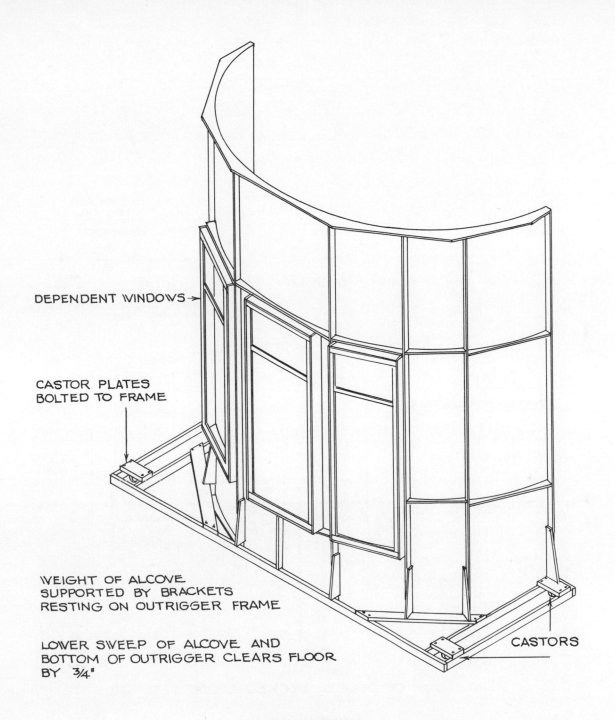

DEPENDENT WINDOWS

CASTOR PLATES
BOLTED TO FRAME

WEIGHT OF ALCOVE
SUPPORTED BY BRACKETS
RESTING ON OUTRIGGER FRAME

LOWER SWEEP OF ALCOVE AND
BOTTOM OF OUTRIGGER CLEARS FLOOR
BY ¾"

CASTORS

OUTRIGGER

PLATE 71

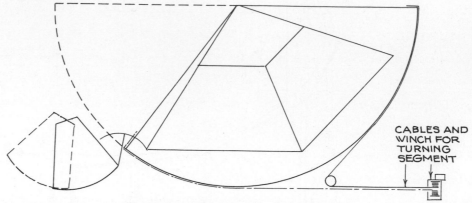

PLAN OF SEGMENT STAGE

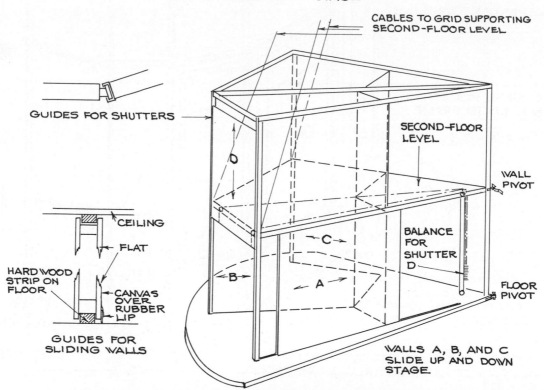

CABLES AND WINCH FOR TURNING SEGMENT

CABLES TO GRID SUPPORTING SECOND-FLOOR LEVEL

GUIDES FOR SHUTTERS

SECOND-FLOOR LEVEL

WALL PIVOT

CEILING

FLAT

HARDWOOD STRIP ON FLOOR

CANVAS OVER RUBBER LIP

GUIDES FOR SLIDING WALLS

BALANCE FOR SHUTTER D

FLOOR PIVOT

WALLS A, B, AND C SLIDE UP AND DOWN STAGE

DIAGRAM OF DOUBLE-DECKED SEGMENT STAGE

PLATE 72

of a conventional sort without extending them past the revolve onto the stationary part of the stage floor; but perhaps the most serious disadvantage is the difficulty of placing both interior and exterior settings on it at the same time. This can only be done when it is possible to build the exterior up over the top of the interiors, or when the exterior is of such a nature that buildings or dense shrubbery and trees can be used to mask the interiors. It should not be concluded, however, that the permanent revolve is a needless expense and almost useless as a shifting device. It is beautifully adapted to formalized or stylized structures that can be permanently mounted on it and revolved in full view of the audience to bring different facets of the design into focus. It is equally successful when used in conjunction with fragmentary settings mounted against black drapes. The drapes are suspended from a batten parallel with the proscenium and at a point where they will divide the revolve in half. Two settings can be in place on the revolve at one time, one in back of the proscenium, the other upstage of the blacks ready to be revolved into playing position. The shift consists of raising the blacks, making a half turn of the revolve, and then lowering the blacks. The first setting can then be struck and a third scene assembled while the action is taking place in the second.

The temporary revolve is capable of great variety both in size and in the manner in which it is used. Since this type of revolve is a disc superimposed on the stage floor, it is sometimes considered necessary to conceal its height and form by building up the surrounding floor areas to the same level. More frequently, however, no effort is made to conceal its circular shape. The use of the revolve is not confined to a single disc large enough to carry several settings. Two or three much smaller revolves are sometimes employed to shift different parts of the same setting. A revolve placed on either side of the stage can carry two side walls placed back to back and at the same time provide adequate floor space for the furniture required for two settings. A production of *Talent and Its Admirers* at the Simonov Theatre in Moscow made excellent use of three small discs to handle the numerous settings required by the play. One small disc was placed downstage left and another downstage right. Each was divided into thirds by a vertical framework covered with black draperies. Against these draperies and supported by the framework were placed parts of three settings. The third and largest of the discs was placed upstage center.

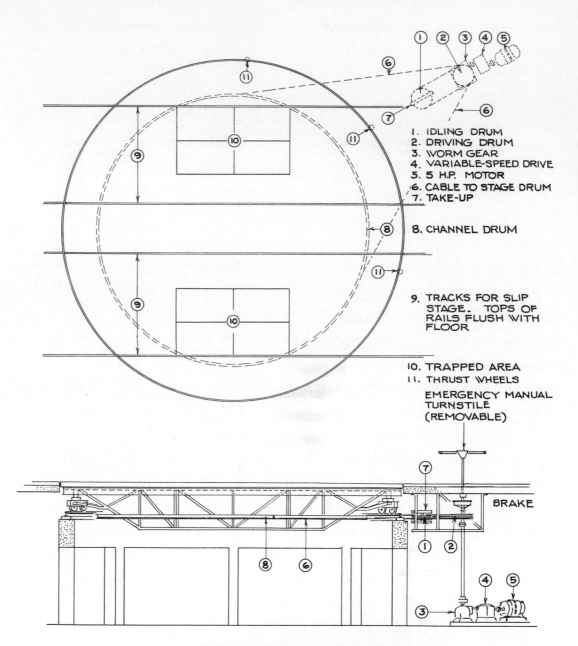

1. IDLING DRUM
2. DRIVING DRUM
3. WORM GEAR
4. VARIABLE-SPEED DRIVE
5. 5 H.P. MOTOR
6. CABLE TO STAGE DRUM
7. TAKE-UP

8. CHANNEL DRUM

9. TRACKS FOR SLIP STAGE. TOPS OF RAILS FLUSH WITH FLOOR

10. TRAPPED AREA
11. THRUST WHEELS

EMERGENCY MANUAL TURNSTILE (REMOVABLE)

BRAKE

PLAN AND SECTIONAL ELEVATION OF
A CABLE-DRIVEN REVOLVING STAGE

PLATE 73

The supporting framework on this unit divided it in half, and parts of two settings were placed on it. Against the background of black draperies the fragmentary set pieces stood out in bold relief, and the discs were turned in plain view of the audience by stagehands concealed behind the units.

A variation of the revolve that has been used extensively is the semicircle. As indicated by the name, this is literally one-half of a circular disc. It is usually designed as a shifting device that is incorporated within the structure of a large setting and revolved to bring a small scene into view without the necessity of dismantling or shifting the master setting. Its use in the Iowa University Theatre production of *Mr. Roberts* made it possible to achieve the rapid shifts required in moving from the large exterior deck scenes to the small interior cabin scenes. The setting was so designed by B. J. Kidd that the wall area beneath the captain's bridge was mounted along the straight side of the semicircle. The interior scenes were placed on the opposite side. A half-revolution of the semicircle brought the interiors into view in a matter of seconds. Masking black drapes were lowered to conceal the remainder of the ship.

More elaborate variations of the revolve—such as the concentric ring and disc or elevator and revolve combinations—while suitable for some types of musical revues, are much too expensive and complicated in both use and maintenance to be considered suitable for the educational theatre.

chapter IX

the rigging of scenery

S PECIFICALLY the word "rigging" applies to the assembly, joining, and adjustment of the parts of a setting that are to be shifted by flying. However, common acceptance and usage have broadened the meaning to include all of the activities associated with the initial assembly of a setting when it is first taken to the stage. Both the time required for rigging and the ease with which it can be accomplished depend upon how thoroughly the technician has analyzed the production in respect to the sequence of construction. This is especially important since the period immediately preceding the technical and dress rehearsals invariably finds extensive use being made of the stage space by director, actors, and members of the lighting, property, and sound crews. If the order of construction has been properly planned, the various parts of the setting requiring extensive rigging can be taken to the stage in advance of others, thus allowing plenty of time for rigging without interfering with other uses of the stage.

RIGGING SEQUENCE

The varied nature of stage settings, coupled with the diversity of equipment by which it will be handled, makes it impossible to establish an order of procedure for rigging that can be applied with equal success to all productions. Each production will present problems that are peculiar to itself and that demand some unusual variation in the manner by which the rigging is accomplished. However, under average circumstances, the sequence of rigging operations follows the outline given below.

1. The ground plan of each setting is chalked or taped off on the stage floor.

2. Scenery is moved from shop to stage in the order required for its rigging.

3. Units of scenery or special pieces of lighting equipment that will be shifted by flying are rigged first.

4. All practical, weight-bearing, three-dimensional units are tested in place for proper fit and alignment.

5. All two-dimensional units are placed in position and joined.

6. All three-dimensional pieces that fit into or against the two-dimensional units are tested in place for proper fit and alignment.

7. All flown units are lowered into position and adjusted.

8. All backings, groundrows, cutouts, and set pieces are placed in position and marked.

9. All lashing and bracing hardware is checked for proper placement and ease of operation.

10. After final adjustments are made the position of the setting is marked on the stage floor with identifying colored scene paint or chalk.

11. The setting is struck and its various parts stored in predetermined spaces nearest their point of use.

12. The back of each unit is marked with act and scene number for ready identification.

RIGGING MATERIALS

The principal tools and materials required for the rigging of scenery are essentially the same as those required in its construction. In addition there will be need for such joining materials as rope, wire, cables, chains, and occasionally clamps.

ROPE

Rope is one of the technician's most useful tools and joining materials. His uses for it are many and varied: scenery is joined, flown, pulled, guided, and restrained by it; actors can be lifted, lowered, and pulled by it. The smooth functioning of a complicated rigging can be completely dependent upon rope. Through its use in tackle rigging manual power can be increased. Perhaps its greatest value lies in the safety and protection afforded to the backstage personnel by the proper use of good quality, well-preserved rope. It is therefore only sensible that the technician take every step possible to inform himself of the nature, limitations, and maintenance of such a vital material as rope.

Judging the condition of a rope by its appearance is difficult; to an untrained person an old piece of rope looks very much like any other. A general rule for judging the condition of manila rope is the following: if the rope feels slightly oily, if it is a little stiff and awkward to handle, and if one gets more than the average number of rope splinters from it, it is likely to be in good condition. But if it seems dry, soft, pliable, and a pleasure to handle, look out! It is probably old and unsafe for heavy use. More specifically, when inspecting a rope, look for worn or frayed areas where it might have been damaged by abrasive action. Look for broken strands, cuts that could weaken it, or discolored spots that might indicate chemical damage. If but one area is damaged in an otherwise sound length of rope, cut out the damaged spot and splice. Sometimes after a rope has been used it will develop a tendency to kink; it is then said to be out of balance. This is caused by additional twisting imparted to the rope by the rigging and can be corrected by twisting the rope in the opposite direction. An easy way to do this is to tie one end of the line to a batten of the counterweight system and raise it until the rope hangs free of the floor. Usually it will then spin of its own accord until it is free of kinks; if not, it is easy to give it the necessary countertwist while it is hanging in this position.

Rope is made from four different materials: vegetable, animal, mineral, and synthetics. Rope used on stage is generally made from vegetable matter. Our best hard-fiber ropes are made from a plant called manila, grown in the Philippines. The stalks of this plant, which contain the fibers, are stripped and either hand- or machine-whipped to remove all foreign matter. After being washed, dried, and graded, the fibers are lubricated and formed into hanks called "roping." The roping is twisted from left to right to form the yarn, and the yarns are twisted in the opposite direction, from right to left, to make the strands. The strands are finally twisted from left to right to "lay" the rope.

ROPE SIZES AND STRENGTHS.   The following specifications are for three-strand rope with standard lay. In selecting a rope that would be safe to use for a given load, allow a 5 to 1 safety factor; that is, if the weight to be raised is 100 pounds, select a rope that has a breaking strain of 500 pounds or better.

Diameter	Net Weight of 100 Feet	Minimum Length in One Pound	Minimum Breaking Strength
$\frac{1}{4}''$	1.96	51.0	450
$\frac{5}{16}''$	2.84	35.2	1000
$\frac{3}{8}''$	4.02	24.9	1350
$\frac{1}{2}''$	7.36	13.6	2650
$\frac{5}{8}''$	13.1	7.65	4400
$\frac{3}{4}''$	16.4	6.12	5400

How to Take Proper Care of Your Rope

1. *Remove rope from coils properly.* Lay coil flat on floor, with inside end at the bottom. Reach down and pull inside end up through the coil. Uncoil regular right-laid rope in a counterclockwise direction.

2. *Store rope properly.* A dry unheated room with free air circulation is the best place to store rope. Keep loose coils off the floor—preferably hung on a wooden peg.

3. *Dry rope properly after wetting.* Rope should never be stored wet. Always make sure it is thoroughly dry before storing. Moist rope, stored, is almost sure to mildew.

4. *Keep rope clean.* When rope becomes dirty, wash it with clean water and dry thoroughly before storing. Dirt on the surface and embedded in rope acts as an abrasive on strands and fibers.

5. *Protect rope from chemicals.* Acids and alkalis are highly injurious to rope. So are many drying oils, such as linseed. Storage battery solutions, washing compounds or solutions, and paint, all injure rope.

6. *Avoid kinks.* When rope is repeatedly twisted in one direction, kinks are certain to develop unless twist in the opposite direction is repeatedly thrown in—or out—of the rope. Kinks pulled through restricted space, such as a tackle block, will seriously damage rope.

7. *Don't overload rope—it's costly and dangerous.* Use a 5 to 1 safety factor based on the minimum breaking strength of your rope. In figuring the safety factor make due allowance for the age and condition of a rope.

8. *Slack off guys.* When ropes are used as guy lines and other supports exposed to weather, they should be slacked off in wet weather. Otherwise damage may result to the rope as well as to what it is supporting.

9. *Avoid sharp angles or bends.* While fiber is somewhat elastic and, used as a sling or lashing, will "hug" an object, sharp corners and angular bends put a heavy extra strain on the outer fibers of a rope.

10. *Reeve ropes correctly.* Remember that small sheaves or pulleys put maximum strain on rope and increase the friction load in the block. Never use a smaller sheave than is recommended for the size of rope you are using.

11. *Don't treat your rope.* A good rope is properly lubricated by its manufacturer for the useful life of the rope.

12. *Avoid unnecessary wear and abrasion.* The outer fibers of a rope, no less than the inner ones, contribute to its strength. When they are worn—by chafing or dragging over rough, gritty, or splintered surfaces—the rope is weakened. When rope must rub over cleats, winch heads, etc., make sure they are smooth.

13. *Splice correctly.* When a relatively small section of a rope has been worn or damaged, cut the section out and splice it together, with either a short or a long splice, depending on the uses you give it.

14. *Avoid sudden jerks or strains.* A common piece of twine that may be difficult to break with a pull can easily be broken with a snap. A similar principle applies to rope, especially when it has had considerable use. Sudden jerks on tackle, slings, or lashings may result in breaks that would never have occurred with a steady pull.

15. *Reverse rope ends.* Particularly in tackle use, reverse the rope end-for-end periodically, so that all parts will receive equal wear. Should it become badly worn on a short section, shorten the rope or cut out the section and splice. A good splice is safer than a damaged section.*

ROPE KNOTS

When a rope is used it is generally necessary to employ a knot of some type to fasten it to an object or to another rope. To support, guide, pull, or lift an object safely and efficiently by means of rope demands a knowledge of basic knot types (Plate 74). The terms used in describing a knot are as follows: the end is the part of the rope used in forming the knot; the standing part is the portion between the knot and the opposite end; the bight is the loop or bend usually formed between the end and the standing part (it forms the basis of many knots); the knot itself is the interlacing of the end of a rope with itself or with another rope, or to an object, to form a temporary union.

THE OVERHAND KNOT (FIG. 95).   This is the simplest of all knots, and forms the basis for many more complicated knots. Pass the end over the standing part to form a loop; then pass the end through the loop from under the standing part and pull it tight.

THE FIGURE-EIGHT KNOT (FIG. 96).   Larger than the overhand and much easier to untie, this knot is used on the end of a rope to keep it from unserving or to prevent the end of a rope from slipping through a block or pulley. Form a

* The material on rope sizes and strengths and on the care of rope is by courtesy of the Plymouth Cordage Company of Plymouth, Mass.

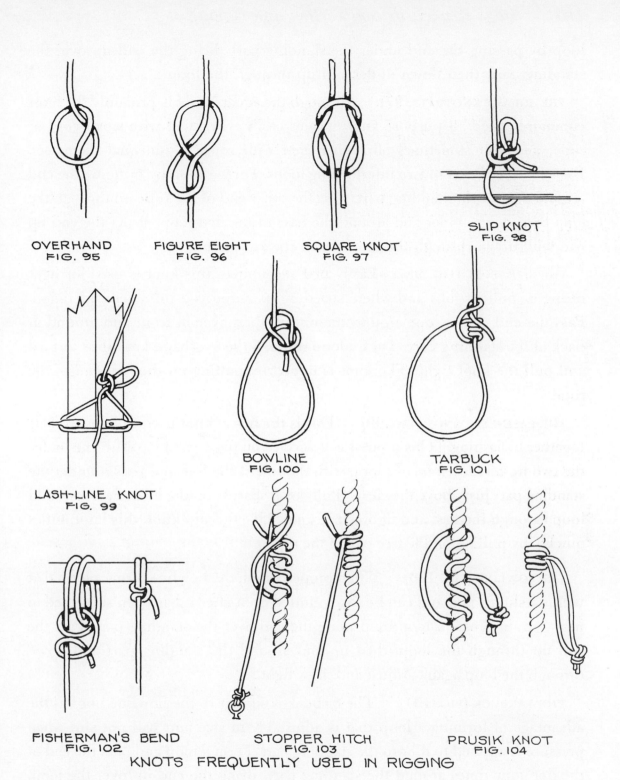

OVERHAND
FIG. 95

FIGURE EIGHT
FIG. 96

SQUARE KNOT
FIG. 97

SLIP KNOT
FIG. 98

LASH-LINE KNOT
FIG. 99

BOWLINE
FIG. 100

TARBUCK
FIG. 101

FISHERMAN'S BEND
FIG. 102

STOPPER HITCH
FIG. 103

PRUSIK KNOT
FIG. 104

KNOTS FREQUENTLY USED IN RIGGING

PLATE 74

loop by passing the end under the standing part. Bring the end up over the standing part, then down under and up through the loop.

THE SQUARE KNOT (FIG. 97).   Although the square knot is probably the most commonly used all-purpose knot, it jams easily when tied with small cord or rope, and will sometimes slip when tied with ropes of unequal diameters. Basically it consists of two interlocking loops. Form a loop by bringing the end around against the standing part. Pass the other end of the rope up through the loop then down under and around the base of the first loop. Bring the end up over and down through the loop. Draw the knot tight.

THE SLIP KNOT (FIG. 98).   Easily tied and untied, this knot is used for light lifting or pulling jobs and where speed of operation is a prime consideration. Pass the end of the rope around the object, then over in front and around in back of the standing part. Tuck a loop through the overhand knot thus formed and pull the knot tight. The knot is untied by pulling on the free end of the rope.

THE LASH-LINE KNOT (FIG. 99).   This is the tie-off knot used to join two flats together by lashing. (This process is described on page 183.) Pass the line under the two tie-off cleats; form a loop with the end of the line and pass it under the standing part just above the cleats. Pull down sharply on the loop. Pass a second loop through the first and tighten the knot. Like the slip knot, this knot unties quickly by pulling on the free end of the rope.

THE BOWLINE (FIG. 100).   When properly tied, the bowline forms a loop that will not slip or jam and can be easily untied even after it has been subjected to heavy strain. Form a loop by passing the end over the standing part. Pass the end up through the loop, then up and around the standing part and down through the loop again. Adjust and draw tight.

THE TARBUCK (FIG. 101).   The tarbuck is similar to the bowline but has the advantage of forming a loop that is adjustable in size and will not slip when pressure is applied to it or to the standing part. Form a loop and pass the end of the line four times around the standing part. Bring the end up over the loop, and form a half hitch around the standing part. Adjust and tighten all loops to bring maximum contact with the standing part of the knot.

THE FISHERMAN'S BEND (FIG. 102).   This knot is used extensively for attaching snatch lines or ropes to a pipe batten preparatory to flying scenery. Form two loops around the batten. Pass the end around the standing part and through both loops. Draw the knot tight. Make a second half hitch around the standing part and pull tight.

THE STOPPER HITCH (FIG. 103).   This is a pressure knot—the greater the pull, the greater the pressure exerted by the knot. One end of a short length of line is anchored to the locking rail by an eye bolt. The stopper hitch is used as a safety feature by tying it around the operating line of a counterweight unit that is temporarily out of balance. Pass the free end of the rope around in back of the operating line, then over the standing part. Make four or more turns with the end around the operating line below the first turn. Tighten the knot by adjusting the turns and sliding them up until they jam against the first turn.

THE PRUSIK KNOT (FIG. 104).   Like the stopper hitch, the prusik is a pressure knot that can be tied around a line or set of lines that is already under load. It is used as a substitute for a clew plate or as a means of attaching a second line. Form an endless loop by tying together, with an overhand knot, the two ends of a short length of rope. Place the loop in back of the operating line. Pass one end of the loop two or more times around the operating line and under the other half of the loop. Pull tight and adjust the loops for maximum contact.

WIRE

Several types of wire are used for various stage purposes.

STOVEPIPE WIRE.   This is an annealed lightweight iron wire. It has no great strength and should not be used for rigging. It is used primarily in the construction of properties and for hanging wall decorations.

GALVANIZED IRON WIRE.   Wire of this type is sold in various gauges or diameters. Like stovepipe wire, it is comparatively easy to work but should not be used to suspend heavy scenery. One of its most frequent uses is as a substitute for misplaced pins from pin hinges.

PIANO WIRE.   This wire is made from spring steel and has remarkable tensile strength for its diameter. It is frequently used for suspending scenery when the means of support must be as unobtrusive as possible. Every precaution should be taken to prevent the wire from kinking, as this reduces tensile strength.

RIGGING PRINCIPLES

TACKLE RIGGING

Tackle is described by Webster as "an assemblage of ropes and pulleys arranged for hoisting or pulling." In stage terminology tackle rigging applies to the use of rope and pulleys to fly scenery or to obtain special effects. In its simplest form a tackle rigging may consist of a rope passing over a single pulley to change the direction of pull or of an applied force. More complicated arrangements of ropes and pulleys can increase the mechanical advantage by 2, 3, 4, etc., depending upon the type of rigging employed (Plate 75). This means that, if the rigging being used has an advantage of 2 to 1,100 pounds, disregarding the friction loss, could be lifted by applying a 50-pound pull on the fall. (The fall is the part of the rope handled by the operator, on which the initial force is applied.)

The ordinary tackle used in moving or lifting heavy objects consists of two blocks and a rope. One block, the stationary block, is mounted in a fixed position; the other block, to which the load will be attached, is a movable block. These blocks may house one, two, three, or four grooved wheels, called sheaves, mounted on a common axel. The number of sheaves in the blocks and the way the rope is reeved (the manner of passing a rope through the blocks) will determine the mechanical advantage offered by a particular rigging.

Just why rope passing around a series of grooved wheels should increase the lifting power at the movable block over that exerted on the fall is perplexing to some. However, the principle is not difficult to understand if the tensions exerted on the movable block are counted. As an example, look at the rigging of a single whip shown by Fig. 106 on Plate 75. A single-sheaved block is mounted in a fixed position. Over this sheave passes a rope. As one end of the rope is pulled the other moves up at the same rate of speed. There is no mechanical advantage with this rigging, just a change of direction. But now suppose that an object too heavy to be lifted by a direct pull must be raised to a gallery. Exactly the same equipment can be employed, but by changing the manner of rigging its lifting power can be increased 100 percent. Tie one end of the line to the gallery, pass the other end of the rope through the block, attach the load to the block, and pull up on the fall. With this rig, called the running block, two

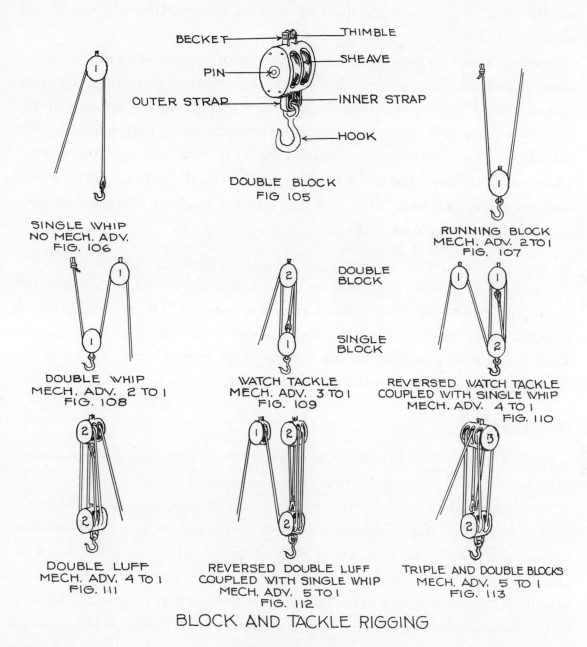

BECKET
THIMBLE
PIN
SHEAVE
OUTER STRAP
INNER STRAP
HOOK

DOUBLE BLOCK
FIG 105

SINGLE WHIP
NO MECH. ADV.
FIG. 106

RUNNING BLOCK
MECH. ADV. 2 TO 1
FIG. 107

DOUBLE WHIP
MECH. ADV. 2 TO 1
FIG. 108

DOUBLE BLOCK

SINGLE BLOCK

WATCH TACKLE
MECH. ADV. 3 TO 1
FIG. 109

REVERSED WATCH TACKLE
COUPLED WITH SINGLE WHIP
MECH. ADV. 4 TO 1
FIG. 110

DOUBLE LUFF
MECH. ADV. 4 TO 1
FIG. 111

REVERSED DOUBLE LUFF
COUPLED WITH SINGLE WHIP
MECH. ADV. 5 TO 1
FIG. 112

TRIPLE AND DOUBLE BLOCKS
MECH. ADV. 5 TO 1
FIG. 113

BLOCK AND TACKLE RIGGING

PLATE 75

tensions are exerted on the moving block, one by the force applied to the fall, and the other by the part of the line tied off to the gallery. Hence the mechanical advantage is 2 to 1.

Some friction loss always occurs with the use of any tackle rigging, and due allowance should be made for it in determining the actual force required to lift a given load. This is done by allowing a 10 percent friction loss for each sheave over which the rope must pass. As an example, assume that a load of 200 pounds is to be raised by a double luff (Fig. 111). Since the rope passes over four sheaves in this rigging, the total friction loss is 40 percent. Add the friction loss to the total to be lifted, and divide by the mechanical advantage, thus

$$40\% \text{ of } 200 \text{ lbs.} = 80 \text{ lbs.}$$
$$200 + 80 = 280$$
$$280 \div 4 = 70\text{-pound pull required to lift this load.}$$

It should be kept in mind that, as the mechanical advantage increases, the speed with which the moving block travels is reduced. The moving block of a double whip travels but half the distance and at half the speed that the fall is taken up; with a double luff the moving block moves but a quarter of the distance and at one-quarter the speed of the fall.

SPOTLINING

Spotlining is employed when it is necessary to fly some piece of equipment or scenery located on stage where it cannot be serviced by either counterweight or sandbag equipment. Spotlining is one of the simplest and most frequently used of all special stage riggings. It consists of a rope that runs from the controlling point at the locking rail or pin rail, to the grid, over a loft block or pulley, across the grid, and over a second block that has been placed in such a position that the line falls to the floor on the desired spot (Plate 76). Normally no mechanical advantage is offered by this rigging, but it does provide a change in the point of location of the pulling force. If the object being raised is heavy, a sandbag can be attached to the fall at a point beneath the first block. Since it is impossible to keep an object in proper alignment when it is suspended from a single line, a second line is used to correct this fault. This second rope runs from the object to the grid and across its own loft blocks to a point where it can be tied off to the fall of the first line. This arrangement keeps the flown object in trim, and provides the operator with a single controlling line.

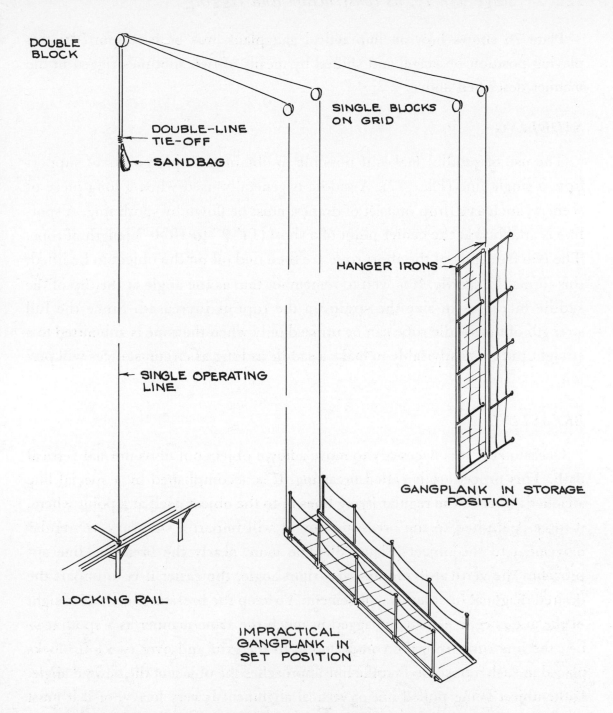

DOUBLE BLOCK

DOUBLE-LINE TIE-OFF

SANDBAG

SINGLE BLOCKS ON GRID

HANGER IRONS

SINGLE OPERATING LINE

GANGPLANK IN STORAGE POSITION

LOCKING RAIL

IMPRACTICAL GANGPLANK IN SET POSITION

DIAGRAM FOR RIGGING A DOUBLE SPOTLINE

PLATE 76

Plate 76 shows how an impractical gangplank was both supported in its playing position on stage, and shifted by means of two spotlines rigged in the manner described above.

SADDLING

The use of saddles makes it possible to obtain multiple points of support from a single line (Plate 77). A saddle is generally used when a long piece of scenery, such as a drop or a set of drapes, must be flown by spotlining. A spotline is attached at the center point of a short (14'-0" to 18'-0") length of rope. The two free ends of the short rope are then tied off on the object to be lifted; this forms the saddle. It is well to remember that as the angle at the top of the saddle increases in size the strain on the rope is increased. Since the full strength of the saddle rope can be utilized only when the rope is submitted to a straight pull, it is advisable to make a saddle as long as circumstances will permit.

BREASTING

Occasionally it is necessary to move a flown object out of its normal vertical path. This procedure is called breasting. It is accomplished by a special line attached either to the regular flying lines or to the object itself at a point where, if force is applied to the breasting line, it will impart a sideways or angular movement to the object (Plate 78). The more nearly the breasting line approaches the vertical flying line at a right angle, the easier it is to impart the desired diagonal or sideways movement. To keep the breasting line out of sight of the audience, it is usually rigged in much the same manner as a spotline—i.e., the line runs from the control point to the grid and over two loft blocks placed in such a position that the line approaches the object at the desired angle. If the object being pulled out of vertical alignment is very heavy, or if it must move any great distance, it may be necessary to attach a block and tackle to the end of the breasting line to provide some mechanical advantage. Obviously, the farther an object is pulled out of vertical alignment, the more its weight is transferred to the breasting line. Notice the rigging used on the bucket in *High Tor* to move it upstage, where is appeared to be overhanging the cliff (Plate 78).

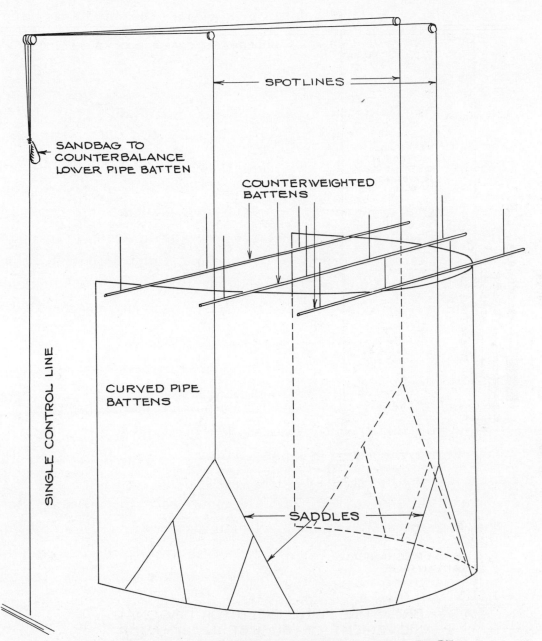

SPOTLINES

SANDBAG TO
COUNTERBALANCE
LOWER PIPE BATTEN

COUNTERWEIGHTED
BATTENS

SINGLE CONTROL LINE

CURVED PIPE
BATTENS

SADDLES

MULTIPLE SADDLES USED TO TRIP BASE
OF SMALL CYC

PLATE 77

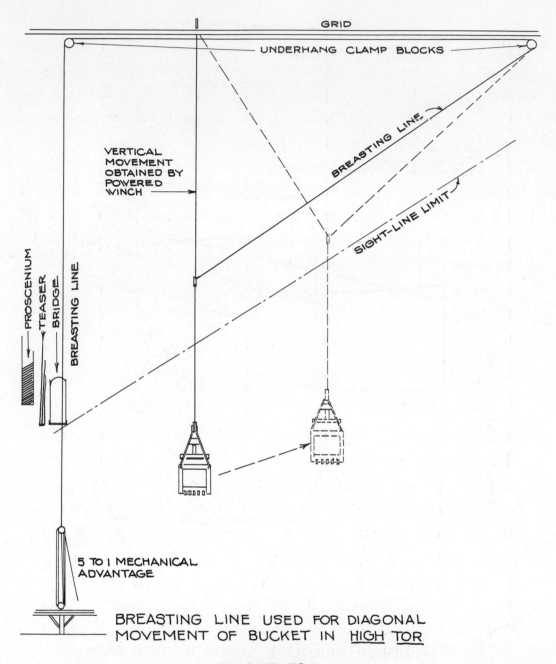

GRID

UNDERHANG CLAMP BLOCKS

BREASTING LINE

SIGHT-LINE LIMIT

VERTICAL
MOVEMENT
OBTAINED BY
POWERED
WINCH

PROSCENIUM

TEASER

BRIDGE

BREASTING LINE

5 TO I MECHANICAL
ADVANTAGE

BREASTING LINE USED FOR DIAGONAL
MOVEMENT OF BUCKET IN HIGH TOR

PLATE 78

TRIPPING

Flying scenery in theatres with unusually low grids presents the problem of raising the scenery high enough to get it out of sight. Tripping is a method of rigging that can sometimes be used to solve this particular problem. Tripping is accomplished by a set of lines placed upstage of the flown unit and attached either at the bottom of the units or to a special trip batten located at about mid-height of the flown unit. By means of these lines an unframed unit can be folded or doubled back on itself until it is raised out of sight. Certain types of framed units, such as the back wall of a setting, can be handled in much the same manner by tipping them from a vertical to a horizontal position. Such a wall must be properly reinforced by several vertical stiffening battens to withstand the strain placed on it by this method of handling.

The lines used for tripping can be attached to an empty batten of the counterweight system, provided a free batten is available just upstage of the flown unit; or it may be necessary to rig a special set of spotlines that can be used for the same purpose. See Plate 59.

MULING

Through the use of loft blocks mounted on special brackets the direction of a rigging line can be changed. This process is called muling. Since the working space above the grid may be obstructed by trusses, supports, light conduits, and cables of the counterweight system, it is frequently necessary to guide special rigging lines around them. To avoid excessive wear, noise, and the possibility of fouling, ropes or steel cables must feed into the sheave of a loft block parallel with the flange on the sheaves (Plate 79). Triangular-shaped brackets made of $\frac{3}{8}''$ x $2''$ strap iron are bolted to the grid, and to these are clamped standard loft blocks mounted in a horizontal position. By adjustment of the brackets a line or set of lines can be guided into their loft blocks at the proper angle and without rubbing against any obstruction. The muling required for a flown cyclorama as shown in Plate 79 illustrates this principle.

SWIVEL AND HOOK

Scenery placed on stage at an angle other than parallel with the battens of the counterweight system can be flown from a single batten by the aid of a swivel

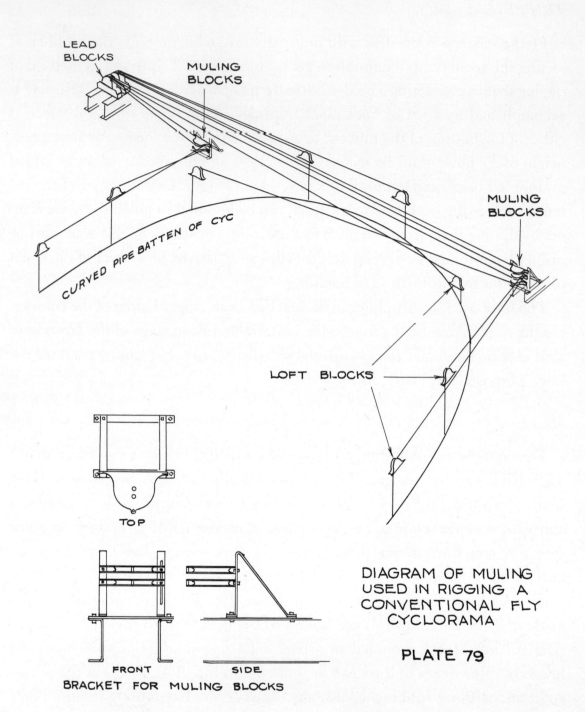

LEAD BLOCKS

MULING BLOCKS

MULING BLOCKS

CURVED PIPE BATTEN OF CYC

LOFT BLOCKS

TOP

FRONT   SIDE

BRACKET FOR MULING BLOCKS

DIAGRAM OF MULING
USED IN RIGGING A
CONVENTIONAL FLY
CYCLORAMA

PLATE 79

and a strap-iron hook (Plate 80). Assume that it is desirable to shift one side wall of a setting by flying but only one batten is available for the purpose. Horizontal stiffeners are added to the wall section so that it may be handled as a rigid unit. A short length of $\frac{1}{4}''$ steel cable is clamped to the batten directly above the stage position of the wall. The cable is fastened to the center of a short section of $1\frac{1}{2}''$ pipe and clamped tightly into position. To each end of the pipe are tied $\frac{3}{8}''$ snatch lines that feed down through hanger irons bolted to the top rails of the flats and are tied off to foot hanger irons placed on the lower flat rails. Pipe bridle and snatch lines must be placed to one side of the wall center to avoid an even balance. The longer and heavier side of the wall is supported by a vertical strap-iron hook made from $\frac{1}{4}''$ x $\frac{3}{4}''$ strap iron bolted to the outer stile. The top of the hook is bent to fit over the pipe batten, and must extend past the top of the flat far enough to provide a level trim for the wall when it is flown. To shift a wall rigged in this manner, unlash and unbrace the unit, raise the batten a little so that the section of wall supported by the snatch lines will clear the floor by 6'' or 8'', lift the free end of the wall, walk it around until it is parallel with the batten, engage the hook over the batten, and raise the unit to high trim. Since both the hook and the swivel extend above the top of the flats, this type of rigging cannot be used on settings fitted with ceilings. It is especially suitable for shifting heavy backings or fragmentary units intended for use without a ceiling.

CONTROL OF THE UNBALANCED ARBOR

During some scene shifts it may be necessary to unfasten a flown unit of scenery from the counterweighted batten that supported it. This creates the special problem of what to do with the counterweight left unbalanced high above the stage floor. The brief time allowed for shifting scenery precludes the possibility of sending a crew member to the grid to unload the arbor, even if the matter of safety were ignored. Four methods of rigging have been developed to solve this type of problem.

1. *The substitution of counterbalance for the weight of the scenery.* If the scenery is not excessively heavy a sandbag of equal weight can be snapped onto the lowered batten before the scenery is unfastened (Plate 81, Fig. 113). The process can be expedited by attaching a special $\frac{3}{4}''$ snatch line to the pipe

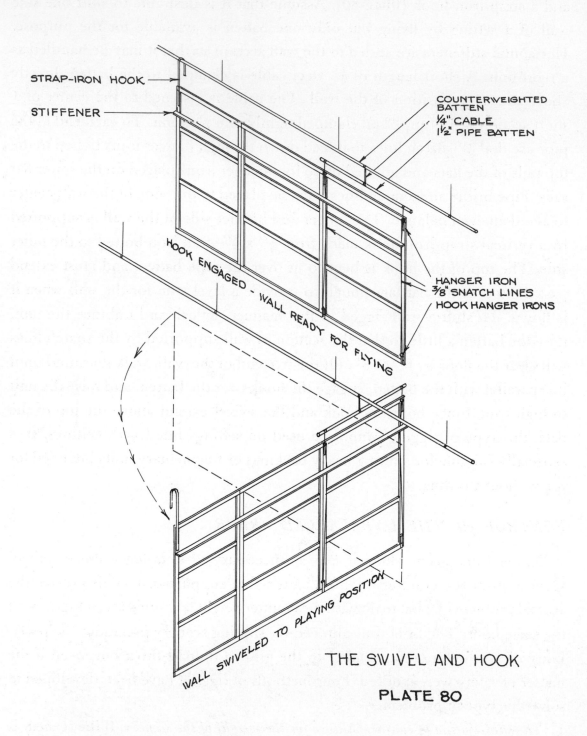

STRAP-IRON HOOK

STIFFENER

COUNTERWEIGHTED BATTEN
¼" CABLE
1½" PIPE BATTEN

HOOK ENGAGED · WALL READY FOR FLYING

HANGER IRON
⅜" SNATCH LINES
HOOK HANGER IRONS

WALL SWIVELED TO PLAYING POSITION

THE SWIVEL AND HOOK

PLATE 80

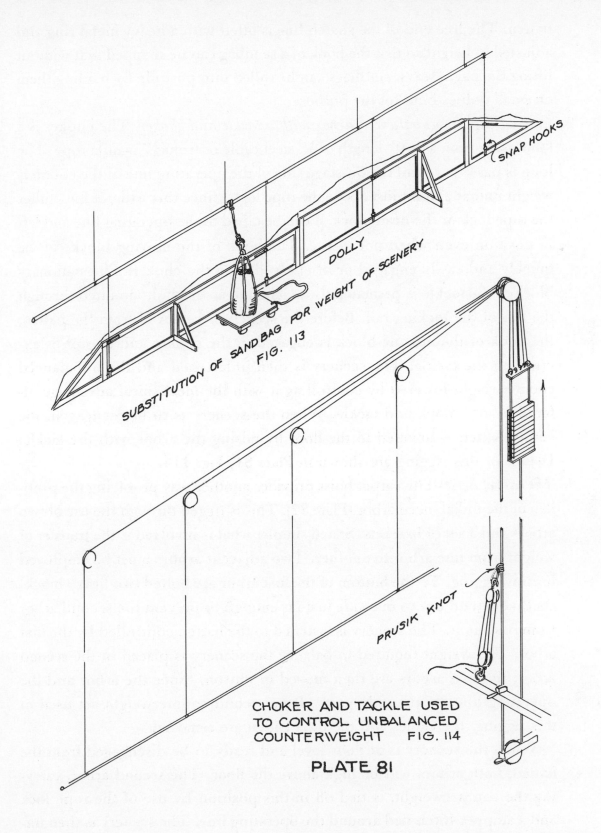

SNAP HOOKS

DOLLY

SUBSTITUTION OF SAND BAG FOR WEIGHT OF SCENERY
FIG. 113

PRUSIK KNOT

CHOKER AND TACKLE USED
TO CONTROL UNBALANCED
COUNTERWEIGHT   FIG. 114

PLATE 81

batten. The free end of the snatch line is fitted with a heavy metal ring and adjusted in height so that the hook of a sandbag can be snapped to it without lifting the bag. Heavy sandbags can be rolled into position by hauling them on small dollies built for the purpose.

2. *Controlling the unbalanced arbor with a tackle and choker.* The choker is a loop made from a 3'-0" length of $\frac{1}{4}$" steel cable or from $\frac{3}{8}$" manila rope. The loop is passed around the on-stage side of the operating line of the counter-weight unit at a point just above the rope lock. Since this will not foul either the rope lock or the head block, it can be taped to the operating line and left in position even when not in use. The hook of the moving block can be quickly and easily engaged or disengaged from the choker. The stationary block of the tackle is permanently attached to an eye bolt mounted through the top of the locking rail. Before the scenery is removed from the batten, the hook of the moving block is engaged in the choker and tension is exerted on the tackle. The scenery is then unfastened and the unbalanced counterweight lowered by controlling it with the mechanical advantage offered by the block and tackle. When the scenery is to be reëngaged, the empty batten is lowered to the floor by raising the arbor with the tackle. Details of this rigging are shown in Plate 81, Fig. 114.

3. *The carpet hoist.* The carpet hoist provides another way of solving the problem of the unbalanced arbor (Plate 82). This is rigged through the use of two arbors and a set of brackets. Stated simply, what is involved is the transfer of weight from one arbor to another. Two adjacent arbors must be employed for this rigging. To the bottom of the first arbor are bolted two heavy brackets that extend out to one side just far enough to prevent the second arbor from passing it. The scenery is fastened to the batten controlled by the first arbor. The weight required to balance the scenery is placed in the second arbor; the two arbors are then moved in unison. Since the arbor and the operating line are the only parts of the second counterweight set used in this rigging, the cables and the pipe batten are removed.

When the scenery is at floor level and ready to be disengaged from the batten, both arbors will be high above the floor. The second arbor, carrying the counterweight, is tied off in this position by use of the rope lock and a stopper hitch tied around the operating line. The scenery is then un-

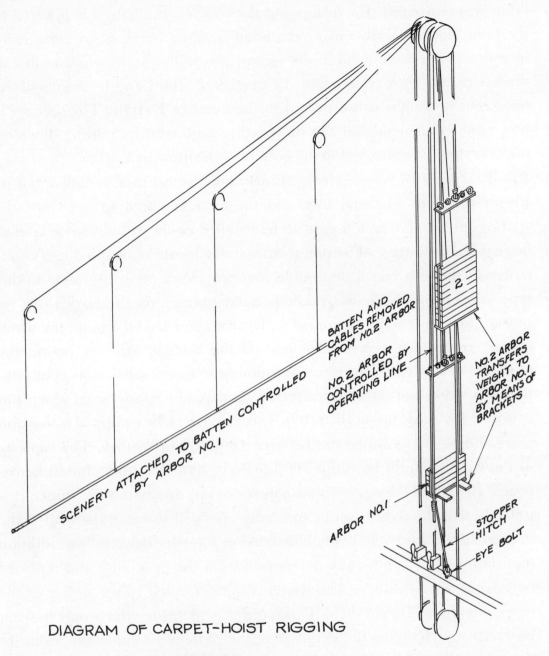

BATTEN AND
CABLES REMOVED
FROM NO.2 ARBOR

NO.2 ARBOR
CONTROLLED BY
OPERATING LINE

NO.2 ARBOR
TRANSFERS
WEIGHT TO
ARBOR NO.1
BY MEANS OF
BRACKETS

SCENERY ATTACHED TO BATTEN CONTROLLED
BY ARBOR NO.1

ARBOR NO.1

STOPPER
HITCH

EYE BOLT

DIAGRAM OF CARPET-HOIST RIGGING

PLATE 82

fastened, permitting the empty batten to be raised out of sight and the empty arbor to be lowered. On reëngaging the scenery, the batten is lowered to the floor, automatically raising the arbor until its brackets are once more in contact with the bottom of the second arbor. The scenery is attached to the batten, the lock released on the number 2 arbor, and by means of the brackets the weight is transferred to the number 1 arbor. The scenery is now counterbalanced and can be raised to high trim by pulling down on the operating line attached to the bottom of the number 2 arbor.

4. *Use of the powered winch.* Heavy scenery must sometimes be flown; but its weight increases frictional loss, and the force required to overcome the starting inertia may be too great to be handled easily without some kind of mechanical advantage. The power-driven winch can be coupled to a counterweight set with very little trouble, and provides a perfect solution to this type of problem. There is a portable electric winch on the market that requires only a single rope attached to the arbor and served around the windlass to control an unbalanced load. If the budget will not permit the purchase of this excellent piece of equipment, a very satisfactory, but nonportable, substitute can be made from a good quality hand-driven winch and a reversible electric motor (Plate 83). The winch must be equipped with worm gears and have a gearing ratio between 18 to 1 and 25 to 1. The capacity of the winch should be about 1000 pounds, and the drum should be between 10″ or 14″ long, with a diameter of approximately 6″. Since it is unlikely that the winch can be manually operated to move the load at the desired speed, it can be easily converted to a power drive by the addition of a motor. The hand crank is removed from the gear shaft and replaced by a large V-belt pulley. The winch is then coupled to the pulley of the reversible motor by a V-belt. The speed at which the winch operates can be varied by changing the diameter of the pulleys on either the motor or the winch. Two $\frac{1}{4}$″ steel cables run from the winch to the counterweight arbor. The end of one cable is clamped to the drum and the cable served onto it from right to left. It then runs to the grid, over a loft block, and is clamped off to the top of the arbor. As the winch turns in a counterclockwise direction, the cable feeds onto the drum, thereby raising the arbor. One end of the second cable is fastened to the opposite end of the drum,

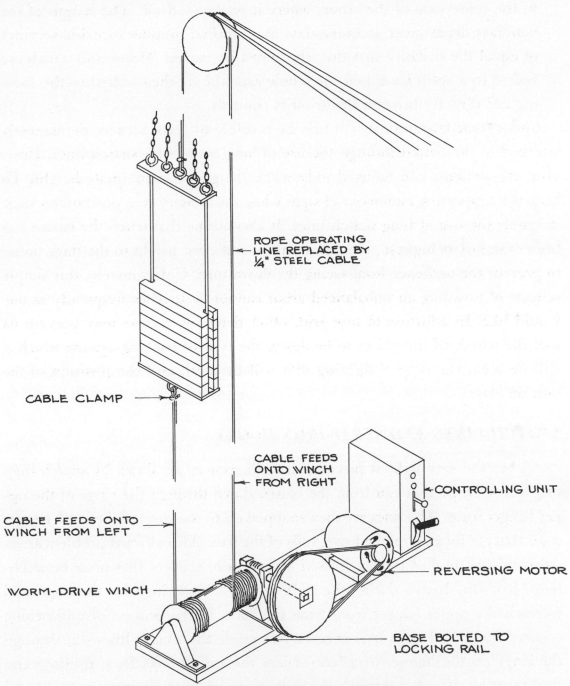

ROPE OPERATING
LINE REPLACED BY
¼" STEEL CABLE

CABLE CLAMP

CABLE FEEDS
ONTO WINCH
FROM RIGHT

CONTROLLING UNIT

CABLE FEEDS ONTO
WINCH FROM LEFT

REVERSING MOTOR

WORM-DRIVE WINCH

BASE BOLTED TO
LOCKING RAIL

POWER-DRIVEN WINCH ADAPTED TO
COUNTERWEIGHT SYSTEM

PLATE 83

but is served onto it from left to right. This cable then runs from the drum to the underside of the arbor, where it is clamped off. The length of the windlass drum must accommodate the required number of cable servings to equal the distance that the arbor must be moved. Motor and winch are bolted to a solid base, and the whole assembly is then bolted to the locking rail directly beneath the arbor it controls.

Under some circumstances it may be possible to leave scenery permanently attached to the batten through the use of long piano wire snatch lines. However, this scheme can be used only when the grid has adequate height. To keep the supporting batten out of sight while the scenery is in position on stage demands the use of long snatch lines. It also means that when the batten has been raised to its highest point there will be sufficient height to the stage house to prevent the audience from seeing the flown unit. Unfortunately, this simple scheme of avoiding an unbalanced arbor cannot be used as frequently as one would like. In addition to low grid, other deterring factors may prevent its use: the nature of the object to be flown, the type of backing against which it will be seen, the type of lighting that will be used, and the position of the unit on stage.

SNATCH LINES AND STRAP-IRON HOOKS

All but the very lightest pieces of framed scenery are flown by snatch lines of $\frac{3}{8}''$ or $\frac{1}{2}''$ rope that run from the batten down through the rings of the upper hanger irons. The lines are then snapped off to the rings of the hook hanger irons that are located on the lower rails of the flats. An awkward problem arises when this method of rigging is used on pieces of scenery that must be unfastened from the batten during the shift, or that are too high for the stagehand to reach the upper hanger irons from the floor. In the process of unfastening scenery from the batten it is necessary to guide the snatch lines out through the rings on the hanger irons to prevent the snap hooks from fouling; and they must be threaded through the same rings when the scenery is reëngaged to the batten. This problem can be solved by the use of a ladder, by tipping the scenery forward until the hanger irons can be reached, or by the substitution of special horizontal strap-iron hooks for the upper hanger irons (Plate 84). The first two solutions are impractical, since they require too much time

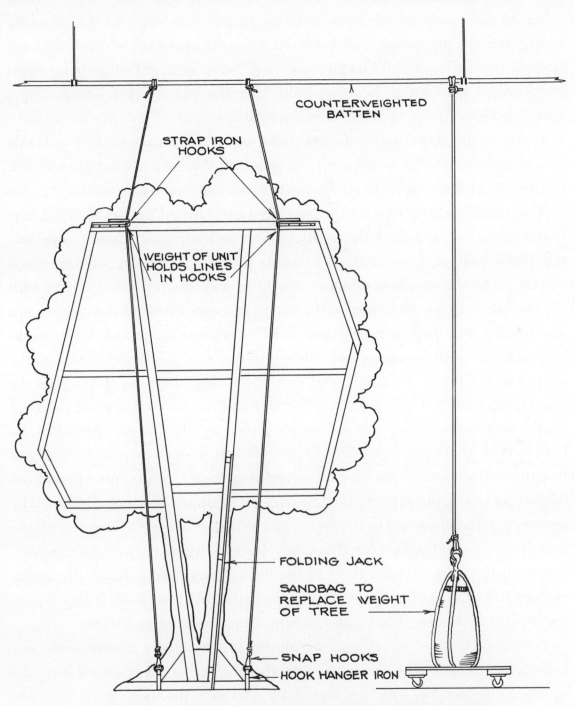

COUNTERWEIGHTED
BATTEN

STRAP IRON
HOOKS

WEIGHT OF UNIT
HOLDS LINES
IN HOOKS

FOLDING JACK

SANDBAG TO
REPLACE WEIGHT
OF TREE

SNAP HOOKS
HOOK HANGER IRON

SUBSTITUTION OF STRAP-IRON HOOKS FOR
UPPER HANGER IRONS

PLATE 84

during a shift; but by the use of horizontal hooks the same result can be achieved as rapidly as lashing or unlashing a flat. Strap-iron hooks are easily made, they are inexpensive, and they have proved remarkably effective. Each hook is made from a 2'-0" length of $\frac{1}{4}$" x $\frac{3}{4}$" strap iron, with the shaft drilled to receive at least three $\frac{3}{16}$" stove bolts. The hook is about 8" deep, with a space of about 2" between the shaft and the inner side. Place the hooks horizontally on the upper rails and bolt them into position about 1'-6" outside of a straight vertical line between the point on the batten where the snatch line is tied and the position of the lower hook hanger iron.

The initial rigging of a unit of scenery to be shifted in this manner is as follows: measure and mark the position of the unit on stage; lower a pipe batten and adjust it, if necessary, so that its position coincides with the floor marks; place the unit face down on the floor with the top rails aligned with the marks; tie two snatch lines to the batten and space them the same distance apart as the two hook hanger irons. The free ends of the snatch lines should be equipped with strong spring snap hooks. Place the snatch lines in the throats of the horizontal hooks and snap the spring hooks to the rings of the hook hanger irons. Counterbalance the unit and raise it to a vertical position. As the unit is raised the snatch lines are pulled tightly into the throats of the hooks. With the scenery standing in position and braced, the snatch lines can be easily unfastened by slacking off on the lines a little, unsnapping them from the hanger irons, and flipping the lines free of the upper horizontal hooks. The scenery can be refastened to the batten just as easily: lower the batten until the snatch lines touch the floor, flip the snatch lines to engage the horizontal hooks, and snap the lines into the rings of the hook hanger irons. Raise the batten enough to put some tension on the lines to prevent them from falling free of the horizontal hooks. The scenery can now be unbraced and flown.

When this method of rigging is employed, it is necessary to control the unbalanced counterweight during the time that the scenery is removed from the batten. This may be done by any of the methods discussed earlier in this chapter for controlling the unbalanced arbor (pages 227–232).

special construction and rigging problems

As we have remarked before, each theatre production may present new problems involving construction principles and methods of rigging. As these problems and their solutions will vary from one production to another, so will they vary as they are adapted to different stages. There will be differences in stage plans and dimensions, in physical equipment of shops and stages, and in the operating budgets of each organization. These differences make it unlikely that the solution to any special problem can be used without modification to solve a similar problem controlled by a different set of circumstances. The ability to improvise, to "make do" with what he has, and to adapt established principles of construction or rigging to the solution of a new problem is one of the most important traits of a first-class technician. He should have a flair for invention and a willingness to experiment with new methods of doing things, even if this often means additional work and occasionally failure. Only in this way is he likely to develop a technique or invent a device that will contribute substantially to the fund of knowledge that helps raise the general standard of stage productions.

The examples of construction and rigging found in this chapter are not the result of paper projects. They have been given the most rigorous testing by actual use on stage during the run of a production. They are given here, not with the idea that they can or should be copied, but to illustrate how a principle can be adapted or modified to solve a particular problem. These examples may give the reader a suggestion or an idea that can be shaped to his own use.

CONSTRUCTION AND BRACING OF FRAGMENTARY SETTINGS

The suggestive or fragmentary setting is one possible answer to the problems presented by a play which requires several settings. Such a partial setting reduces the time required for construction, is less expensive, and is easier to shift and store than a complete setting. At the same time it is likely to present unusual problems in both construction and bracing.

The drawings of the railway coach on Plate 85, one of the six settings needed in producing *Point of No Return* present a good example of problems met in constructing and bracing fragmentary scenery. Without the benefit of the side walls which would normally be used to help support the curved ceiling, some other scheme of bracing had to be devised. The double-faced seats would be too heavy and bulky to shift easily, and the number of windows in the back wall would make this unit awkward to handle. All of these problems were solved by mounting the setting on a wagon and by using modified jacks.

Two rigid platforms taken from stock, one 5'-0" x 10'-0" and the other 5'-0" x 5'-0", were bolted together end to end to form a wagon 5'-0" wide, 15'-0" long and 7" high. The back wall was constructed as an oversized window flat. Each window was made as a separate unit and attached to the window openings by means of its 4" thickness pieces. Galvanized wire screen was stretched across the back of each window as a substitute for glass. The wall was braced by four rigid jacks screwed to 2" x 4" blocks attached to the wagon tops. Each jack had been modified by attaching a concave sweep to its top. The concave shape of the car roof was obtained by nailing sheets of corrugated cardboard to the supporting sweeps of the jacks.

The back-to-back car seats were supported by two frames made from 1" x 3" stock, and were covered on the downstage side by a single sheet of $\frac{1}{4}$" plywood. The seats themselves were made as individual units from 1" x 4" stock on edge, covered with $\frac{1}{4}$" plywood, and screwed between the two supporting frames at the proper height and angle. The backs were formed by nailing single sheets of $\frac{1}{4}$" plywood to the edges of the supporting frames. Both seats and backs were padded with moss and cotton batten and covered with dark green rep. The assembled seats were placed on the platform with their upstage faces

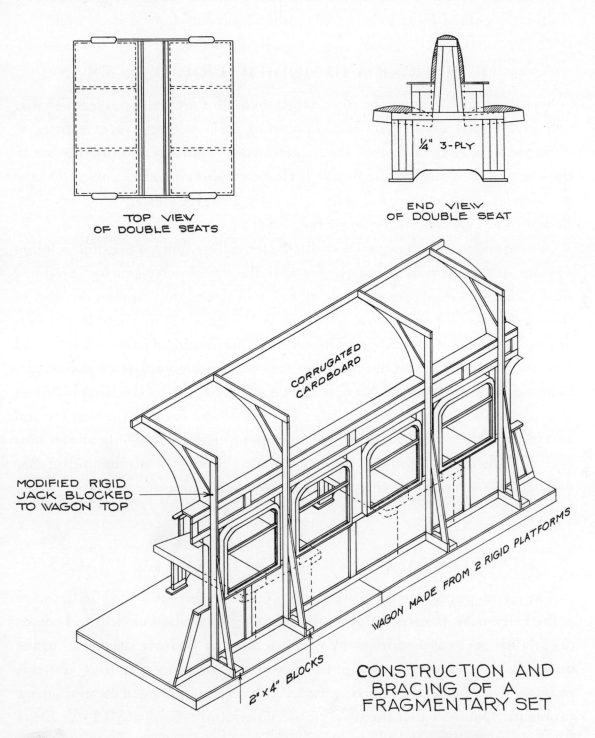

TOP VIEW
OF DOUBLE SEATS

END VIEW
OF DOUBLE SEAT

¼" 3-PLY

CORRUGATED
CARDBOARD

MODIFIED RIGID
JACK BLOCKED
TO WAGON TOP

2" X 4" BLOCKS

WAGON MADE FROM 2 RIGID PLATFORMS

CONSTRUCTION AND
BRACING OF A
FRAGMENTARY SET

PLATE 85

flush against the back wall and screwed into position. Their weight, stability, and height helped them to serve as additional bracing for the back wall.

OUTRIGGER AND MODIFIED RIGID JACKS

Scenic designers are constantly on the lookout for architectural features that will give added interest and atmosphere to their settings. Such features as cornices, beams, slanting roof lines, and dormer windows add interest to settings where their use can be justified. However, these features complicate the problem of construction and shifting to such a degree that in some cases the designer may be forced to forego their use.

Where adequate stage space is available for rolling units, a possible solution to some of these problems may be found in the use of outriggers and modified rigid jacks. The outrigger is a skeletal wagon designed to fit against the back of the scenery it will be used to shift. It may be designed to any shape and is usually made of 2″ x 4″ framing and mounted on conventional rubber-tired swivel castors. The flooring on the outrigger may be either complete or partial, depending on circumstances. Scenery can be attached to it by screwing it against the side of the frame or by attaching a batten to the back of the scenery and locking it to the outrigger top by means of pin hinges. Plate 86 illustrates how both a slanted ceiling and a dormer window, used in a production of *The Crucible,* were constructed and shifted by means of jacks mounted on an outrigger.

HINGED STAIR UNIT MOUNTED ON LIFT JACKS

The reconstruction of the Shakesperian Old Globe theatre used on the stage at the University Theatre at Iowa follows the original plans closely and consequently has no visible stairway by which actors can go from stage level to the inner-above level within view of the audience. Providing a stairway for this purpose that could be shifted quickly and quietly presented several major problems. One was that the level of the inner-above floor was 10′-0″ above the main stage. This would require a stairway at least 9′-4″ high which would be both awkward and heavy to handle. Another was that the only way such a stairway could be placed in position during the action of the play was to move

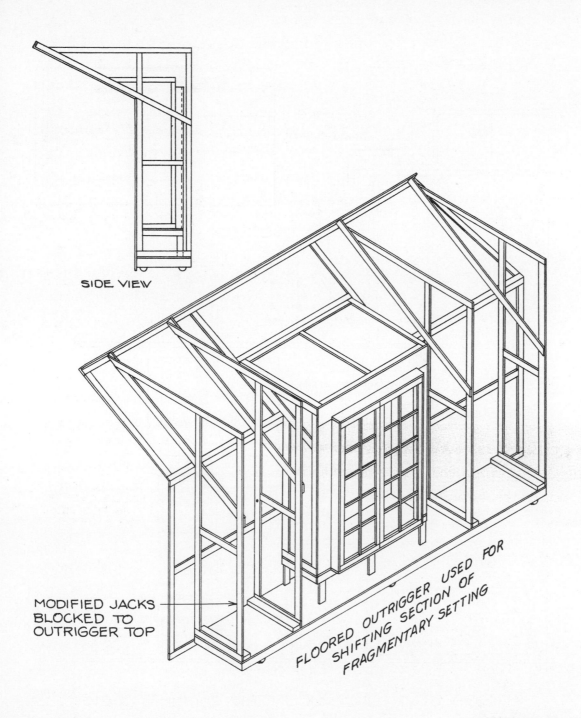

SIDE VIEW

MODIFIED JACKS
BLOCKED TO
OUTRIGGER TOP

FLOORED OUTRIGGER USED FOR
SHIFTING SECTION OF
FRAGMENTARY SETTING

PLATE 86

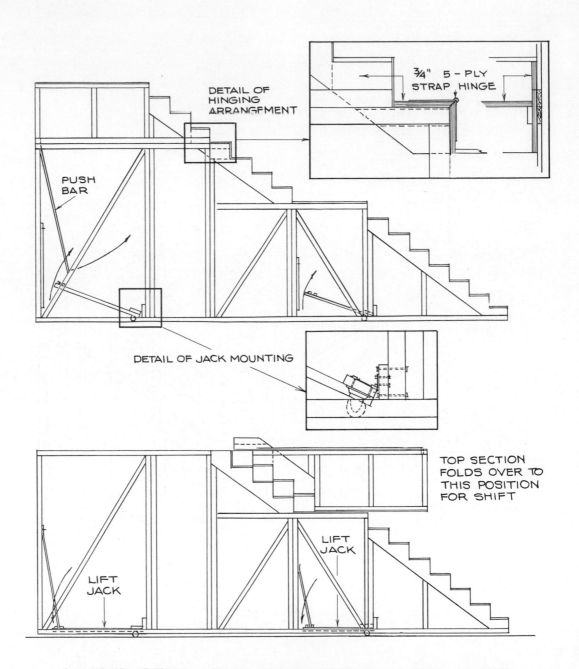

DETAIL OF HINGING ARRANGEMENT

¾" 5-PLY STRAP HINGE

PUSH BAR

DETAIL OF JACK MOUNTING

TOP SECTION FOLDS OVER TO THIS POSITION FOR SHIFT

LIFT JACK

LIFT JACK

HINGED STAIR UNIT MOUNTED ON LIFT JACKS

PLATE 87

it through the inner-below while the middle stage curtains were closed. This operation was complicated by the fact that the clearance from the stage floor to the underside of the trusses supporting the inner-above floor was only 8'-2".

The obvious solution to the problem of shifting quickly was mounting the stairway on castors; but a unit that was 18'-6" long, 9'-4" high and only 3'-0" wide would be extremely unstable if its weight and that of the actors was to be borne by castors at all times. The use of two lift jacks placed within and at either end of the stairway solved this problem. The stairway could rest solidly on its own base during the time it was used and could be raised onto the jack for shifting (Plate 87).

The top four steps were made as a separate unit and hinged to the lower section at the junction of the riser and tread of the twelfth step. When this upper section was folded over onto the lower section the overall height was only 7'-0", which allowed ample clearance when the unit was rolled through the inner-below. The height of the stairway made it necessary to hinge a length of 1" x 3" to the underside of the upper section to facilitate the opening and closing of that unit. By pushing on this 1" x 3" a stagehand could tip the top section over to a position where its weight could be taken by a second stagehand standing on the lower step section, who could then "walk it down." By reversing this procedure the top could be placed in position for action.

Notice that the lower section of the stairway, while made as a single rigid unit, is so planned and constructed that sawing through the horizontal members will reduce the structure to five separate step-and-landing sections for independent use. Although this was the original intention, it has never been done, because so many uses were found for the unit as it stood that it was decided to keep it as it was. It has been variously used as an off-stage stairway, a rolling tower stand for lights, a rigging platform and a paint boomerang.

REVERSIBLE UNIT MOUNTED ON LIFT JACKS

In Obey's play, *Noah,* three of the five scenes take place on the deck of the Ark. The limitations placed on the size of the Ark by the stage dimensions resulted in a setting that noticeably restricted the action of the actors and made it difficult for the director to obtain the variety in stage movement he felt the play demanded.

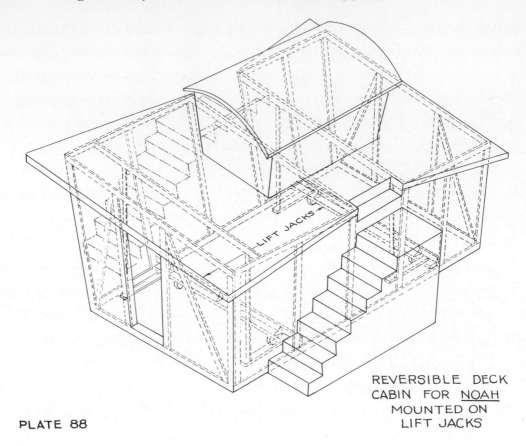

LIFT JACKS

REVERSIBLE DECK
CABIN FOR NOAH
MOUNTED ON
LIFT JACKS

PLATE 88

In an effort to overcome these problems the designer and the director planned to change the position of the Ark between scenes. By reversing the direction in which the Ark was apparently sailing, the major acting areas would also be changed, and at the same time the compositional arrangement of the setting would be altered. Such a scheme could be accomplished in several ways: (1) Two separate Arks could be constructed; each would be a duplication of the other as far as design was concerned, but one would be a reverse of the other. (2) A single double-faced setting could be built and mounted on the revolve. (3) A single reversible unit could be built and mounted on lift jacks. Since cost, available storage space, and length of scene shifts had to be considered, it was decided that the reversible unit would be the most logical choice. The use of the revolve as a shifting device was thereby eliminated—an important consideration, since the stage had to be cleared for the opening and closing scenes.

Plate 88 illustrates the general principle of construction and the placement of the two lift jacks used in shifting it. Since the roof of the deckhouse had to support the capering of both "animals" and humans, and since there was to be much running up and down both stairways, the lift jacks were employed instead of mounting the whole structure on a wagon. The jacks permitted the cabin to be lowered to rest on its own base during the playing of the scenes, thus eliminating any tendency the unit might have had to creep or roll.

The framing of the side walls and the base of the cabin were made from 2″ x 4″ fir. A much lighter structure could have been built by using $1\frac{1}{4}$″ x 3″ white pine, but this would have doubled its cost. In this particular case the weight of the heavier lumber was not a factor for consideration, since the cabin was to be shifted by rolling. The two stairways on either side of the cabin were built as separate units and bolted to the slanting side walls of the cabin; they were shifted as an integral part of the cabin.

The mast of the Ark was an independent structure and was placed along the deck 12′-0″ forward of the cabin. The mast, a tapered, three-dimensional column 16′-0″ high, was given a broad stable base by having it anchored, in a most unnautical fashion, to the center of a 4′-0″ x 6′-0″ hatch. The mast and hatch were the only other elements of the design, besides the cabin, that were too large and awkward to be shifted by running. Two small lift jacks mounted inside the hatch converted it into a rolling unit that was easily shifted. The gunwales of the Ark were two-dimensional cutouts made as reverse duplicates to be shifted by running.

DETACHABLE LIFT JACKS

The conventional lift jack is one of the most useful of the scene-shifting devices at the disposal of the technician. By means of it units of scenery that are too heavy, too irregular in shape, or too awkward to shift manually can be lifted onto castors and easily moved by rolling. Under normal circumstances the lift jacks are concealed from the audience by placing them within or behind the unit they are designed to shift.

A variation that makes the lift jack even more useful is the detachable jack. This jack was designed to meet an unusual problem that arose in connection with a production of *The Grass Harp*. One of the settings required in this play is a tree house supported between two trunks of a divided tree. The floor

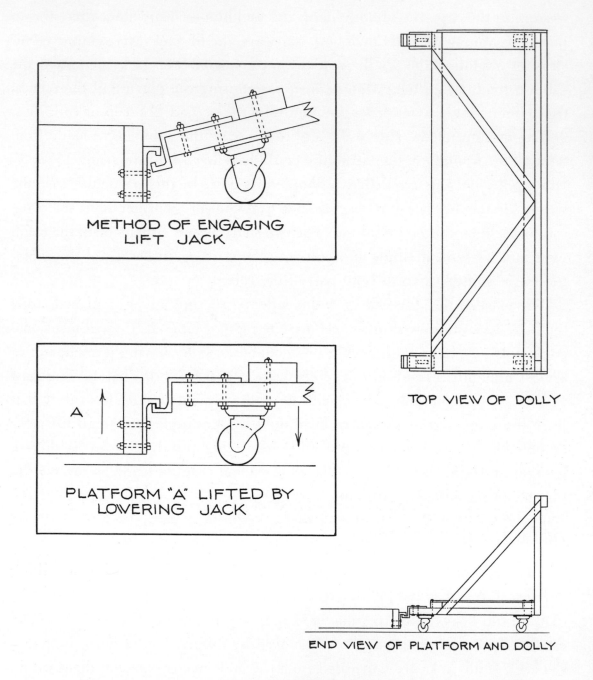

METHOD OF ENGAGING
LIFT JACK

PLATFORM "A" LIFTED BY
LOWERING JACK

TOP VIEW OF DOLLY

END VIEW OF PLATFORM AND DOLLY

DETACHABLE LIFT JACK

PLATE 89

level of the tree house was 9'-0" above the stage floor, and it had to be large enough and strong enough to support the weight and movement of six actors. As it was designed, the tree had a spread of 23'-0" between the outermost branches and stood 19'-0" high. The base that locked the two trunks together was comparatively small—only 7'-0" wide and 11'-0" long. Standard lift jacks could not be used because the base was too small to conceal them. Even mounting the base on a heavy wagon seemed ill-advised, since the rubber tired castors would have compressed under the weight of tree and actors, possibly causing an objectionable swaying of the whole tree form. The problem of moving the finished tree from the shop to the stage, a distance of 120'-0", and of shifting it during performances, was met by designing a lift jack that could be attached and detached from the tree base (Plate 89).

Four sets of heavyweight brackets were made from $\frac{3}{8}$" x 4" strap iron. Each set consisted of two hooks, one to be bolted to the base of the tree frame, the other to be bolted to the jack dolly. Two dollies, each 8'-0" long and 3'-0" wide, were made of 2" x 4" framing and mounted on four swivel castors with 3" rubber-tired wheels. An upright hand-bar mounted on the back of the dolly made it easy for a stagehand to operate. The mounting position of the hooks on both the tree base and the dolly was critical. It was necessary to place them in such a position that they could be engaged only when the off-stage side of the dolly was raised. Using the forward set of castors as a fulcrum and the dolly as a lever, the base of the tree frame could be raised about one inch from the stage floor when the dolly was lowered to rest on its four castors. The two dollies were rolled into position on either side of the tree base, the brackets engaged, and both dollies were then lowered. The entire weight of the tree was thereby transferred to the castors.

Although the hand-bar on each dolly was made long enough for two stage-hands to use it, it was discovered that only one operator on each dolly was required to shift the tree.

APPARITION EFFECT

The apparition scene, in which an apparently solid substance disappears to reveal objects beyond it, is an old trick in the theatre. That it can still prove effective was demonstrated convincingly in an experimental production of a new script entitled *Black Blizzard,* by Sherwood Collins.

The play, laid in the mid-1930's, centers about the struggles of a Kansas farmer and his family against the ravages of prolonged drought and dust storms. Although the main action of the play was treated realistically, a poetic quality was introduced through the medium of flashbacks. These spoke of man's ravishing the land and retold much of the romantic pioneer history of the area. They made use of ten historical figures such as the Buffalo Hunter, the Homesteader, the Cowboy, the Quitter, etc. Each appeared out of darkness to give his short monologue and then disappeared into darkness. Since none of these flashback scenes was longer than two or three minutes, it became imperative to devise some scheme of integration that would reduce to a minimum the interruption of the main theme of the play. Several different schemes were proposed; what was finally selected was an adaptation of the old apparition or disappearance scene.

The setting was designed as a composite interior-exterior of the old farm. The interior revealed the living room and a corner of the dining room; the exterior showed the front porch, the second story, and a general outline of the whole house. The second story was used for the apparition scenes. The silhouette of the second floor was made of two-dimensional framing; the center section, through which the historical figures were seen, was covered with sharkstooth scrim. The areas on either side were covered with canvas and were therefore opaque (Plate 90).

Immediately behind the scrim section was placed a 7'-0" by 11'-0" platform with its floor 10'-0" from the stage floor. On this platform small backing flats formed a three-sided booth with the open face against the scrim. A baffle entranceway with black drapes at either end and a small ceiling over the top made this booth completely light-proof.

The success of the apparition effect depends upon how well the light can be controlled. During the playing of all scenes within the living room or on the front porch, and when the sky cyc lights were up, it was necessary to prevent any of this light from striking the back of the scrim and making this part of the second story transparent. It was equally important, during the playing of the apparition scenes, when all other lights were out, to control any spill

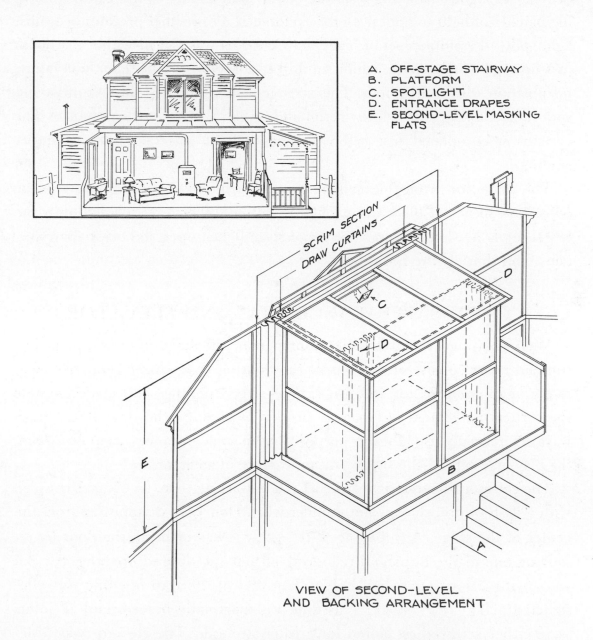

A. OFF-STAGE STAIRWAY
B. PLATFORM
C. SPOTLIGHT
D. ENTRANCE DRAPES
E. SECOND-LEVEL MASKING
   FLATS

VIEW OF SECOND-LEVEL
AND BACKING ARRANGEMENT

RIGGING USED FOR APPARITION
SCENES IN BLACK BLIZZARD

PLATE 90

or reflected light emanating from the booth spot, as this would cause disturbing patches of light to appear on the cyclorama. As a further precaution against light spills, therefore, a set of black draw curtains was rigged within the booth just upstage of the scrim, which could be closed while the actor was taking his position within the booth. This arrangement eliminated the risk of having spill-light filtering through the scrim and revealing the actor's presence. The curtains were opened just before the booth light was raised to its proper reading.

The transition from the realistic scenes on the lower acting levels to the apparition scenes of the historical figures on the upper level required only the few seconds needed to lower one set of stage lights, open the black draw curtains, and dim up the booth spot.

THE DISAPPEARANCE TRAP AND ELEVATOR

Well-equipped theatres have all or part of the stage floor trapped. The trapped areas consist of sections of the flooring that can be removed separately or in combination to form various-sized openings and make possible the vertical movement of actors or properties through the stage floor. Stairways are normally used for this purpose, but in some instances, as in *Don Juan,* the play may call for the sudden disappearance of an actor.

The elevator illustrated on Plate 91 is a fast-acting type. Its use was coupled with a flash of fire, smoke, and thunder when Don Juan disappeared from the center of the stage. An opening 3'-0" x 2'-8" was made in the floor by removing one of the traps and reflooring all but the desired opening. An elevator with a floor area slightly less than that of the trap opening was constructed of $1\frac{1}{4}$" x 3" stock. This unit was diagonally braced, and all joints were either screwed or bolted for greater strength. The elevator was 3'-6" high and had as its basic members two vertical 2" x 6"s centered on either side. To the outer face of each 2" x 6" was bolted a length of 2" x 2" that formed a projecting tongue; these tongues fitted into grooves on the vertical tracks and served as guides for the movement of the elevator. The grooves on each track were formed by bolting two 2" x 2"s to the face of the 2" x 6" just far enough apart to permit the tongues to fit between them. Each vertical track was carefully centered on either side of the trap opening and lag-screwed to the supporting beams of the stage floor. It was necessary to have the tracks solidly braced to hold them equidistant from each other and to prevent their springing apart. This bracing eliminated any chance of the elevator's binding

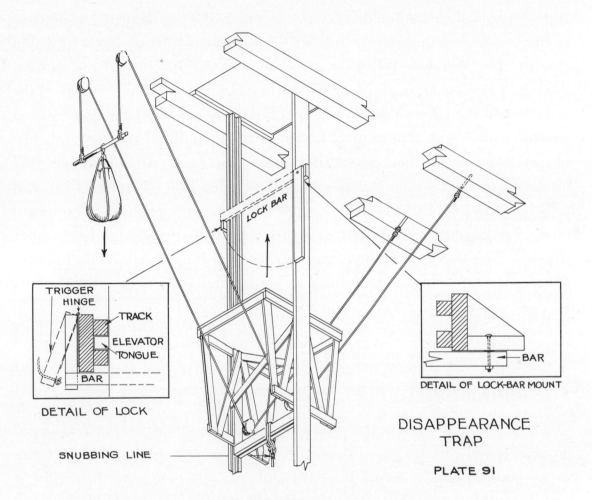

TRIGGER HINGE

TRACK

ELEVATOR TONGUE.

BAR

DETAIL OF LOCK

SNUBBING LINE

LOCK BAR

BAR

DETAIL OF LOCK-BAR MOUNT

DISAPPEARANCE TRAP

PLATE 91

between the tracks or of its becoming disengaged from the guiding grooves. (For the sake of clarity the diagonal bracing is omitted from the accompanying drawing.)

Power for the operation of the elevator was provided by a double-whip tackle rigging and a sandbag counterbalance. Two separate lines of $\frac{1}{2}''$ manila rope ran from a pipe yoke up over two single blocks attached to the floor beams, passed down under two additional blocks on the bottom of the elevator and up again to the floor beams, where they were tied off. This rigging provides a 2 to 1 mechanical advantage and reduces by about half the weight required to counterbalance the elevator and its load. This weight was sufficient to hold the top of the empty elevator flush with the stage floor. Until it was time for its use, the elevator rested upon a 2″ x 4″ lock bar, one end of which was pivoted from one track and supported on the other by a 2″ x 4″ hinged trigger attached to the opposite track. A length of $\frac{1}{4}$″ sashcord was attached to the free end of the trigger, passed over a pulley, and then down to within reach of the operator. When the actor stepped to the center of the elevator top, the trigger was released on a given cue. The additional weight of the actor forced the elevator to fall rapidly until the angle of the supporting lines became more acute. The more nearly these lines paralleled the elevator's line of travel, the greater became their upward thrust, thus gradually slowing the elevator's speed. By the time the elevator had fallen about 8 feet it had slowed sufficiently to permit the actor to step off onto a landing platform. The weight of the sandbag then propelled the empty elevator back to stage level. Since the upward movement of the empty elevator was rapid, a snubbing line was attached to the bottom to prevent its projecting above the stage floor, the lock bar was pivoted into position and the trigger engaged.

Plate 91 illustrates the moment when the elevator has been freed of its load and is starting upward to its stage position.

THE POWER-DRIVEN ELEVATOR

The elevator needed in the production of *The Faithful Shepherdess* served an entirely different purpose than that employed in *Don Juan*. Here the figure of the god Neptune must rise in a slow and stately fashion from the depths of a well—and just to make the problem more interesting, he carried in his arms the body of the shepherdess Amaryllis. (Neptune weighed 255 pounds, Amaryllis 110, the elevator 86 pounds—a total of 471 pounds.) Since it was necessary for these actors to move from the elevator to the stage floor, there would be a shifting of weight and of the points of strain on both the elevator and its guiding tracks. This necessitated a different method of construction, rigging, and guiding than that used for a disappearance trap.

The size of the trap opening and of the elevator was determined by the length of the reclining figure of Amaryllis as she was held in the arms of Neptune. This resulted in an elevator 5′-0″ long, 3′-0″ wide, and 3′-6″ high. To

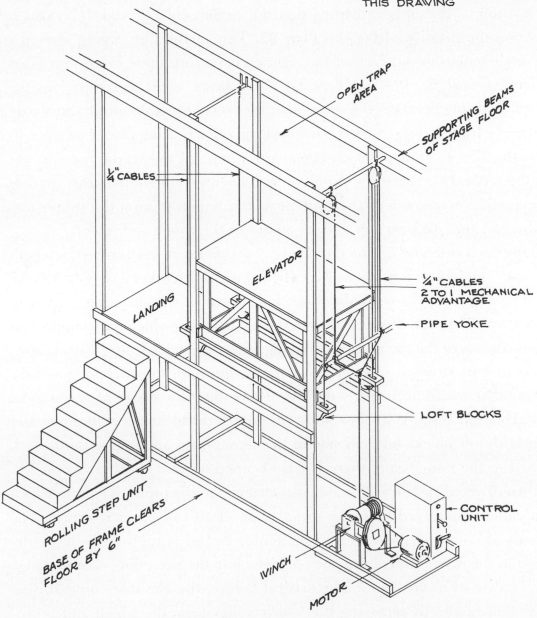

NOTE. ALL DIAGONAL BRACES USED
ON FRAME WERE OMITTED FROM
THIS DRAWING

OPEN TRAP AREA

SUPPORTING BEAMS OF STAGE FLOOR

¼" CABLES

ELEVATOR

LANDING

¼" CABLES
2 TO 1 MECHANICAL ADVANTAGE

PIPE YOKE

LOFT BLOCKS

ROLLING STEP UNIT

BASE OF FRAME CLEARS FLOOR BY 6"

CONTROL UNIT

WINCH

MOTOR

POWER DRIVEN ELEVATOR SUSPENDED FROM
UNDERSIDE OF REVOLVE

PLATE 92

keep its weight at a minimum, the elevator was built of 1″ x 4″ lumber with diagonal bracing of 1″ x 3″ white pine stock. On the four corners of both top and bottom the lengthwise pieces were joined to the cross members by notched joints, the ends extending past the corners by $1\frac{1}{2}″$ and $3\frac{1}{2}″$. This is shown on the detail drawings on Plate 92. This method of joining formed a right-angle extension on each of the eight corners. Into these extensions fitted the four vertical 2″ x 4″ guideposts. These posts were lag-screwed to the heavy supporting beams of the stage floor; they served to both guide and steady the elevator from its four corners. Diagonal and cross bracing placed on the outside of the 2″ x 4″ guideposts held them firmly in place and yet did not interfere with the vertical movement of the elevator. The lower horizontal cross bracing was extended to one side of the guideposts far enough to form the supporting members for the platform required for mounting the winch and motor.

Along each side and on the underside of the elevator was fastened a length of 2″ x 4″. Four steel loft blocks were aligned with each other and bolted to the 2″ x 4″s. These blocks were placed as close as possible to the outer corners of the elevator. Through these blocks ran the rigging lines which gave support on all four corners of the elevator. The rigging lines were made from $\frac{1}{4}″$ steel cable, not because its strength was needed, but to avoid both the stretching and the creaking that would accompany the use of rope lines for a load of this weight. Each cable ran from its anchor point on the overhead floor beam down and under both loft blocks on each side of the elevator, up and over a third block fastened to the floor beam; there it was clamped off to a short length of $1\frac{1}{2}″$ pipe. An inverted saddle of $\frac{1}{4}″$ cable was clamped to the pipe yoke, from which ran a cable that served onto the drum of an electrically driven winch. The methods of coupling the winch to the motor and of mounting them are described in the discussion of the powered winch in the preceding chapter (page 232). In case of either motor or electrical failure, the elevator could still be operated manually by removing the V-belt pulley from the winch and substituting the hand crank—an operation that required only a few seconds.

THE CLOUD MACHINE

Much of the fun associated with a production of Aristophanes' play, *The Birds*, came from the use of a modern version of the old Greek *mechane* or sus-

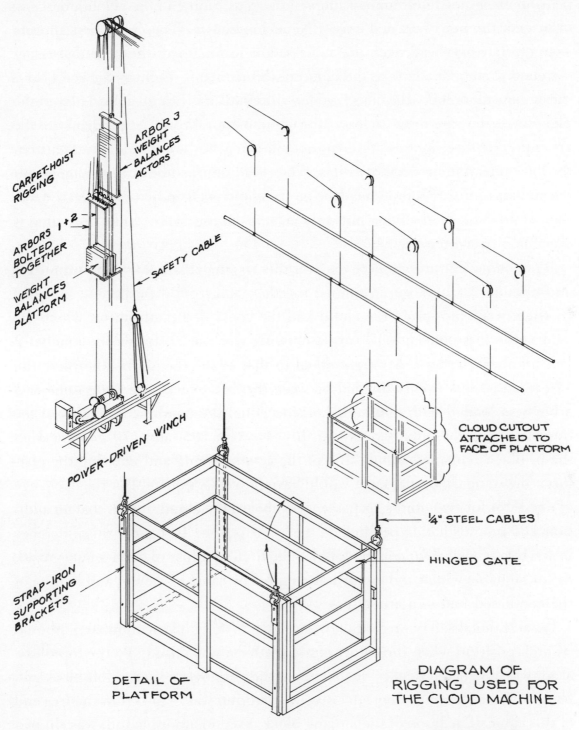

CARPET-HOIST
RIGGING

ARBOR 3
WEIGHT
BALANCES
ACTORS

ARBORS 1 + 2
BOLTED
TOGETHER

WEIGHT
BALANCES
PLATFORM

SAFETY CABLE

POWER-DRIVEN WINCH

CLOUD CUTOUT
ATTACHED TO
FACE OF PLATFORM

¼" STEEL CABLES

HINGED GATE

STRAP-IRON
SUPPORTING
BRACKETS

DETAIL OF
PLATFORM

DIAGRAM OF
RIGGING USED FOR
THE CLOUD MACHINE

PLATE 93

pension machine. Three ambassadors of the gods, riding upon a cloud, descend to inspect the newly created city of Nephelococcugia. The cloud first appears from directly overhead, with the ambassadors leaning over the edge discussing the general state of affairs as the cloud descends. After reaching the stage floor the ambassadors leave the cloud, which rises until it is out of sight. Later in the play, when they are ready to leave, the cloud reappears and settles gently to the ground. The three ambassadors mount and after they are lifted a few feet from the floor one of them decides to stay. The cloud returns to earth once more and the ambassador leaves, but his place on the cloud is taken by two mortals. Here then is a problem involving not only an unbalanced arbor, but a load that is variable in weight as well.

Three adjacent arbors were used in this rigging (Plate 93). The number 1 and number 2 arbors were clamped together, and from the battens controlled by them were supported the cloud and the concealed platform on which the actors stood. A conventional carpet-hoist rig was used between the number 2 and number 3 arbors. A weight equal to that of the cloud and the platform, 120 pounds, was evenly divided between the first two arbors. The number 3 arbor was loaded with counterbalance to equal the combined weights of the three heavyweight ambassadors—in this case 215, 205, and 170 pounds! Had the problem remained simply that of the actors leaving and entering the platform, the standard carpet hoist would have proved adequate. But the exchange of one actor for two others, as passengers aboard the cloud, meant that an additional 80 pounds had to be lifted on the last trip aloft. To handle this difference in weight, as well as to compensate for the frictional loss of such a heavy load, the old reliable winch and motor was coupled by cable to the top and bottom of the combined first two arbors.

An additional safety precaution was used in locking off the number 3 arbor at its high position when the empty cloud platform was raised. To the top of the arbor was attached a steel cable that ran to the grid, over a special loft block and back down to the stage floor. A heavy welded ring was clamped to the free end of this cable. The hook of the moving block, used in a double luff, was slipped into the ring and tension was exerted on the tackle. The fall of the tackle was then tied off to an eye bolt on the locking rail. This rig, coupled with the rope lock and a stopper hitch tied to the operating line, safely held the 590 pounds in place.

The cloud platform was made as two units, the weight-bearing platform and the cloud silhouette. As the diagram shows, the platform was constructed like any standard rigid platform, except that to its sides were bolted 2″ x 4″ uprights that formed the supports for the protective guard rails and the hinged gate. In order that the weight of both the platform and the actors could be flown under compression, two U-shaped strap-iron brackets were bolted in place around each end of the platform. Four steel cables ran from the brackets to the two pipe battens from which the platform was suspended. The cloud silhouette was made as a canvas-covered two-dimensional framed cutout screwed to the down-stage side of the platform. The part of the canvas cloud which extended below the base of the platform was left unframed so that it would not interfere when the platform rested on the stage floor.

No effort was made to conceal the supporting steel cables. The stylized designs used in this production seemed to justify decorating the cables with knotted ropes liberally entwined with flowers and vines.

THE CARPET HOIST USED WITH A DOUBLE-WHIP TACKLE RIGGING

A variation of the cloud machine just described was the swing used in the same play by the god's messenger, Iris (Plate 94). Unlike the slow and leisurely entrance of the ambassadors, the director wanted the entrance of Iris to be breath-taking and swift. In addition, he wanted Iris to appear first in her swing in the upper right-hand corner of the proscenium arch, swing diagonally across the stage, and, in a series of diminishing arcs, come to rest on a prescribed spot on the stage floor. She was then to dismount, and the empty swing would be raised out of sight, to return for her later in the play.

Occasionally some particular stage effect cannot be obtained by any one rigging technique; and a combination of rigging principles are required in order to achieve it. This was the case with Iris' swing, which employed a spotline, breasting line, tackle rigging, rope-line carpet hoist, a metal yoke, and saddles.

On the grid directly above the spot where Iris was to land, which was almost

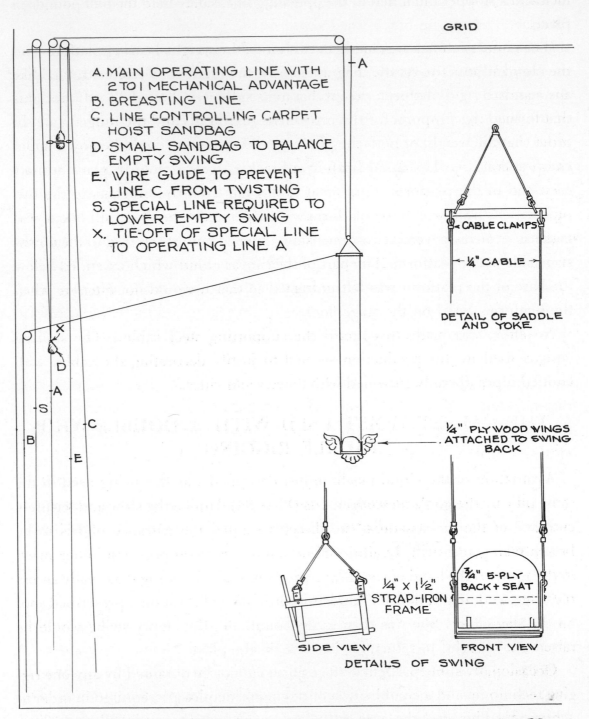

GRID

A. MAIN OPERATING LINE WITH 2 TO 1 MECHANICAL ADVANTAGE
B. BREASTING LINE
C. LINE CONTROLLING CARPET HOIST SANDBAG
D. SMALL SANDBAG TO BALANCE EMPTY SWING
E. WIRE GUIDE TO PREVENT LINE C FROM TWISTING
S. SPECIAL LINE REQUIRED TO LOWER EMPTY SWING
X. TIE-OFF OF SPECIAL LINE TO OPERATING LINE A

CABLE CLAMPS

¼" CABLE

DETAIL OF SADDLE AND YOKE

¼" PLYWOOD WINGS ATTACHED TO SWING BACK

¼" x 1½" STRAP-IRON FRAME

¾" 5-PLY BACK + SEAT

SIDE VIEW

FRONT VIEW

DETAILS OF SWING

DIAGRAM ILLUSTRATING A COMBINATION OF RIGGING PRINCIPLES

PLATE 94

center stage, was placed one of the two loft blocks required for the rigging of a spotline. The second block was located on the grid above the locking rail, so that the operator could see past the end of the lowered cyclorama and observe the movement of the swing. The spotline was rigged as a double whip to give the operator a 2 to 1 mechanical advantage. Notice in the diagram that one end of the line, A, is attached to the grid; the line then passes through a single movable block, up over the center loft block, over the head block, and down to the stage floor at the locking rail. A single cable runs from the movable block to a connecting link, to which is centered and clamped a short cable saddle. This saddle is fastened to both ends of a short iron bar yoke fitted with two heavy welded rings at each end. From the second set of rings on the yoke two cables run down to the small chain saddles on each side of the swing. These saddles made it easy to adjust the angle of the chair seat and eliminated any tendency for the swing to tip. As an additional precaution the swing was fitted with a back, arms and safety belt—making it impossible for Iris to fall out even had she fainted.

A breasting line, B, was run from the locking rail over a pulley, fastened to the stage house wall 25'-0" from the floor, and tied off to one of the rings on the yoke. This kept the swing facing the audience and provided the means of moving it from side to side.

A special line, S, was required to lower the empty swing to the stage floor. The failure of the empty swing to return without help to the floor was due in part to the friction loss caused by the operating line's passing over three blocks, but principally to the weight of the operating line between the stage floor and the point where it passed over the head block. This special line ran from the locking rail to the grid, over a block, then back down to where it was tied off to the operating line at X. Pulling on the special line lifted the weight of the operating line, and the swing could then be lowered as rapidly as was needed.

Although Iris in this production weighed only 105 pounds, the friction loss from the tackle rigging used amounted to approximately $30\frac{1}{2}$ pounds. This meant that the operator was lifting about 67 pounds, even with the 2 to 1 mechanical advantage offered by the double whip. Since he could not control this much weight safely, or move it at the speed asked by the director, a 40-pound sandbag carpet hoist was coupled to the operating line of the double whip. A separate line, C, was used to control the sandbag and to tie it off at its high position when the empty swing was to be raised. A metal ring was tied to each side of the sandbag. Through one passed the operating line of the double whip; through the other passed a wire guide that kept the bag from swinging or pivoting around the other lines and fouling them. Notice that the special line was tied off to the operating line at a point below the metal ring on the sandbag. By raising the operating line until the tie-off at X came in contact with the ring, it was possible to transfer the 40-pound weight to the double-whip rigging.

The crew members who were to operate the swing were carefully trained, and the rigging of the swing was tested repeatedly before it was used in rehearsal. A sandbag which equaled the weight of Iris was strapped into the swing and put through a series of tests that were much more severe in all respects than anything required in the performance routine. Frequent inspections of the rigging were maintained for possible signs of wear or strain. Only after the crew had been thoroughly trained and the rigging repeatedly tested did the actress try out the swing for the first time. She became accustomed to the feel of the swing gradually; she was raised, lowered and swung from side to side at increasing heights and speed until the performance routine was achieved.

SUPPORTING TRUSSES

Educational theatres may differ radically from each other in many ways, but in one respect there is a great similarity—they all produce Shakespeare. If their productions of the bard have progressed beyond the "drapery background" type of setting, there is a good possibility that their thinking has been focused upon the problems involved in building a setting that is representative of an Elizabethan playhouse. Foremost among these is the problem of how to support a wide inner-above stage and leave the inner-below area directly beneath free of supporting columns or posts. Coupled with this are the problems of keeping the cost down and of devising a platform arrangement that will be easy to assemble, strike, and store. A modified reconstruction of the Old Globe Playhouse, built from the plans shown here, has been in use at the University Theatre at Iowa for the past 15 years.

The weight-bearing and bracing units used in this particular reconstruction consist of the following: diagonal-bracing stairways, off-stage landing platforms, weight-bearing supports, trusses, and the inner-above platform flooring.

The bracing stairways are made as dependent step units (see Plate 45). They not only provide access to the landing platform, but when locked to both platform and stage floor they also serve as diagonal bracing. This eliminates any possible side sway of the assembled platform structure.

Each of the off-stage landings is 5'-0" wide and 7'-0" long. The top of each is made as a rigid platform with 2" x 4" frames covered with tongue and groove flooring. To each lengthwise side of the platform top is bolted a set of preassembled legs that raises the platform top 10'-0" from the floor. Each set of legs carries identification marks that correspond with similar marks on the platform —a precaution that avoids assembly by the trial-and-error method. Temporary cross bracing between each set of legs is made by nailing 1" x 3" members into place.

Bolted to the on-stage side of each landing are the supporting frames for the joists. These are made of doubled 2" x 4" stock. As can be seen in Plate 95, this provides a frame with four 4" x 4" supporting legs diagonally braced on either side of a doorway and joined together by three horizontal cross members. One of the 2" x 4"s from each leg extends 1'-6" above the top horizontal 2" x 4" and serves as a support to which a truss is bolted.

The four trusses make it possible to span a distance of 20'-0" without central supports. A truss can be described as an assemblage of members or beams so combined and reinforced by triangular bracing as to form a rigid framework. In this case each truss is 21'-0" long and 1'-6" wide, or more accurately, 1'-6" from top to bottom. Two 21'-0" lengths of 2" x 4" were laid out parallel with each other and separated by cross members of the same-sized stock. These were joined by battening 1" x 4" stock over each of the butt joints formed by the 2" x 4"s. Fitting tightly against the edges of the 1" x 4" cross members are diagonal braces of 1" x 4". Both sides of each truss are treated in the same manner.

The flooring that rests on top of the trusses consists of five rigid platforms, each 4'-2$\frac{3}{16}$" wide and 10'-0" long. With the trusses in place, the flooring sections are raised on end and skidded into position on top of the trusses. The first section is bolted to the side of the landing platform, the second is then bolted to the first, the third to the second, and so on, until all flooring sections are not

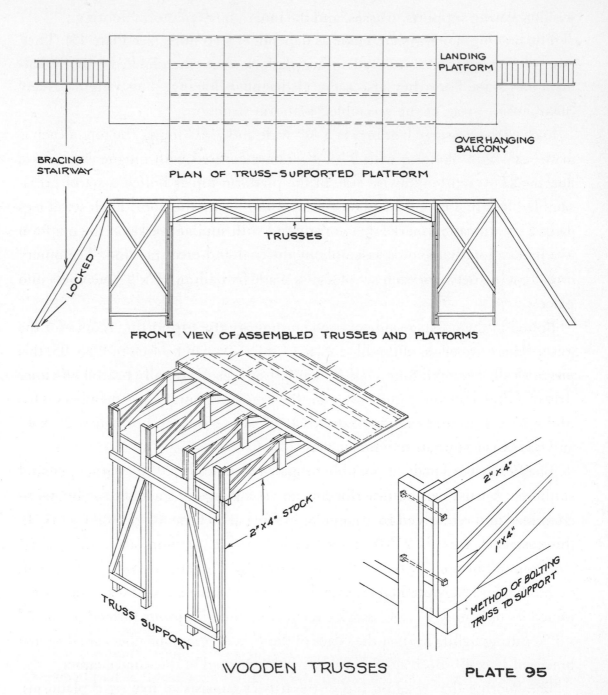

LANDING
PLATFORM

OVER HANGING
BALCONY

BRACING
STAIRWAY

PLAN OF TRUSS-SUPPORTED PLATFORM

TRUSSES

LOCKED

FRONT VIEW OF ASSEMBLED TRUSSES AND PLATFORMS

2"X 4" STOCK

2" X 4"

1"X 4"

METHOD OF BOLTING
TRUSS TO SUPPORT

TRUSS SUPPORT

WOODEN TRUSSES

PLATE 95

only bolted together but bolted to the side landings as well. This method of joining the various parts of the structure gives it surprising rigidity. Since the flooring sections extend 3'-0" past the downstage truss, they form an overhanging balcony for the inner-above. As an additional lock to prevent their tipping up at the back, the upstage end of each section is cleated to the side of the upstage truss.

Assembly of the platforms on stage moves rapidly if the operational steps listed here are followed. (1) Measure and mark the exact position of the landing platform on the stage floor. (2) Rig a double-luff tackle from a pipe batten that is directly above the center of the inner-above area. This can be used to help right the landing platforms as well as to lift the trusses into place. (3) Turn the landing platform upside down and bolt the leg sections into place, reinforcing them by nailing on cross-bracing members. (4) Turn the platforms right side up and position them on their marks, attach the bracing stairways, and bolt the supporting frames to the on-stage sides of the landing platforms. (5) Rig a saddle on the double luff, and raise the trusses into place. (6) The floor sections are next skidded into place and bolted. (7) Remove the tackle rigging from the pipe batten. The platform structure is now completely assembled and ready to receive the masking flats that will complete the setting.

Occasionally, when the nature of the design calls for the use of a second floor level, good use is made of this platform structure in other productions. Both the captain's bridge in a production of *Mr. Roberts* and the second floor of the Hilliard home in *Desperate Hours* used these platforms to advantage in Iowa productions.

RIGGING FOR HORIZONTAL MOVEMENT OF DRAPERY TREES

In a production of *Emperor Jones,* designed by Richard Knaub, trees were constructed from 30'-0" lengths of black drapery material that had been given three-dimensional form by attaching them at top and bottom to circular wooden sweeps and suspending them from the pipe battens of the counterweight system (Plate 96). These drapery trees were supplemented by back projections of jungle forms thrown on a translucent muslin drop. The combination formed a convincing imaginative jungle in which Jones finds himself hopelessly lost. The director

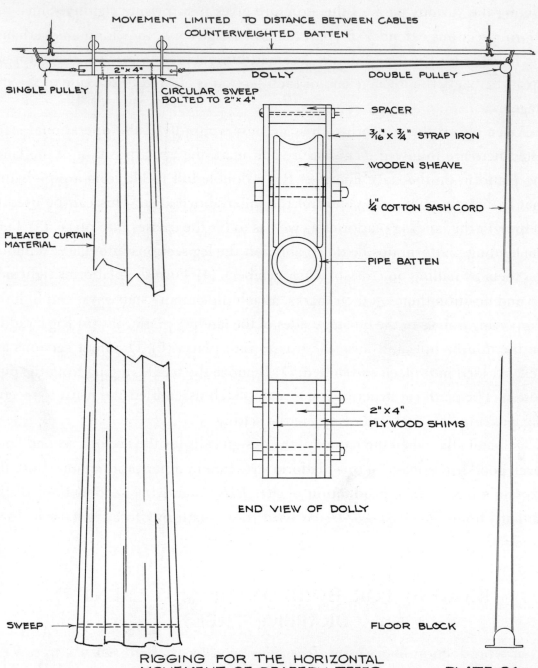

MOVEMENT LIMITED TO DISTANCE BETWEEN CABLES
COUNTERWEIGHTED BATTEN

DOLLY

DOUBLE PULLEY

SINGLE PULLEY

CIRCULAR SWEEP
BOLTED TO 2"x 4"

2"x 4"

SPACER

$\frac{3}{16}" \times \frac{3}{4}"$ STRAP IRON

WOODEN SHEAVE

$\frac{1}{4}"$ COTTON SASH CORD

PLEATED CURTAIN
MATERIAL

PIPE BATTEN

2"x 4"

PLYWOOD SHIMS

END VIEW OF DOLLY

SWEEP

FLOOR BLOCK

RIGGING FOR THE HORIZONTAL
MOVEMENT OF DRAPERY TREES

PLATE 96

asked if it would be possible, at the climax of one scene, to have several of these drapery trees move horizontally and actually converge on the cowering figure of Jones.

The construction and rigging for this effect was fairly simple. A dolly was made for each tree that was to move, consisting of a 3'-0" length of 2" x 4" suspended from one of the counterweight pipe battens by means of two wooden sheaves attached to the 2" x 4" by brackets made of $\frac{3}{16}$" x $\frac{3}{4}$" strap iron. The sheaves were turned by lathe to fit the contour of the pipe batten, and were made from wood to reduce any sound that might be heard as the dolly rolled along the batten. The top circular sweep of each tree was bolted to the underside of the dolly. This kept the tree sweeps parallel with the floor and prevented their tipping. An operating line of $\frac{1}{4}$" sash cord ran from a floor block over a double pulley and a single pulley placed at opposite ends of the batten; the free ends of the operating line were attached to each end of the dolly. This rigging gave the dolly and the tree freedom for a horizontal movement of about 10'-0", which was the distance between the cable supports of the pipe batten.

It was thought at first that it might be necessary to use guy lines from the battens to the stage floor to keep the operating lines from moving or swinging the pipe battens, but they were not needed when care was used in placing the floor block directly beneath the double block mounted on the batten. The straight-down pull on the operating line needed to move the trees had no tendency to impart a swinging motion to the batten.

GEAR-DRIVEN REVOLVING DISC

Sidney Howard's play, *Yellow Jack,* calls for the use of a small revolving disc to be mounted on top of a platform and turn in full view of the audience. Ordinary means of turning the revolve could not be used in this instance. A cable drive was impractical because of the elevated position, and walking the revolve around with pull rods was out of the question with the curtain open. Two gears and a hand crank gleaned from the local junk yard made highly satisfactory equipment for accomplishing this effect (Plate 97).

The cost of the materials for the disc, which was to be 8'-0" in diameter, was held to a minimum by utilizing one of the rigid platforms taken from stock. By building 2" x 4" triangular frames that fell within the desired circumference of

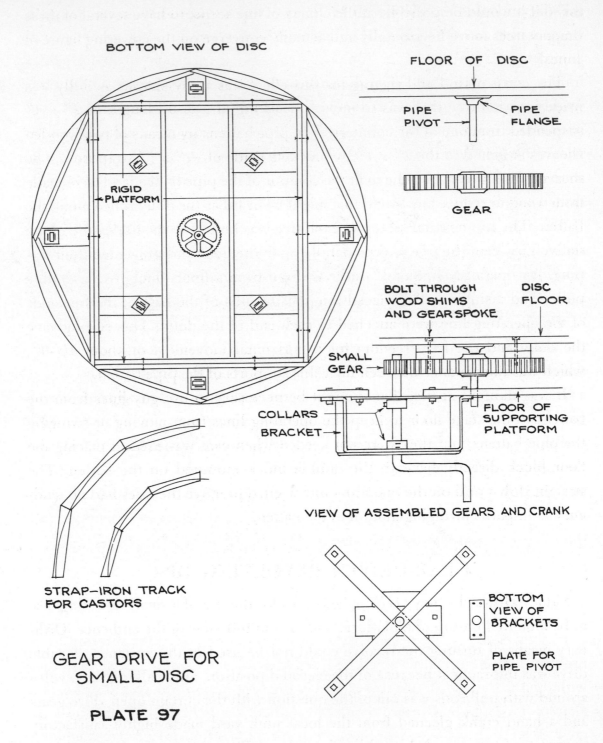

BOTTOM VIEW OF DISC

RIGID PLATFORM

FLOOR OF DISC

PIPE PIVOT

PIPE FLANGE

GEAR

BOLT THROUGH WOOD SHIMS AND GEAR SPOKE

DISC FLOOR

SMALL GEAR

COLLARS

BRACKET

FLOOR OF SUPPORTING PLATFORM

VIEW OF ASSEMBLED GEARS AND CRANK

STRAP-IRON TRACK FOR CASTORS

BOTTOM VIEW OF BRACKETS

PLATE FOR PIPE PIVOT

GEAR DRIVE FOR SMALL DISC

PLATE 97

the disc and covering them with $\frac{3}{4}''$ fir 5-ply flooring cut to a circular shape, it was possible to bolt them to the four sides of the 4'-0'' x 7'-0'' platform and complete its circular shape. Four rigid castors, one to each of the triangular frames, were placed an equal distance in from the circumference, with their wheels at a right angle to a radius line. Four additional castors were mounted in the same manner to the rigid platform. Since the flooring of the platform on which the disc was to turn was not too smooth, two sets of sheet-iron tracks were made, from short straight sections of $\frac{1}{8}''$ x 4'' strap iron with mitered ends, drilled so they could be screwed to the platform top.

The axle, or pivot, was made from a pipe flange and a short length of 1'' pipe securely fastened to the exact center of the disc on the underside. The pipe extended through a hole drilled in the top of the supporting platform. This prevented the disc from creeping out of position as it was turned.

The larger of the two gears (12'' in diameter) was shimmed up and bolted to the underside of the disc, with the pivot pipe projecting through the arbor in the gear. An 8'' square hole was cut in the flooring of the supporting platform at a point where the small gear and crank could be positioned to engage the larger gear. After the disc had been placed in position on the platform the smaller gear and the crank were put into place. Two sets of strap-iron brackets that fitted around the crankshaft had been designed so they could be screwed into position from the underside of the platform. Horizontal adjustment of the two gears was made by proper placing of the brackets, while two adjustable collars around the shaft and between the brackets made the vertical adjustment of the gears easy.

VARIATIONS IN CASTOR MOUNTING FOR A REVOLVING DISC

In some settings the design may necessitate an entirely new solution for a problem that is normally solved in a much simpler fashion. This was the case with the revolving gun turret required in the production of a new script called *Flowers of Victory,* by Richard Smith. Most of the action of this play involved the crew of a tank destroyer who had taken up its position in the wreckage of a French village. The only way the crew had of entering the destroyer was through a hatch in the top of the 37 MM gun turret. This, of course, meant that the turret could not be constructed as a regular revolving disc with a solid base and a central pivot point; the base of the turret had to be open, allowing the crew to drop through into the body of the destroyer.

Although the gun turret was only 3'-0" in diameter, eight rigid castors were used to obtain the desired effect. Four of them served to carry the weight of the turret and gun, and on them the gun turret revolved. The other four were needed to hold the turret centered within the circular opening cut in the top of the tank destroyer (Plate 98).

This assembly consisted basically of but two parts: the supporting table mounted inside the body of the destroyer on which both sets of castors were bolted, and the turret and gun itself. The 3'-0" square table top was open in the center and was literally nothing but a frame of 1" x 6" with halved jointed corners. It was supported by 1" x 4" legs diagonally braced for stability; the base of each leg was blocked and screwed to the floor of the destroyer. The castors on which the turret revolved were placed upside down and bolted to the 1" x 6" in the center of each table side. The wheel of each castor was placed at a right angle to a line from the center of the table. In the corners of the table were placed the four guiding castors. Since they had to be mounted in a horizontal position so that the wheels would bear against the sides of the turret, they were bolted to wooden brackets made of 1" x 6". The brackets could be easily adjusted and then screwed into position on the top of the supporting table corners.

The turret was made on the same principle as a three-dimensional column. Two completely circular sweeps were cut from $\frac{3}{4}$" 5-ply fir; the outside diameter of each was 3'-0", the width $3\frac{1}{2}$". The two sweeps were separated by vertical 1" x 4"s spaced about 1'-6" apart around their circumferences. The side of the turret was covered with $\frac{1}{8}$" thick fir plywood. Although the turret extended only 1'-6" above the deck of the destroyer, it was made 2'-6" high, to allow its circular sides to drop far enough below the deck to permit the guiding castors to bear against it.

The only fault of this rigging was that the turret turned too easily. This was corrected in part by changing the position of the weight-bearing castors slightly in order to force the rubber-tired wheels to skid against the movement of the disc. A few counterweights placed between the vertical spacers and strapped

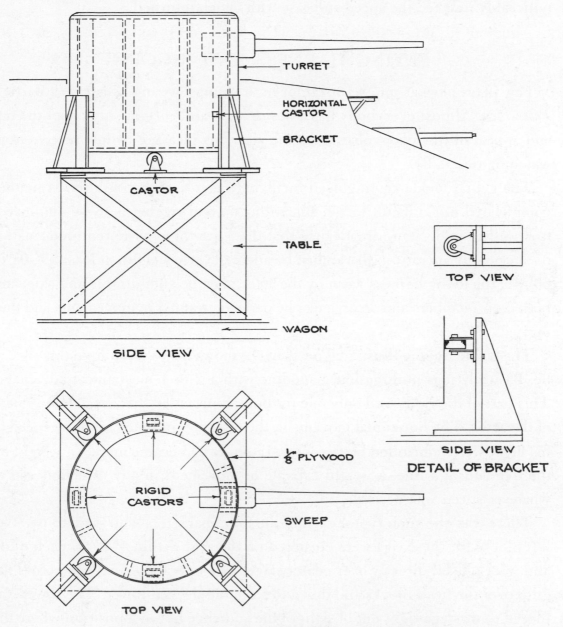

TURRET

HORIZONTAL
CASTOR

BRACKET

CASTOR

TABLE

WAGON

SIDE VIEW

TOP VIEW

⅛ PLYWOOD

RIGID
CASTORS

SWEEP

SIDE VIEW
DETAIL OF BRACKET

TOP VIEW

VARIATIONS IN CASTOR MOUNTING

PLATE 98

to the top of the lower sweep gave the turret the much needed weight and noticeably reduced the speed and ease with which it turned.

FLYING HARNESS AND RIGGING

Few plays have as much appeal for both youngsters and oldsters as Barrie's *Peter Pan.* Almost everybody has a desire to fly and certainly a part of the fun and appeal of this play comes from the vicarious pleasure people receive from watching others fly.

The actual tackle rigging used for flying Peter and the children is neither complicated nor difficult to rig. But if this type of rigging is to be employed, it is well to understand in advance that there are three basic requirements for its successful operation: there must be adequate grid height, at least 55'-0" to 60'-0"; the flying harness worn by the actor must be comfortable and safe; and both crew members and actors must be perfectly trained in movements and timing.

The tackle rigging illustrated on Plate 99 shows how very simple this rig can be. Basically it is nothing but a spotline with a 2 to 1 mechanical advantage. This part of the rig served only one purpose: it provided the vertical movement of the actor. The horizontal movement, the direction of swing, and the speed of his flight were controlled by the actor. Literally he became merely a weight on the free end of a line, a weight capable of movement in any direction and at whatever speed was desired.

There was one such rig for each of the four characters who were to fly. The loft blocks for these rigs were clustered on the grid within 4'-0" of each other and were placed directly over center stage. The operating lines ran across the grid, over the head blocks and down to a double-decked tower. The tower was placed downstage right out of sight of the audience but in a position where the two operators on each of the decks could see past the ends of the lowered cyclorama and had an unobstructed view of the stage.

The harness was made of heavy canvas reinforced by webbing and leather. It was designed as a one-piece garment to be laced down the side; the two adjustable shoulder straps then laced to the front of the jacket, as did the two crotch straps. The padded and chamois-covered crotch straps were placed in much the same position as the crotch straps of a parachute harness. There was no chafing

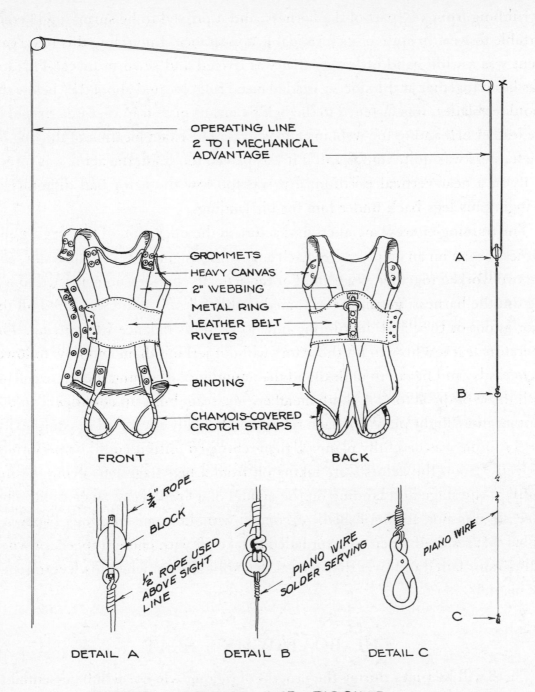

OPERATING LINE
2 TO 1 MECHANICAL
ADVANTAGE

A

B

C

GROMMETS
HEAVY CANVAS
2" WEBBING
METAL RING
LEATHER BELT
RIVETS

BINDING

CHAMOIS-COVERED
CROTCH STRAPS

FRONT

BACK

¾" ROPE
BLOCK
½" ROPE USED
ABOVE SIGHT
LINE

PIANO WIRE
SOLDER SERVING

PIANO WIRE

DETAIL A

DETAIL B

DETAIL C

FLYING HARNESS AND RIGGING

PLATE 99

or rubbing from any part of the harness, and it proved to be surprisingly comfortable to wear in spite of its formidable appearance. Encircling this basic garment was a wide band of leather that was riveted and sewn in place. This too was laced together at the side. A welded metal ring, located about $2\frac{1}{2}''$ below the shoulder blades, was fastened to the belt by means of a strap that was riveted to the leather belt and to the webbing and canvas. The exact location of the ring on the harness was quite important: if it was placed too high, the actor was forced to fly in a near-vertical position; if it was too low the actor had difficulty in swinging his legs back under him for his landings.

The training of crew members and actors in the operation of the rigging and harness began on an empty stage. Each actor was assigned his own operator, and the two worked together as a team. For the actor the first lesson consisted of trying out the harness, getting accustomed to the feel of it as he was lifted off the floor a foot or two, and discovering how to keep his balance while flying. The operators learned how to lift the actors without jerking them and how to lower them easily, and began to understand the importance of timing their movements with those of the actors. As both members of a team built up confidence in one another, the "flight plan" for each rehearsal gradually increased in complexity. Each routine was carefully planned, then rehearsed until it could be performed perfectly. Soon the actors were taking off from a bed stage left, flying the full width of the stage and landing on the mantel of a fireplace at stage right. This final act was not accomplished, of course, without some hilarious backward flights that resulted when an actor failed to take off with enough speed, or when an operator failed to lower the actor at that split second when his feet touched the mantel.

THE BOATSWAIN'S SEAT

There will be times during the process of rigging when it will be essential to work at a height from the stage floor that cannot be reached even with the use of an extension ladder. The boatswain's seat provides the answer to this problem. This device consists of a short board seat slung from two saddles and supported by the moving lower block of a watch tackle (Plate 100). The workman, seated in the chair, raises and lowers himself by operating the fall. When he reaches his

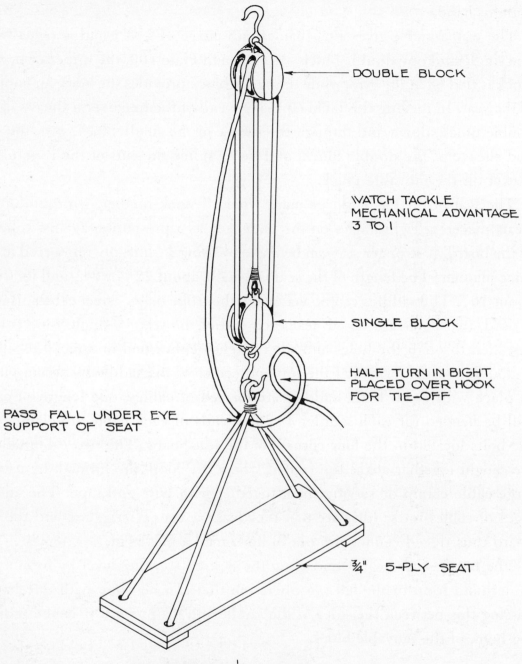

DOUBLE BLOCK

WATCH TACKLE
MECHANICAL ADVANTAGE
3 TO 1

SINGLE BLOCK

HALF TURN IN BIGHT
PLACED OVER HOOK
FOR TIE-OFF

PASS FALL UNDER EYE
SUPPORT OF SEAT

¾" 5-PLY SEAT

BOATSWAIN'S SEAT

PLATE 100

working level, he ties the fall to the hook of the movable block, thus freeing both his hands.

The watch tackle gives a mechanical advantage of 3 to 1 and is rigged with one single and one double block. As shown in Plate 100, the upper or double block is tied off at the grid, while the single block provides the hook for support of the seat. In reeving this tackle, pass one end of the line over a sheave of the double block, down and through the sheave of the single block, over the second sheave of the double block, and tie or splice the end of the rope to the becket on the movable block.

The seat of the chair can be made from 1″ stock lumber, with reinforcing cleats placed at right angles on the underside as a precaution against splitting of the board. A stronger seat can be made by using $\frac{3}{4}$″ fir 5-ply reinforced in the same manner. The length of the seat is usually about 22″ or 24″ and its width about 10″. The saddles can be made of either rope or $\frac{3}{16}$″ steel cables. If rope is used, two holes are bored near each end of the seat. A single rope is then threaded through the holes and the two ends either tied or spliced together. A double loop is formed at the top and center of the saddle by serving them in place with cord. If the saddles are formed of cables, one length of cable will be needed for each saddle. The free ends of each cable are clamped to eye bolts located in the four corners of the seat board. The two cable saddles are caught together at the top center, where two loops are formed, by using a large cable clamp or serving them together with wire and tape. The advantages of cables for saddles are that they make a stronger rigging, and the seat board thus rigged cannot slip out of horizontal adjustment.

The boatswain's seat is tied off at the desired working level by forming an underhand loop in the fall (an operation that can be done with one hand), passing this between the sides of the saddle and dropping it over the projecting hook of the movable block.

backstage organization and management

THE last few days immediately preceding the opening of a production are traditionally depicted as nerve wracking and harrowing. Movie and TV script writers have done an excellent job of showing this period filled with frantic all-night sessions, exhausted actors and crew members, crisis heaped upon crisis, and a supervising director on the verge of a nervous breakdown. Unfortunately, within a field as universal as that of play production, there will always be a small percentage of individuals whose warped sense of the dramatic so far outweighs their common sense that their dress rehearsals are like those just described—chaotic. However, this is the exception rather than the rule, and it is easy to put the blame right where it belongs—lack of proper organization and planning.

The dress rehearsal period is intended for one purpose: synchronizing and polishing all elements into a production with unity. This presupposes that the elements of scenery, props, lights, and costumes have all been completed according to the plan of their individual work schedules and are ready to be integrated. There is then an orderly sequence of operations that avoids last-minute congestion and confusion. As an example, the technician's work schedule may have called for all construction to be finished by the 20th; the next three days are allowed for painting; the 24th and 25th are set aside for assembly, rigging, and preliminary work on lighting; the 26th and 27th are to be devoted to assembling properties, trimming sets, and to final adjustments on lighting. Should the scene shift be especially complicated, a part of the 27th could well be used for a technical rehearsal, which is best described as a performance without benefit (or hindrance) of audience or actors. Just as the technician's work schedule has pinpointed possible troublesome details in advance and provided time for their correction, the costumer's schedule may have set aside a time for a dress parade that provides the actors with an opportunity to try out their costumes and makeups against the scenery and under the lights in advance of dress rehearsals. There is then time to make any necessary changes or adjustments before dress rehearsal begins. If the mechanical aspects of the production have been worked out in advance, there is no reason why the first dress rehearsal should not be devoted to the purpose for which it was intended: namely, the polishing of the production.

THE STUDENT STAGE MANAGER

The stage manager is the key to backstage organization. He is usually one of the more experienced and older students, selected as much for his tact, diplomacy, and ability to get along in trying situations as for any other qualities. He becomes the director's representative backstage and is responsible for the smooth running of the production through the rehearsal period and during the run of the play.

Unlike the professional stage manager, who is in attendance at all rehearsals from the time of casting till the close of the production, the stage manager of the educational theatre usually assumes his duties only shortly before the first technical rehearsals. Just how soon and how long he attends rehearsals will depend upon the complexity of the production and the director's need for his services. It is obvious that the value of the student manager to the director is in direct proportion to his knowledge of the script, the actors, and the established stage business. Such knowledge can be assimilated only through attendance at a series of rehearsals. During this period while he is learning the script, he is busy making notes on a series of details that it will later become his responsibility to supervise: the sequence of scenes, opening and closing curtain cues, and at what points the director wants the act breaks and intermissions. His notes will also include all of the information required for compiling his actor's check list, and at what time music and sound cues are required. He will make a furniture plan for each scene, note where each major prop must be placed, and whether doors and windows are closed or open at the beginning of a scene. He is aware of any special effects involving either lighting or sound, and he will know the cues for them, and how they are to be timed to the stage business.

Because of his knowledge of the production the stage manager can, in the absence of the director, provide the technician and lighting specialist with needed information during the rigging and lighting of the production. He is able to show the technician where each item of furniture is to be placed for a special piece of stage business; he can explain why certain parts of the setting may need additional bracing; or he can show the lighting specialist which acting areas must receive special attention. Since the stage manager frequently serves as head of the stage crew, he helps the technician plan the details of each shift and make individual crew assignments. By the date of the first technical rehearsal the stage manager has become thoroughly conversant with every phase of the production; he knows how, where, and when each physical aspect of the play will occur. He has become an able backstage assistant to the director.

ACTOR'S CHECK LIST

During the rehearsal period and the run of the production there is little time for the stage manager to use an elaborate set of notes. However, any chart or diagram that will provide him with needed information at a glance can prove extremely helpful. Such a chart is the actor's check list. This chart takes two forms, a simplified version that is checked by the actors as they enter the theatre and a more detailed chart that is again checked by the actors when they report to the stage for their entrances.

The simplified version is a listing of characters by order of appearance on stage, followed by the actor's name, his phone number, and a series of spaces representing the dates of dress rehearsals and performances (Plate 101). This list is posted by the stage entrance or near the dressing rooms, where it is checked by the actors as an indication that they have arrived at the theatre and are busy with their makeups and costumes.

The second chart is posted on the bulletin board near the stage manager's desk; a check opposite an actor's name on this chart indicates that he has reported to the stage and is ready for his entrance. This chart is more detailed

CHARACTER	ACTOR	PHONE	REHEARSAL			PRODUCTION DATES						
			10/13	10/14	10/15	10/16	10/17	10/18	10/22	10/23	10/24	10/25
HELEN POTTS	RUTH CANFIELD	7392										
HAL CARTER	ED WELLS	X 3291										
MILLIE OWENS	JOAN HUMMER	5219										
BOMBER	BOB HALL	4716										
MADGE OWENS	ALICE BONNER	X 2241										
FLO OWENS	DEE YOUNG	X 2340										
ROSEMARY SIDNEY	VIRGINIA DE LILLO	7418										
ALAN SEYMOUR	KENNETH HILL	5521										
IRMA KRONKITE	PEGGY SPRAGUE	6593										
CHRISTINE SCHOENWALDER	MARAGRET KEYS	3361										
HOWARD BEVANS	WILLIAM KELLY	4432										

PICNIC

ACTOR'S CHECK LIST

PLATE 101

					PICNIC									
CHARACTER	ACTOR	PHONE	PLAYING TIME	ACT BREAK	REHEARSAL			PRODUCTION DATES						
ACT I			34 MIN.	10 MIN	10/13	10/14	10/15	10/16	10/17	10/18	10/22	10/23	10/24	10/25
POTTS	CANFIELD	7392												
CARTER	WELLS	X 3291												
MILLIE	HUMMER	5219												
BOMBER	HALL	4716												
MADGE	BONNER	X 2241												
FLO	YOUNG	X 2340												
ROSEMARY	DE LILLO	7418												
ALAN	HILL	5521												
IRMA	SPRAGUE	6593												
CHRISTINE	KEYS	3361												
ACT II			35 MIN.	12 MIN.										
MILLIE	HUMMER													
MADGE	BONNER													
FLO	YOUNG													
IRMA	SPRAGUE													
CHRISTINE	KEYS													
ROSEMARY	DE LILLO													
POTTS	CANFIELD													
HOWARD	KELLY	4432												
CARTER	WELLS													
ALAN	HILL													
ACT III SCENE I			11 MIN.	2 MIN.										
HOWARD	KELLY													
ROSEMARY	DE LILLO													
CARTER	WELLS													
MADGE	BONNER													
ACT III SCENE II			17 MIN.											
FLO	YOUNG													
MILLIE	HUMMER													
POTTS	CANFIELD													
ROSEMARY	DE LILLO													
IRMA	SPRAGUE													
CHRISTINE	KEYS													
BOMBER	HALL													

ACTOR'S CHECK LIST
STAGE MANAGER'S COPY

PLATE 102

than the first; it not only carries all of the information listed on the first but lists the names of the characters and actors in the order of their appearance for each act and scene. Also listed is the playing time for each act and scene and the time required for each scene shift and intermission (Plate 102).

These charts inform the stage manager at a glance whether all actors have reported to the theatre, whether each is ready for his entrance, and who should be on stage for the opening of each scene. By consulting this chart both cast and crews can be kept informed regarding the length of time remaining before their next appearance or assignment.

STAGE MANAGER'S SCRIPT COPY

The stage manager's need to make extensive use of a play script will vary from production to production. With a comparatively simple play that has few light or sound cues there is little need for a script once the play has progressed past the dress-rehearsal period. On elaborate productions the stage manager may find it simpler to follow the dialogue on stage, line by line, in his own script. Along the margins of each page are his penciled notes calling his attention to the proper place for warning cues and action cues for lights, sounds, music, entrances, or special effects. The action cues are usually underscored in colored pencil so that they may be easily spotted.

TIME SCHEDULE

One of the most valuable charts kept by the stage manager is the time schedule. By noting the exact time when the curtain is opened or closed, this chart provides a simple way for the manager to keep an accurate record of the playing time for each act or scene. If this record is correct, it will automatically give the total elapsed time for each act break—the difference between the closing time of one scene and the opening of the next. If it is considered desirable, the actual scene shift can be more accurately timed by noting the elapsed time between the closing of the curtain and the moment when the last crew head reports to the stage manager that his crew has completed its assignment and is "set." Usually space is reserved on the chart to note the cause for any delay that might affect the overall time of the act break. A misplaced prop, a flickering spotlight, or a difficult costume change may cause a delay of from

PRODUCTION — PICNIC					DIRECTOR — GEE		
DATE	ACT	CURTAIN UP	CURTAIN DOWN	PLAYING TIME	ACT BREAK	SHIFT	DELAY
WED 10/16	I	8:10	8:44	34	10		
	II	8:54	9:29	35	12		2 MIN. REFOCUS SPOT
	III-1	9:41	9:52	11	2		
	III-2	9:54	10:11	17			
	TOTAL			1:37	24		
TOTAL PRO. TIME 2 HRS. 11 MIN.							
				STAGE MANAGER — TILTON			

TIME SCHEDULE

PLATE 103

one to several minutes. If these delays are recorded and their causes noted, proper steps can be taken to overcome them (Plate 103).

Keeping an accurate time record of the production is not a needless piece of busy work; it provides the director, the house manager, and all crew heads with needed information. It provides the director with a perfect method of checking the playing time of one performance against another. It can be done scene by scene and act by act, or by comparing total elapsed playing times. Detecting when actors have been racing their lines or unnecessarily prolonging stage business becomes a simple matter of comparing performance records. Faults of this type can be easily corrected if the director knows exactly when it occurred and how long it lasted. "What time is the play over?" is a question asked of the house manager many times a night by taxi drivers or others who are meeting friends after the play. If there is an emergency call for a member of the audience, knowing just when there will be an act break helps the house manager locate the individual with a minimum of disturbance to the rest of the house. When heads of prop, costume, light, and sound crews know just how long the stage crew requires to complete a shift, their own assignments can be planned accordingly. If the time of the shift is very short, say 1 or 2 minutes, this may mean that additional crew members will be needed or a different method devised to complete their assignments in the allotted time.

THE STAGE CREW

Selecting the members to form the stage crew is a responsibility of the scene technician. Frequently the stage manager will be called into conference by the technician and the two of them will discuss each shift in detail, deciding on the desired number of crew members. On simple one-set productions a stage manager, an assistant manager, and a curtain man may be all that are needed. On heavier productions with several settings a full crew of eight, ten, twelve, or more may be required. Usually the crew is divided into three sections, each assigned to handle the scenery on some particular part of the stage such as stage right, center rear, or stage left.

At this point, just before the first technical rehearsal, the technician calls the crew together to explain the general scheme of shifting and to make individual crew assignments. Certainly one of the easiest ways of accomplishing this task is to draw a floor plan of each setting on a blackboard, explaining in detail the order in which the setting will be struck and just where each unit of scenery will be stored. Since the word "shift" implies the dismantling of one set and the assembly of another to take its place, the technician will explain where the various parts of the second set have been stored and in what order they should be assembled. Individual assignments can be given at this time. If the crew is inexperienced, it is best to discuss one shift at a time, preferably just before the crew members go to the stage to try out their assignments. The crew should be reassembled at the completion of the shift and each step reviewed. Sometimes it may be necessary to alter the operational steps or to change individual assignments; and always there are questions to be answered and suggestions to evaluate.

It is advisable to have the heads of both the lighting crew and the property crew present at these briefing sessions. Frequently their crew assignments are so interrelated with those of the stage crew that it is impossible to plan the shift without taking them into consideration. One point should be stressed at these first meetings: the importance of coöperation between crews, and a complete understanding by all crew members of the sequence of steps to be performed in accomplishing the shift. A quick quiet shift can be obtained only if all crew members know when, how, and where their assignments must be completed.

THE OPERATIONAL SEQUENCE OF A SCENE SHIFT

The pattern used in planning the shifts of most conventional settings generally follows the outline below. Note that the order of the strike involves the removal of all upstage units first, moving progressively from the back wall down to the tormentors. If this pattern is followed and the scenery is stacked in that order, it is automatically in the right order for reassembly.

1. The stage manager warns the crew members to take their respective positions shortly before the close of the curtain.
2. The main curtain is closed.
3. Switching on the stage work lights is the silent command for the strike to begin.
4. The cyclorama is raised. This operation both protects the cyc and clears the stage floor for the free movement of scenery, props, and lights.
5. The ceiling is raised.
6. The prop crew removes all decorative and practical props from the walls

of the set. Floor props are pulled into the downstage center area to clear them from the folding or the movement of the walls.

7. The stage crew strikes all backings, cutouts, and set pieces.

8. The light crew disconnects and removes all light fixtures from set walls. All floor and table lamps are disconnected and removed.

9. The stage crew removes all three-dimensional architectural trim (removable doors, windows, fireplaces, etc.).

10. The rear wall is struck.

11. The larger floor props are removed.

12. The side walls are unbraced and struck.

13. The large floor props for the second setting are moved to downstage center.

14. The side walls are run in and braced.

15. The back wall is joined to the side walls and braced.

16. Three-dimensional architectural trim is placed in position.

17. Floor props are placed. Light fixtures and decorative props are fitted to the set walls.

18. The ceiling is lowered.

19. Backings, set pieces, and cutouts are placed in position.

20. The cyclorama is lowered.

21. All backstage lights are tested.

22. Prop, light, and costume crew heads report to the stage manager that their assignments are completed and they are "set."

23. The crews clear stage, the stage manager gives the command of "Places," checks with the control board operator, and, if he is ready, gives the cue for the opening of the scene.

There is always a possibility of combining several of these operations so that they can be performed at the same time. On the strike, for instance, operations 4 to 9 could be carried out simultaneously, and on the assembly steps from 14 to 20 could be combined.

THE PROPERTY CREW

The property master and his crew have assembled or constructed all the required props under the supervision of the director and designer. The director must pass on their acceptability for stage business, while the designer is concerned about their correctness as to period, form, and color. Once properties have been approved they become the responsibility of the property master and his crew. Details regarding their placement on stage and manner and order of shifting them are determined at early briefing sessions with the stage manager. He will see to it that the shifting of the props is coördinated with the other activities of the scene shift.

The property master will use many tricks to reduce the time required for the removal or assembly of props. When possible, and if it can be done without damage, heavy floor props can be stacked on a low dolly and wheeled to and from the stage. Props can also be loaded on wagons and rolling platforms used for shifting scenery. Two chairs can be stacked seat to seat and carried as one, or they can be laid on a sofa or table and all carried at once. Small decorative props placed on tables, buffets, shelves, etc., must be cleared before the latter can be moved. This can be done rapidly by two crew members who make a circuit of the set, collecting all such items and placing them in a large container such as a wicker clothesbasket. Wall hangings, pictures, and fixtures are all marked for ready identification with their proper positions on the set walls. "Spike marks" of chalk, scene paint, or tacks on the stage floor are frequently used to spot the floor props in exactly the correct position. If spike marks are inadvisable for some reason the position can be established by two measurements taken from some distinctive feature of the setting. For example, a table can be aligned with the door in the right wall and a window in the rear wall.

Hand properties, at least those that are carried on or off stage by the actors, are usually dispensed and collected from a table placed off stage near the main entrance of the setting. A crew member assigned to this table, whose principal duty is to collect the props from the actors as they leave the setting, will eliminate the exasperating job of locating missing hand props after a performance.

THE LIGHT CREW

Details concerning the division of the light crew into various sections were discussed in Chapter I. The floor and bridge crews are the only sections of the light crew, besides the control board operator, that are likely to be directly involved with the actual scene shift. As such, their duties and the order in which they are to be accomplished fall under the supervision of the stage manager, who must coördinate them with the other activities of the shift.

The actual duties of the light crew during the shift are few, compared with those of the stage or property crew. Although they may be considered minor in respect to the number of assignments per crew member, they are nonetheless important. Failure to disconnect and remove light fixtures from the setting can delay the stage crew many seconds, just as a barrier of horizon strips can block the movement of scenery either on or off the stage. Electrical cables must be disconnected from all wagons before those units can be moved, and all electrical cables that lie on the floor must be coiled out of the way in order to prevent their fouling rolling scenery and to avoid damage to the cables themselves.

The busiest man on the light crew during a shift is likely to be the control-board operator. He must clear the board of all controlling units used in the preceding scene and reset additional units to their proper reading for the scene coming up. If the time of the shift will permit it, and the control board is backstage, he will test each instrument as he puts it on reading. Should the control board be located in the orchestra pit or at the rear of the auditorium, the testing operation is done with the aid of the house phone and one of the floor crew members who checks each backstage light. The one exception to the testing of crucial acting lights is from instruments mounted in the auditorium. Since nothing looks much worse than a series of circular blobs of light thrown momentarily on the main curtain, the testing of these instruments is conducted before the audience assembles.

THE COSTUME CREW

Unless there are fast costume changes that demand temporary onstage dressing rooms, the shift is not likely to be much affected by the activities of the costume crew. However, temporary dressing rooms occupy valuable space otherwise available for storage of scenery or props and do concern the stage manager. It becomes his duty to designate the area that can best be used for the purpose.

Occasionally, even with the aid of dressers, a particularly complicated costume and makeup change cannot be accomplished within the specified time of the shift. In such cases the costumer will notify the stage manager, who will make proper allowances for it on the time schedule.

SUMMARY OF THE STAGE MANAGER'S DUTIES AND OPERATIONAL CHECK LIST FOR UNIVERSITY PRODUCTIONS

Since the duties of the stage manager are so numerous and varied, some kind of a list should be prepared for the student manager, summarizing the principal duties and responsibilities expected of an efficient stage manager. Where this practice has been established, there is a noticeable decrease in the number of mistakes that occur because the student was unaware of what was expected of him. Some additions or deletions would have to be made in this list to make it conform to the pattern of production used by different producing organizations; but, whatever the schedule may be, it is well to have it down in black and white so that it may be given out at the time the stage manager is appointed. Information contained on the chart of a stage manager's duties and the operational check list used at the University Theatre at Iowa follows.

STAGE MANAGER'S DUTIES

1. Secure a copy of the play and study the script before attending rehearsals. Use this script for underscoring warning cues, action cues, sound cues, light cues, etc.
2. During the absence of the director or any staff member backstage, the stage manager has full authority over actors and crew members.
3. The length of time the stage manager attends rehearsals preceding the first technical rehearsal depends upon the director's need for his service and the complexity of the production. In all cases he must attend rehearsals, in advance of the technical rehearsals, a sufficient number of times to become familiar with the sequence of scenes, the actors, stage business, use of props, and placement of furniture.

4. Make out an actor's check list containing the name of the actor, the character he plays, and his telephone number. (See example.) Post a copy of the list on the board by the dressing-room doors. Insist on all actors checking in as they enter the theatre. Post the stage manager's copy of this list on the bulletin board by your desk on the stage.

5. Make out a crew check list containing the names, telephone numbers, and addresses of students serving as crew heads, control-board operators, curtain man, etc.

6. Draw a plan of the property and furniture layout for each scene. Pay attention to each key prop such as a fan, letter, etc., that must be placed by the prop crew before the opening of the scene. Check, and note on your plan, the position of doors and windows. Are they to be open or closed for the beginning of the scene?

7. Check sound effects controlled from backstage. Telephone buzzers are usually operated backstage by the prompter. All other sound effects are usually controlled from the light booth by members of the sound crew, using the public address system.

8. Become familiar with the operation of the following stage equipment before the first rehearsal.
   a. House lights.
   b. Lights controlled from the stage manager's desk.
   c. Warning bell for audience.
   d. Controls for the main curtain.
   e. Asbestos curtain.
   f. Controls for the revolving stage.
   g. Fire hose and fire extinguishers.
   h. Fire doors.
   i. Cyclorama.
   j. Backstage work lights.
   k. House phone system.
   l. First-aid supplies.

9. Keep an accurate time schedule of all dress rehearsals and performances, showing opening and closing times of each scene, elapsed time between scenes and acts, and the reason for any delay during a scene shift.

SAMPLE

	Curtain Up	Down	Playing Time	Shift	Delay
Act I	8:10	9:00	50	5	1 min. props
Act II	9:05	9:45	40	12	Intermission
Act III	9:57	10:32	35		
			125	17	

Total Playing Time	2 hours and 5 minutes
Total Shift Time	17 minutes
Total Production Time	2 hours and 32 minutes

OPERATIONAL CHECK LIST

1. Check the forestage to see that no classroom equipment or rehearsal furniture has been left on the apron in front of the asbestos.

2. Make certain that the beam work lights over the auditorium are out. It is easy to overlook these with the auditorium lights on.

3. Give the first warning call to the actors 30 minutes before the curtain, a second call 15 minutes later. Last call is given at 8 o'clock, when all actors who open the play should be on stage.

4. Between the first and last warning calls, the stage manager should check all scenery, lights, and props for the opening act.

5. As the actors come to the stage from the dressing rooms have them check their names on the actor's check list which is posted to the left of the stage manager's desk. After an actor has checked in for a scene do not permit him to leave the stage without notifying you or your assistant.

6. Under no circumstances should the play be opened until the majority of the audience is seated. Information on the condition of the house is obtained by calling the ticket office or by word from the director.

7. At 8 o'clock, the asbestos curtain is raised and tied off. It will not be lowered again, except in an emergency (it can be used as a substitute for the main curtain should it fail) until the end of the play.

8. The usual curtain time is 8:10, but this varies a little, depending upon the length of the play and whether the audience is slow in assembling and getting seated.

9. After receiving word from either the house manager or the director that the audience is in and seated, the command "Places" is given. All crew

members clear stage and the actors take their positions for the opening scene.

10. Turn off all backstage work lights. This is easy to overlook, especially if the bridge and cyc lights are on. Flick the work lights off and on several times as a silent warning to those who may not have heard the call of "Places." This should remind you to turn them off.

11. Call the control-board operator for a last-minute check on lights, and if he is ready ask for the house lights to be dimmed out.

12. When the house lights are completely out, give the cue for the opening of the curtain. Should the director want the play to open on a black stage, it will be necessary to notify the control-board operator when the curtain is open since it will be impossible for him to see it.

13. Enter on the time schedule the exact time that the curtain was opened.

14. The curtain is closed at the end of the act on a cue determined by the director during the dress rehearsals.

15. Enter on the time schedule the exact time when the curtain closed at the end of the scene.

16. Do not turn on the work lights backstage for the scene shift until the auditorium lights are up. This can create a bad light spill across the apron or under the front curtain.

17. During dress rehearsals the stage crews will not begin a shift until the command "Strike" is given by the stage manager; the director may want to repeat a part, or all of an act. During the run of the performance, the switching on of the work lights is the silent command for the shift.

18. When the director has chosen to close a scene by dimming or blacking out all stage lights, the stage manager must notify the control-board operator when the front curtain is closed. This will be his cue to bring up the house lights. When scenes are to be handled in this manner the stage manager must see that all backstage lights not controlled by the board are out, including the light over the stage manager's desk, the prompter's lights, etc.

19. The usual time between acts is about 5 to 6 minutes, and for a shift of scenery or props between scenes of an act 3 minutes or less. The act break selected by the director for the intermission is usually about 10 to 12 minutes.

20. Three minutes before the end of the intermission sound the audience warning chimes three times.

21. Note the exact closing time of the play on the time schedule. Compute the total playing time and total shift time. Give the director a copy of this record.

22. Before leaving the theatre after a rehearsal or performance, make sure that the cyclorama has been raised, the fire doors above the grid closed, the asbestos lowered and all backstage lights turned off.

glossary

APRON.   The part of the stage floor extending beyond the proscenium arch into the auditorium; forestage.

ARBOR.   A metal frame that holds the counterweights used to balance the weight of flown scenery; synonymous with carriage and cradle.

ASBESTOS CURTAIN.   A fireproof curtain hung just upstage of the proscenium arch to prevent the spread of fire.

BACK-FLAP HINGE.   See *Hinge.*

BACKING.   Any type of two- or three-dimensional scenery placed in back of an opening to screen the backstage area from the audience.

BATTEN CLAMP.   A piece of stage hardware used to attach drops or borders to a pipe batten.

BLOCK.   A grooved pulley or sheave housed in a wooden or metal frame provided with a hook, eye, or strap by which it may be attached to other objects.

BOARD FOOT.   A unit of measure by which lumber is sold. Each unit represents a piece of lumber 1″ thick, 12″ wide and 12″ long.

BOBINETTE.   A very lightweight cotton netting.

BOLT:

   CARRIAGE.   A threaded shaft with a round head. The shaft graduates into angular shoulders just beneath the head; these prevent the bolt from turning when driven into wood.

   MACHINE.   A threaded shaft with a square or hexagonal head.

   STOVE.   A threaded shaft with a head that is slotted like a screw.

BOOK CEILING.   See *Ceiling.*

BOOMERANG.   A multileveled rolling platform on which workmen can stand.

BORDERS.   Strips of fabric hung horizontally above the stage to mask overhead space and equipment.

BRACE CLEAT.   A metal plate 2″ wide by 4″ long drilled with holes; used in conjunction with a stagebrace and a stage screw to brace scenery.

BREASTING.   The process of pulling a flown object out of its normal vertical path by means of a special line and blocks.

BUTT HINGE.   See *Hinge.*

BUTT JOINT.   See *Joint*

CARPET HOIST.   A type of rigging used to transfer weight from one counter-weight arbor to another by means of special brackets.

CARRIAGE.   (1) The supporting member of a run of stairs. (2) Synonym for arbor and for cradle.

CARRIAGE BOLT.   See *Bolt.*

CASING.   The enclosing framework around a door or window opening.

CEILING:

   BOOK.   A ceiling piece so constructed and rigged that its two halves fold face to face for compact storage in the flies.

   ROLL.   A ceiling piece so constructed that it can be easily dismantled and rolled into a compact bundle.

CEILING PLATE.   A metal plate $2\frac{1}{2}″$ wide and 7″ long, fitted with a metal ring and drilled to receive bolts. Used in joining the cross battens to the length-wise battens of ceilings.

CEL-O-CLOTH.   A thin sheet of cellophane with a backing of loosely woven threads. Used as a substitute for glass.

CEL-O-GLASS.   Screen wire that has been treated with a coating of cellophane to make it completely translucent. Used as a substitute for glass.

CELLULOSE ACETATE.   A chemical compound having the appearance and most of the properties of glass. Occasionally used as a substitute for glass; more frequently used in making curved slides for projectors.

CLOUT NAIL.   A nail with a tapering wedge-shaped shaft used for joining key-stones and corner blocks to flat frames. The points of these nails are easily bent or clinched for a stronger anchor.

COLUMN.   A supporting shaft or pillar.

CONTINENTAL PARALLEL.   See *Parallel.*

CORNER BLOCK. A $\frac{1}{4}''$ thick piece of plywood in the shape of a right triangle with 10″ sides, used to reinforce and join right-angle butt joints.

CORNER PLATE. An L-shaped right-angle metal plate used to reinforce the butt joints of a window or door unit.

COTTON CANVAS DUCK. The most commonly used covering material for flat frames.

COTTON REP. An inexpensive, heavy-duty, ribbed cotton material obtainable in colors.

COUNTERWEIGHT, MULTIPLE SPEED. Used in flying scenery; employs a 2 to 1 mechanical advantage in its rigging. The batten moves twice as far and twice as fast as the arbor.

COUNTERWEIGHT SYSTEM. A method of raising scenery vertically by means of steel cables, blocks, pipe batten, and weights placed in an arbor.

CRADLE. A metal frame for holding counterweights. Synonym for arbor and carriage.

CURTAIN:

DRAW. A curtain that parts in the center; each section pulls to the sides in back of the proscenium arch.

FLY. A curtain that is opened and closed by raising and lowering it by means of the counterweight system or rope-line rigging.

MAIN. The front curtain that separates the stage from the auditorium.

ROLLER. A curtain that is opened by winding it around a long wooden roller which is usually attached to the lower hem.

TAB. A two-sectioned curtain rigged to open diagonally, presenting a decorative draped effect.

CUT-LINE. A special line used to hold the asbestos curtain in the open position. Cutting or releasing this line will automatically lower the asbestos.

CYCLORAMA:

FLY. A U-shaped expanse of light blue canvas enclosing the acting area on three sides. It is raised and lowered by the counterweight system. Used for sky effects.

TRIP. Similar to a fly cyc, but so rigged that it will fold as it is raised, thus requiring less grid height.

LINNEBACH.   Serves the same purpose as the fly or trip cyc but operates differently. It is suspended from a curved track and moves horizontally to store in a rolled position around a truncated cone. Named after the inventor, Adolph Linnebach.

DADO JOINT.   See *Joint.*

DESIGNER'S PLANS.   Scaled mechanical drawings for exact representation of a setting. They include the ground plans, front elevations, detail, and sight-line drawings.

DESIGNER'S SKETCH.   Usually a colored perspective drawing showing the proposed setting as it will appear to a member of the audience seated about halfway back in the auditorium.

DETAIL DRAWINGS.   Mechanical drawings, made to a large scale, showing the top, front, and side views of three-dimensional objects.

DIAGONAL BRACE.   A brace made of 1″ x 2″ lumber and placed at an angle between the stile and rail of a wide flat to strengthen the frame.

DOLLY.   A small low platform mounted on wheels or a single roller; used in moving heavy objects.

DOME, PLASTER.   Similar in shape and use to a cyclorama but made of steel screening and covered with plaster. It cannot be shifted. It may partially or completely enclose the acting area on three sides.

DOUBLE LUFF.   An arrangement of rope and pulleys used to provide a mechanical advantage of 4 to 1.

DOUBLE WHIP.   An arrangement of rope and pulleys used to provide a mechanical advantage of 2 to 1.

DOWELED JOINT.   See *Joint.*

DOWNSTAGE.   The front of the stage, toward the audience.

DRAPERIES, STAGE.   A set of draperies used to mask the backstage area when no scenery is being used.

DRAPERY HANGERS.   Steel sockets and hooks used to support door and window draperies. Hooks are attached to a drapery pole, sockets to the scenery.

DRAW CURTAIN.   See *Curtain.*

DROP.   A large unframed expanse of cloth supported by a heavy wooden batten at the top with a lighter batten at the bottom to hold the material free of wrinkles.

DROP, CUTOUT.   A standard drop with sections removed to give it a distinctive shape.

DUTCHMAN.   A strip of muslin 5″ wide that is glued and tacked over the hinges and crack formed when two flats are hinged together.

EYE BOLT.   A threaded shaft with one end formed into a solid ring.

FALL.   That part of the rope of a tackle rigging to which the power is applied in hoisting.

FALSE PROSCENIUM.   A decorative silhouette usually made of two-dimensional scenery, placed just upstage of and parallel with the regular proscenium arch.

FLAT:

ARCHWAY.   A flat frame with the structural members arranged to form a door or window opening with a curved or shaped top.

DOOR.   A flat frame with the structural members so arranged as to form a door opening.

IRREGULAR.   Flats whose shape is other than rectangular.

JOG.   A narrow plain flat; usually any flat less than 3′-0″ wide.

PLAIN.   A rectangular frame covered with an unbroken expanse of canvas, muslin, or compositional material.

WINDOW.   A flat with its structural members placed to form a window opening.

FLIES.   The space above the acting area where scenery can be flown for storage.

FLOAT.   To lower standing scenery to a horizontal position on the floor by blocking the lower rail and allowing the flat to fall.

FLOOR CLOTH.   A covering of heavy canvas for the stage floor, usually dark brown in color.

FLY CURTAIN.   See *Curtain.*

FLY CYCLORAMA.   See *Cyclorama.*

FLY GALLERY.   A platform attached to the sidewall of the stage house about 15′-0″ to 25′-0″ from the floor. Used by workmen when flying scenery by the rope-line and sandbag method.

FLYING.   Shifting scenery by raising it vertically over the acting area by rope-line rigging or the counterweight system. The fastest and quietest method of shifting.

FOLDING JACK.   See *Jack*.

FORESTAGE.   The part of the stage floor extending beyond the proscenium arch into the auditorium. Synonym for apron.

FOOTIRON, HINGED.   A steel brace used in bracing the bottom of scenery. The two legs of this brace can be adjusted to different angles.

FOOTIRON, RIGID.   A right-angle steel brace fastened to the bottom of scenery to brace or lock it to the stage floor.

FRONT ELEVATION.   Scaled mechanical drawing representing a front view of the setting as it would appear when drawn in a single plane.

GRID, GRIDIRON.   A framework of metal or wooden beams extending over the stage area and located about 6'-0" below the roof of the stage house. On it are bolted the head and loft blocks of the counterweight or rope-line rigging systems.

GROUND PLAN.   A scaled mechanical drawing representing the top view of a setting in position on stage.

GROMMET.   A reinforcing metal eyelet used to protect the edges of a hole cut in fabric.

GUN TACKLE.   An arrangement of rope with one single and one double pulley that provides a mechanical advantage of 3 to 1.

HALVED JOINT.   See *Joint*.

HANGER IRON.   A steel strap $1\frac{1}{8}''$ wide by $7\frac{1}{2}''$ long fitted with a metal ring. Used in flying scenery.

HINGE:

BACK-FLAP, LOOSE-PIN.   Hinges designed especially for joining flats. They come in two sizes, $1\frac{1}{2}''$ by $3\frac{1}{2}''$ and $2''$ by $4\frac{3}{8}''$. Pins can be easily removed to separate flats.

BACK-FLAP, TIGHT-PIN.   Same as above except that the pins cannot be removed.

BUTT.   Each half, or leg, of this hinge is rectangular in shape and wider than it is long.

STRAP.   The legs of this hinge are elongated and tapering.

HEAD BLOCK.   Several grooved wheels, or sheaves, turning on a single axle and housed in a common metal frame. It is bolted to the eye beams above the grid.

HOOK HANGER IRON.   A steel strap with a metal ring attached to one end, the other end shaped to receive the lower rail of framed scenery. Used in conjunction with a hanger iron for flying scenery.

JACK:

FOLDING.   A triangular frame of 1″ x 3″ placed on the back of scenery to brace it. It is hinged so as to fold parallel with the scenery as an aid in shifting and storage.

MODIFIED.   A 1″ x 3″ frame built to brace irregularly shaped scenery and conforming to its shape.

RIGID.   Made in the same way as a folding jack, but held rigidly at right angles to the flat frame by hinges placed on both sides of the jack.

JACKKNIFE STAGE.   A large platform mounted on rigid castors; one corner is locked to the floor by a pivot pin. The stage moves in a quarter arc to bring the setting in alignment with the proscenium. Two such stages are generally used, one on each side of the stage.

JOG.   See *Flat*.

JOINT:

BUTT.   Two pieces of wood squared off and joined at a true right angle.

DADO.   The end of one piece of wood fits into a slot cut into the side of another. The slot can be speedily cut with a dado attachment for a circular saw.

DOWELED.   Matched holes are drilled into the pieces of wood to be joined. Hardwood pegs, called dowels, are covered with glue and inserted into the holes.

HALVED.   A method of joining two pieces of lumber without increasing the thickness. One-half the thickness is removed from the ends of two pieces of lumber and they are then glued together.

LAP.   The simplest of all wood joints. One piece is laid over another and nailed or screwed in place.

MORTISE AND TENON.   A rectangular hole, the mortise, is cut in one piece of lumber. A projecting peg, the tenon, is cut into the other. The tenon fits into the mortise and is held by glue.

NOTCHED.   This joint is similar to the dado joint except that the notch is cut in the edge of the lumber rather than across the face.

SCARF.   A method of joining two pieces of lumber end to end without increasing the thickness of the lumber at the joint. The 18″ wedges are removed from the faces of both pieces, the cuts are covered with glue, and one piece is placed upon the other and held in place with nails or screws until the glue has dried.

KEEPER OR S-HOOK.   Strap iron shaped into a double hook. One side of the hook is placed over a toggle bar and a stiffening batten is placed in the other side of the hook. Used in bracing scenery.

KEYSTONE.   A piece of $\frac{1}{4}$″ plywood 8″ long, tapered from 4″ wide at one end to $2\frac{3}{4}$″ at the other. Used for joining butt joints between stiles and toggle bars.

LAP JOINT.   See *Joint*.

LASH LINE.   A length of $\frac{1}{4}$″ sash cord used to lace two flats together.

LASH-LINE CLEAT.   Metal cleats attached to the inner edges of flat stiles to engage the lash line when flats are to be joined by lashing.

LASH-LINE EYE.   A metal cleat fitted with a ring at one end and drilled to receive a screw on the other. Provides a method of attaching a lash line to a flat. Line is passed through the ring and knotted.

LASH-LINE HOOK.   A strap of metal drilled to receive two screws and with a hook formed at one end. Used as a substitute for standard lash cleats when the latter cannot be used.

LENGTHWISE BATTEN.   The outside framing members that extend the full length of either a roll or a book ceiling.

LIFT JACK.   A device used for shifting scenery. A lever lifts the weight of the scenery onto castors so that it can be rolled.

LIGHT BRIDGE.   A metal framework about 2′ wide, located upstage from the proscenium arch and extending a few feet past the limits of the arch on each side. It is suspended from the counterweight system so that it can be raised and lowered. On it are mounted spotlights and other lighting equipment.

LINEN CANVAS.   The best, and most expensive, material for covering flat frames.

LINNEBACH CYCLORAMA.   See *Cyclorama*.

LOADING PLATFORM.   A metal gallery supported by the grid. It provides a working platform where counterweights can be loaded into the arbors.

LOCKING RAIL. A metal framework bolted to the wall and floor along one side wall of the stage house. On it are the rope locks of the counterweight system.

LOFT BLOCK. A single-grooved wheel mounted in a metal housing and bolted to the grid. Over these wheels run the ropes or cables of the flying system.

MACHINE BOLT. See *Bolt*.

MAIN CURTAIN. See *Curtain*.

MARQUISETTE. A sheer, somewhat lustrous, cotton netting.

MASKING. Placing either framed or unframed scenery in a position to prevent the audience from seeing the backstage area.

MECHANICAL ADVANTAGE. Increasing an applied force by mechanical means, as through the use of a block and tackle or a winch.

MECHANICAL DRAWING. A type of drawing made with the aid of instruments, generally made to scale.

MORTISE AND TENON JOINT. See *Joint*.

MULING. Changing the direction of a cable or rope by passing it around a specially mounted horizontal block.

MUSLIN. Heavyweight unbleached cotton material used for covering flat frames or in the construction of drops when economy is a prime requisite.

NOTCHED JOINT. See *Joint*.

OPERATING LINE. (1) The rope used to raise and lower the arbor of the counterweight system. (2) The rope used to open or close different types of curtains, such as the draw, tab, or roller curtains.

OUTRIGGER. A skeletal platform of irregular shape mounted on castors with scenery attached to one of its faces.

PAINT FRAME. A large wooden frame to which scenery is temporarily nailed to hold it in a vertical position while it is being painted. The frame can be lowered into a slot in the floor so that all painting is done from the floor level.

PAINT PALLET, ROLLING. A metal-topped rolling work table on which small quantities of paint are mixed.

PARALLEL, CONTINENTAL. A folding platform with a removable top and inside supporting frames. When folded the outside frames form a compact unit.

PARALLEL, STANDARD.   A folding platform with a removable top. The folded supporting frames of this parallel are awkward to handle.

PICTURE HOOK AND EYE.   Lightweight steel sockets and hooks used for attaching objects to scenery that must be shifted rapidly.

PILASTER.   An upright support that is structurally a part of the wall but projects out from it by a distance equal to one-third the width of the support.

PIN RAIL.   A part of the rope-line rigging system consisting of a metal pipe or wooden beam attached to the fly gallery and fitted with removable pins used in tying off the ropes.

PIPE BATTEN.   The part of the counterweight system to which the scenery is attached for flying.

PLATFORM, RIGID.   A weight-bearing platform that may be varied in height by attaching different sets of supporting legs.

PLYWOOD.   A compositional material made of three or more layers of wood glued together, each layer laid with the grain at right angles to that of the others. Sold in sheets 4′ wide in varying thicknesses and lengths.

PROPERTIES:

DECORATIVE.   Furniture or objects on stage that serve no practical purpose but help to give character to the setting.

FLOOR.   All the furniture normally used by the actors.

HAND.   Small objects carried to or from the stage by the actors or handled by them while on stage.

PROSCENIUM ARCH.   The opening in the wall between the stage proper and the auditorium.

PROSCENIUM DOORS.   Doorways located on either side of the forestage and usually on the auditorium side of the proscenium arch.

PULL ROD.   A $\frac{3}{8}''$ iron rod with a handle at one end and a hook at the other, used in pulling wagon stages or turning a revolving disc.

PULL ROPES.   Short lengths of knotted ropes attached to low wagon stages and used in pulling them.

RAIL.   The top and bottom horizontal members of a flat frame.

REEVE.   To pass a rope over a sheave in a block or pulley.

REVOLVING DISC.   A low circular platform supported by the stage floor. Usually designed for a particular production and carries but a portion of a setting.

REVOLVING STAGE.   A circular section of the stage floor that revolves and is supported from beneath. It is usually electrically driven. Used for shifting entire settings.

RIGGING.   All of the activities associated with the initial assembly of a setting when it is first taken to the stage. Rigging also readies a set to be shifted.

RIGID PLATFORM.   See *Platform*.

RISER.   The vertical face of a step.

ROLL CEILING.   See *Ceiling*.

ROLLER CURTAIN.   See *Curtain*.

ROLLING SCENERY.   Scenery mounted on castors or wheels to be shifted manually or by power.

ROPE LOCK.   A lever that activates a pawl housed in a metal frame so as to apply pressure on the operating line of a counterweight unit.

RUNNING.   Shifting or moving scenery manually.

SADDLE, SADDLING.   Obtaining multiple points of support from a single line. Both ends of a short line are tied off to an object and the lifting line is then attached to the center of the saddle thus made.

SANDBAG.   A heavyweight canvas bag enclosed by ropes and filled with sand, used for balance in rope-line rigging.

SASH CORD.   The $\frac{1}{4}''$ thick braided cotton cord used in making lash lines.

SATEEN.   A shiny cotton material, not very strong, but inexpensive.

SCARF JOINT.   See *Joint*.

SCENE DOCK.   The area and racks where two-dimensional scenery can be stored.

SCENE SHIFT.   The striking of one setting and assembly of another.

SCENE SHOP.   The area used for the construction, covering, joining, and painting of scenery.

SEGMENT STAGE.   A pie-shaped rolling platform used in shifting scenery.

SEMICIRCLE.   A low semicircular platform mounted on castors and pivoted from the center of the straight side.

SHARKSTOOTH SCRIM.   A netting with a rectangular weave; it is stronger and has greater opacity than bobinette.

SHEAVE.   A grooved wheel in a block or pulley.

SIGHT LINE.   An imaginary line extending from any seat in the auditorium past the proscenium arch to any position on stage to determine how much of the stage will be visible from that point.

SILL IRON.   A reinforcing length of strap iron, $\frac{1}{4}''$ thick by $\frac{3}{4}''$ wide, joining the two legs of a door flat.

SLIP STAGE.   A very large platform riding on flanged wheels and tracks. It can carry a full setting and all properties.

SNAP HOOK.   A steel hook with a spring trigger that closes its throat. Attached to the end of snatch lines it eliminates the need for rope knots.

SNATCH LINE.   Length of rope, piano wire, or chain used in attaching scenery to a batten of the rope-line or counterweight flying system.

SPOTLINE.   A rope line passing over special blocks on the grid to fall to the stage floor at a given point.

STAGE BRACE.   Used in bracing scenery. Metal loops hold two overlapping lengths of hardwood that can be adjusted in length and locked in position with a thumbscrew. One end of the brace is fitted with a double hook, the other with an angular or curved footiron.

STAGE LEFT.   That part of the stage that lies to the left of the actor as he faces the audience.

STAGE RIGHT.   That part of the stage that lies to the right of the actor as he faces the audience.

STAGE SCREW.   A large steel screw with a handle in place of a slotted head. It can be driven into the stage floor by turning and hand pressure.

STANDARD PARALLEL.   See *Parallel*.

STIFFENING BATTEN.   Length of 1" x 3" or 1" x 4" lumber used to brace and strengthen a series of flats that have been joined by hinging.

STILE.   A vertical outside member of a flat frame.

STOCK SCENERY.   Flat frames, standardized in height, that are kept for possible alterations and reuse.

STOP BLOCK.   Short length of 1" x 1$\frac{1}{2}$" wood used to prevent one flat from slipping past another when making an inside lashing.

STOP CLEAT.   A small metal cleat $\frac{3}{4}''$ x 3" that is screwed to the back of a stile and allowed to project $\frac{3}{4}''$ to insure the vertical alignment of flats joined by an outside lashing.

STOVE BOLT.   See *Bolt*.

Strap Hinge.   See *Hinge*.

Strap Iron.   Strips of malleable iron, $\frac{3}{16}''$ or $\frac{1}{4}''$ thick and $\frac{3}{4}''$ wide, used in making sill irons for door flats.

Straps, Plywood.   Rectangular pieces of $\frac{1}{4}''$ plywood $8''$ long and $2\frac{3}{4}''$ wide. Used for the same purpose as keystones.

Strike.   Command given by the stage manager to signal the beginning of a scene shift. Also used at the close of a production for the operation of dismantling all scenery and stripping it of hardware preparatory to storing it.

Sweeps.   The curved or shaped structural members of an archway flat that give it its distinctive shape.

Swivel and Hook.   Stage hardware used to help in flying scenery placed on stage at an angle other than parallel with the pipe battens.

T-Bar Track.   Vertical metal tracks mounted against the side wall of the stage house to guide the arbors and prevent side sway.

Tab Curtain.   See *Curtain*.

Tackle Rigging.   The method of arranging rope and pulleys for the purpose of lifting or moving heavy objects.

Teaser.   A horizontal masking border that usually matches the main curtain in color and material. It can be raised or lowered to mask the space above settings of different heights.

Tee Plate.   A steel plate shaped like the letter T, used in place of a keystone when greater strength is required.

Template Bench.   A workbench especially suited for the assembly of flat frames.

Tension Pulley.   A special pulley mounted on the T-bar track below the locking rail and around which the operating line passes.

Tie-Off Cleats.   Cleats placed opposite each other on the stiles at the $3'$-$0''$ level, around which the lash line is tied off.

Tip Jack.   A device used for shifting heavy or awkward units of scenery. It is similar to a rigid jack but is mounted on castors with the vertical member at less than a 90-degree angle to its base. Two jacks are required for each unit of scenery to be so shifted.

Thickness Pieces.   Structural members that give the appearance of depth and solidity to all openings in two-dimensional scenery.

TOGGLE BAR.   The inside cross member of a flat frame.

TORMENTORS.   Vertical masking pieces, usually of plain flat construction, placed on either side of the proscenium just upstage of the teaser.

TRACK, CURTAIN.   The hollow supporting frame, either metal or wood, from which the draw curtain is suspended and on which it moves.

TRAP.   A removable section of the stage floor.

TREAD.   The horizontal plane of a step unit.

TRIAL SETUP.   The process of assembling the various parts of a setting for the first time.

TRIM.   Adjusting flown units of scenery so that the lower rails or battens are parallel with the stage floor.

TRIP CYCLORAMA.   See *Cyclorama.*

TRIPPING.   To fold, by special lines, a flown unit such as a drop or a cyc to reduce the amount of height required to raise it above sight lines.

TRUSS.   An assemblage of members or beams combined and reinforced by triangular bracing to form a rigid framework.

TUMBLER.   A vertical length of 1″ x 3″ lumber hinged to two flats of a three-fold unit that will permit three flats of the same width to fold into a compact stack.

TURNBUCKLE.   A steel loop fitted with a threaded eye bolt at one end and a threaded hook bolt at the other. By turning the loop the bolts are drawn together or extended.

TWO-DIMENSIONAL SCENERY.   Framed or unframed scenery that has width and height but no depth other than that of the material from which it is made.

UPSTAGE.   A position away from the audience and toward the back of the stage.

VELOUR.   A heavy deep-piled fabric used for main curtains.

WAGON STAGE.   A platform mounted on castors on which heavy sections of a setting can be shifted.

WALK IT UP.   Raise a framed two-dimensional unit from a horizontal to a vertical position by blocking the lower rails and lifting the upper rails until the stagehands can reach the stiles. They then walk hand over hand along the stiles until the unit is upright.

WEBBING.   Strips of strong fabric used to reinforce the top hem of curtains and stage draperies.

WINCH, POWERED.   A power-driven piece of machinery consisting of a set of gears that turn a drum or cylinder on which a rope or cable is coiled. Used in hoisting heavy objects.

WINDOW STILES.   The vertical members of a flat that form the sides of a window opening.

WORK SCHEDULE.   A calendar of operational steps to be followed in mounting a production.

WORKING DRAWINGS.   The scaled mechanical drawings that show the carpenter what to build and how to built it.

WING NUT.   A threaded nut with extensions or wings on each side that make it possible to tighten or loosen it with the fingers.

selected references

Adix, Vern. *Theatre Scenecraft*. Anchorage, Kentucky: The Children's Theatre Press, 1956.

Burris-Meyer, Harold, and Cole, Edward C. *Scenery for the Theatre*. Boston: Little, Brown, 1951.

Burris-Meyer, Harold, and Cole, Edward C. *Theatres and Auditoriums*. New York: Reinhold, 1949.

Cheney, Sheldon. *The Theatre—Three Thousand Years of Drama, Acting and Stagecraft*. London: Longmans, Green, 1930.

Cornberg, Sol, and Gebauer, Emanuel. *A Stage Crew Handbook*, rev. ed. New York: Harper, 1957.

Davis, Fremont, and Van De Water, Marjorie. *Use of Tools Phototold in 420 Pictures*. Washington: Washington Infantry Journal Press, 1946.

Friederich, Willard J., and Fraser, John H. *Scenery Design For the Amateur Stage*. New York: Macmillan, 1950.

Gassner, John, and Barber, Philip. *Producing the Play and the New Scene Technician's Handbook*. New York: Dryden, 1941.

Gruver, Bert. *The Stage Manager's Handbook*. New York: Harper, 1953.

Hake, Herbert V. *Here's How! A Basic Stagecraft Book*, rev. ed. Evanston: Row, Peterson, 1958.

Henderson, Kenneth A. *Handbook of American Mountaineering*. Boston: Houghton Mifflin, 1942. (Rope knots.)

Hewitt, Barnard, Foster, J. F., and Wolle, Muriel Sibell. *Play Production Theory and Practice*. Philadelphia: J. B. Lippincott, 1952.

Philippi, Herbert. *Stagecraft and Scenic Design*. Boston: Houghton Mifflin, 1953.

Plymouth Cordage Company. *Manual of Rope Usage, How to Put Rope to Work In Industry, and Useful Knots and How to Use Them.* Plymouth: Plymouth Cordage Company, 1948.

Selden, S., and Sellman, H. *Stage Scenery and Lighting,* rev. ed. New York: Appleton-Century-Crofts, 1958.

Southern, Richard. *Changeable Scenery: Its Origin and Development in the British Theatre.* London: Faber and Faber, 1952.

Wade, Robert J. *Designing for TV.* New York: Farrar and Straus, 1952.

Whiting, Frank. *An Introduction to the Theatre.* New York: Harper, 1954.

index

Note: italic numbers indicate illustrations.